MYSTERIOUS MINDS

MYSTERIOUS MINDS

The Neurobiology of Psychics, Mediums, and Other Extraordinary People

Stanley Krippner and Harris L. Friedman,
Editors

PRAEGER

An Imprint of ABC-CLIO, LLC

A B C 🔖 C L I O

Santa Barbara, California • Denver, Colorado • Oxford, England

Copyright 2010 by Stanley Krippner and Harris L. Friedman

All rights reserved. No part of this publication may be reproduced, stored in a
retrieval system, or transmitted, in any form or by any means, electronic, mechanical,
photocopying, recording, or otherwise, except for the inclusion of brief quotations in a
review, without prior permission in writing from the publisher.

Library of Congress Cataloging-in-Publication Data

Mysterious minds : the neurobiology of psychics, mediums, and other extraordinary people /
  Stanley Krippner and Harris L. Friedman, editors.
    p. cm.
  Includes bibliographical references and index.
  ISBN 978–0–313–35866–1 (hard copy : alk. paper) — ISBN 978–0–313–35867–8 (ebook)
1. Parapsychology. 2. Neurobiology. I. Krippner, Stanley, 1932– II. Friedman, Harris L.
BF1040.M97   2010
130—dc22   2009036128

14 13 12 11 10   1 2 3 4 5

This book is also available on the World Wide Web as an eBook.
Visit www.abc-clio.com for details.

ABC-CLIO, LLC
130 Cremona Drive, P.O. Box 1911
Santa Barbara, California 93116-1911

This book is printed on acid-free paper ∞

Manufactured in the United States of America

This book is dedicated to the memory of Stephen Bruce Baumann, Ph.D. (1949–2009), pioneer investigator of the neurobiological aspects of parapsychological phenomena.

Contents

North Siren

Foreword

"The great field for new discoveries," said a scientific friend to me the other day, "is always the unclassified residuum." Round about the accredited and orderly facts of every science there ever floats a sort of dust-cloud of exceptional observations, of occurrences minute and irregular and seldom met with, which it always proves easier to ignore than to attend to. The ideal of every science is that of a closed and completed system of truth. The charm of most sciences to their more passive disciples consists in their appearing, in fact, to wear just this ideal form.

(William James, 1896/1956, p. 229)

Anomalous psychological phenomena, *psi* among them, are certainly part of the dust cloud that surrounds the science of psychology. Unfortunately, psychology is hardly an orderly science, but more like a nebula composed of fashions, trends, and borrowed pieces from other sciences (see Kuhn, 1962). Nevertheless, those who investigate such phenomena are held to the highest standards possible by both friends and critics. Indeed, most serious observers agree that careful investigations into psi phenomena exhibit typical levels of rigor that equal or surpass the expectations of ordinary psychological research.

This in mind, it is a curious fact that the field of psi research is so regularly criticized on the grounds that its experimental findings are not, in the long run, replicable. This, of course, is a valid concern, as explained so well in the chapter by Alcock. Critics, or more properly "counteradvocates," use this argument to dismiss even the most dramatic results of single experiments as well as temporary runs of strikingly successful experiments. It is worth noting, however, that ordinary psychological research is not itself held to this standard. In fact, we have no idea what the replication rate of ordinary psychological research would be if replications were actually carried out and the results published on a regular basis, as they are in psi research.

Despite the high value placed on experimental replications by research methods texts, the American Psychological Association in fact discourages the publication of replication research, to say nothing of its even greater reluctance to publish reports of failed replications (Modgil and Modgil, 1986). One is reminded of the years of supportive findings published on the topic of chemical memory transference in flatworms during the 1950s and 1960s, all of which started with Thompson and McConnell in 1955. It was eventually discovered that these findings were mostly if not completely the products of statistical false positives (so-called alpha errors), but none of the many failed efforts at replication found their way to press. It is said that the discovery that the flatworm had no clothes was finally confirmed by a petition passed informally among respected scientists who had tried and failed to demonstrate the memory transfer effect (Rosenzweig, 1996). Now, the point of all this is that even the most legitimate and unquestionable effects discovered by science, flatworms excluded, parade across the pages of professional journals untrammeled by demands for replication. Yet the best current estimates place the success rates for replications in the combined social and physical sciences at only around 41 percent (Hedges and Cooper, 1994; Modgil and Modgil, 1986), far below what any counteradvocate would accept for psi research. It would seem, then, that critics of psi research force it to meet a standard to which ordinary research itself patently fails to measure.

With these thoughts in mind, perhaps it makes more sense to push ahead and seek an understanding of the psychological and neurobiological processes that accompany putative psi phenomena rather then endlessly trying to demonstrate their existence. The present volume is a pioneering effort in this direction. In these pages the reader will find a rich variety of approaches to the neurobiology of parapsychological phenomena.

Williams and Roll open this volume by presenting an excellent review and analysis of research on psi phenomena and the brain, including extrasensory perception (ESP) and electroencephalograph (EEG) activity, functional brain correlates of psi, cerebral lateralization, and temporal lobe lability. The authors go on to review some data regarding the relationships between psychokinesis (PK) and brain activity, as well as possible explanatory models derived from quantum physics.

Watt and Irwin take a process-oriented approach to understanding ESP, focusing on states of mind and associated brain activity. They summarize the results from experimental measurements with EEG and evoked potentials, as well as functional magnetic resonance imaging (fMRI) findings. They report that effects are associated with temporal and occipital lobe activity as well as overall brain states related to low levels of arousal. Parker reviews several more-or-less successful lines of research with PK, coming to the conclusion that more adventurous designs are called for in order to stimulate theory development, especially as related to the perennial "mind/body" problem.

In comparison, Hageman, Peres, Moreira-Almeida, Caixeta, Wickramasekera, and Krippner offer a fine review of the neurobiological literature bearing on trance states and mediumship, focusing especially on EEG research with some Brazilian mediums whose psychophysiology often is paradoxical. These authors also include a fascinating historical treatment of the topic.

In a rich review of the most current evidence about the brain processes that underlie consciousness itself, Don reports that, among the extraordinary people he has encountered, many had high to very high 40 Hz (gamma band) EEG voltage and unusually high wave coherence. He suggests that high-voltage 40 Hz gamma activity is a feature of people who have conscious access to the underlying unity found expressed in correlation waves. Moreover, he comes to the remarkable conclusion that psi may well be an unconscious and ubiquitous psychological function, exhibited in the electrical responses of ordinary brains as well as those of psychic claimants, but in the former instances it goes unrecognized.

Additional chapters supply a meaningful context for these areas of investigation, including an in-depth examination of clinical reports by Neppe. Freedman enriches our understanding of regional brain activity associated with alleged parapsychological phenomena, emphasizing particularly the importance of the frontal lobes.

Luke and Friedman address the potential value of psychedelic substances as promising pathways for understanding data from anecdotal, anthropological, clinical, historical, and survey sources of psi-related accounts. They also report a number of experiments linking neurochemistry to extraordinary phenomena, and propose plausible neurochemical models that involve β-carboline and tryptamine, dimethyltryptamine (DMT), and ketamine.

This book also includes a masterful critical essay, including examinations of the difficulties facing the assessment of parapsychological research findings by Alcock. Readers who find parapsychology a captivating area of study need to acquaint themselves with Alcock's caveats to comprehend how many additional bases psi researchers need to cover before many mainstream scientists will take them seriously.

Throughout this remarkable collection of essays the reader is offered a tour through what once was a "dust-cloud of exceptional observations" but now is taking on discernable dimensions in the viewfinders of modern neuroscience.

Allan Combs

References

Hedges, L. V., and Cooper, H. M. (1994). *The handbook of research synthesis*. New York: Russell Sage.

James, W. (1956). Address of the President before the Society for Psychical Research. In *The will to believe, and other essays in popular philosophy, and human immortality* (2nd ed.). New York: Dover. (Original work published 1896.)

Kuhn, T. (1962). *The structure of scientific revolutions*. Chicago: University of Chicago Press.

Modgil, S., and Modgil, C. (Eds.). (1986). *Hans Eysenck: Consensus and controversy*. Philadelphia: Falmer Press.

Rosenzweig, M. R. (1996). Aspects of the search for neural mechanisms of memory. *Annual Review of Psychology, 47*, 1–32.

Thompson, R., and J. V. McConnell. (1955). Classical conditioning in planarian, *Dugesia dorotocephala. Journal of Comparative and Physiological Psychology, 48*, 65–68.

Acknowledgments

The editors express their gratitude to the Floraglades Foundation and the Saybrook Graduate School Chair for the Study of Consciousness for their support of the preparation of this book. They also thank Christian Gaden Jensen, who served as the managing editor of the book, Steve Hart for his additional editorial assistance, and Debbie Carvalko, our editor and supporter at Praeger/ABC-CLIO for her visionary concept of the volume. The editors are especially grateful to Robert Vanderhorst, the eminent Canadian artist, for allowing them to use several of his paintings as illustrations.

Introduction

Mysteries are unexplained phenomena and, despite the many notable advances in science, there remains no shortage of mysteries (Brooks, 2009). Unfortunately, people have so much confidence in the undeniable strides that modern science has produced that they often forget there is much more to learn than has thus far been learned. Perhaps some of these mysteries will eventually yield to scientific progress, while others may simply remain unsolved.

Among the most perplexing mysteries are those related to what is often called "mind," that construct that is at once both the center of all experience and, as subjectivity itself, the most difficult of all concepts to grasp in any scientific way. Science utilizes so-called "objective" methods, which may not be able to ever directly grasp subjectivity. Mainstream science requires consensual approaches, as in the need for replication of findings, so that more than an isolated individual's belief is needed to be credible. Many attempts to understand mind have occurred over the millennia, but a consensual definition or explanation has yet to emerge, leading to our titling this book *Mysterious Minds*, as the nature of mind is argued about today with as much rancor as it was in ancient times.

One widely held position on this debate about understanding mind is monist materialism, which assumes that mind is the functioning of the material brain, often reducing mind to a by-product or epiphenomenon of brain that has no independent existence—or even discounting mind as merely an illusion. This position is often portrayed using the analogical computer distinctions between brain as a type of hardware and mind as a type of software (or the brain's so-called operating system) both seen as the same monist materialistic brain viewed from differing perspectives (see Dennett, 1991).

Another position is dualism, which assumes that mind and brain are separate realms, irreducible to each other. In this position, mind is seen as nonmaterial and having properties called "qualia," which may or may not relate in various ways to the brain (see Chalmers, 1996). And there are numerous other positions dealing with mind and brain, all yet reconciled and perhaps irreconcilable.

Among the most fascinating aspects of the mysterious mind is the possibility of alleged parapsychological or psi experiences (e.g., telepathy, psychokinesis, precognition). People have always reported such extraordinary experiences, but there is great divisiveness as to whether such experiences may relate to veridical events or should be discounted for various reasons. In this regard, people often divide into two camps.

On the one hand are those who dismiss parapsychological data as necessarily invalid. Many arguments are brought to bear in rejecting these data, often based on procedural critiques (e.g., the data being methodologically flawed or fraudulent). Another argument is ad hominem (e.g., those who accept such evidence are gullible or deceptive). From this vantage, it is often automatically assumed that all anomalous phenomena of the mysterious mind can be explained away—and any empirical evidence to the contrary would be a priori impossible.

For advocates of psi phenomena, this stance is reminiscent of the stories of Galileo's telescopic discoveries supporting the Copernican theories, which were reportedly rejected by both those refusing to look through his telescope and, more shockingly, those looking and simply not seeing the empirical evidence before their eyes (see Cohen, 1985). In fact, routinely dismissing psi as nonsensical is often evaluated highly in the scientific community, since to accept such claims could be seen as evidence of a lack of scientific skepticism.

In our opinion, however, any such a priori dismissal of psi is not only premature but often based on a limited worldview, one misunderstood as a simple linear system of cause-effect. This linear model is based on so-called material interactions (such as via particles and waves) within a synchronized forward-moving time. This circumscribed view of the material world and how it can be best known by science contrasts with some contemporary scientific paradigms of a universe filled with all sorts of perplexing mysteries, such as quantum entanglements leading to, so-called, "spooky interactions" at a distance that seem to defy conventional notions of time, space, and causation. From this perspective, casual dismissals of psi reflect "scientism," a rigid adherence to an antiquated view of science.

On the other hand, there is undoubtedly widespread "romanticism" among some proponents of psi who embrace many extraordinary beliefs without the benefit of proper discernment. Examples would be advocating the belief systems exemplified in such popular New Age movies as *What the Bleep?* and *The Secret* that, in their most extreme interpretations, imply that whatever one believes to be true will in fact become true. Adherents to such romanticism accept various extraordinary claims not only devoid of adequate empirical evidence, but sometimes of the most rudimentary logic. These belief systems run the alphabetical gamut from accepting astrological charts as valid descriptions of personality to accepting popularized versions of Zen Buddhism that have been stripped of their cultural meanings and often misappropriated to serve agendas other than their original purpose. Such romanticism naively accepts examples of mind's mysteries too readily, often accepting phenomena as valid that can be reproduced by stage magic and sleight of hand.

Is there a proverbial middle way, one that reconciles the dilemmas of both scientism and romanticism, in the understanding of the mysterious mind and its relationship to extraordinary phenomena? We are undergoing a profound scientific revolution in the area of neurobiology (for an overview of neurobiology, see Matthews, 2000) and now possess impressive new technologies for studying the brain and nervous system, which we think are candidates for providing a needed reconciliation between these extreme perspectives. Through quantitative electroencephalography (qEEG), functional magnetic resonance imaging (fMRI), and many other imaging approaches, sophisticated types of brain mapping are able to provide remarkable noninvasive glimpses into the heretofore unknown workings of the brain. Also, we can now peek into the most private of spaces, the brain, in vivo.

In addition, interactive technologies that go beyond just mapping, such as transcranial magnetic stimulation (TMS), are opening ethical avenues for implementing changes within the living human without causing any noticeable damage as its inner functioning is being explored and transformed. These technological advances provide exciting new avenues for researching various aspects of the mysterious mind, including those related to psi, allowing for possible sophisticated answers to questions that have previously eluded scientific investigators. And many futurists anticipate a brave new world of neurobiological transformations that will alter what it means to be human into becoming "transhuman" (e.g., Kurzweil, 1992).

This volume does not attempt to provide any definitive answers to this myriad of questions. As editors, we do not promote any dogmatic position on mind-brain relationships or even on the existence or nonexistence of psi phenomena as actual events. Rather we hope to introduce our readers to many pioneering efforts exploring the mysterious mind through emerging neurobiological perspectives and technologies. Although these efforts can demonstrate patterns of convergence between neurobiological phenomena and the mysterious mind—and may even demonstrate how such technologies could causally alter neurobiology, these forays do not necessarily imply that all such mysteries can be reduced to neurobiological mechanisms. Instead, our distinguished chapter authors have articulated a range of attempts to explore the mysterious mind as associated with several neurobiological concomitants. Their data could be interpreted as supportive of either a dualistic or a monist philosophical stance, as well as of other possible positions.

We also present two notes of caution. First, in a culture that has such great respect and maybe even religious-type awe for science, it is easy to be swayed by findings from impressive technologies. Often, this awe is due more to the technology itself than to the value of the findings. The same data may not have seemed so convincing had it emerged from less complex and impressive technologies. The data derived from these technologies should, however, be viewed as critically as any other data. A series of papers (e.g., Vul, Harris, Winkielman, and Pashler, in press; Barrett, in press) has exposed various artifacts and statistical problems involved in findings derived from such technology.

Second, regardless of how sophisticated the technology, if it is focused on exploring the wrong questions, it will yield nothing of value. Most understandings of the brain as related to mysterious minds, including what is being explored with these impressive pieces of apparatus, focus on neurons, yet neurobiology involves much more than neurons. Indeed, Nicholls (1981) once wrote, "to be interested in glia [a nonneuronal type of brain cell] was almost disreputable, somewhat akin to dabbling in parapsychology or memory transfer" (p. 3), yet now we are just learning that astrocytes, a type of glia that outnumbers neurons in the brain by 10-fold, are what most significantly differentiates human's from other species' brains and may be far more important to higher mental process than neurons (Oberheim et al., 2009).

Truly, neurobiology is just in the beginning stages of incredible opportunities to explore the mysterious mind. Consequently, we have left it to the reader to evaluate whether or not the neurobiological findings presented in this volume, using such technologies as fMRI, TMS, and other approaches, are useful in regard to increasing our understanding of mysterious minds as related to alleged psi and other extraordinary experiences. If so, the reported data may lay the groundwork for eventually delivering long-sought answers to some of humanity's deepest and most fundamental concerns.

Harris L. Friedman and Stanley Krippner

References

Barrett, L. (in press). Understanding the mind by measuring the brain: Lessons from measuring behavior (commentary on Vul et al., 2009). *Perspectives in Psychological Science.*

Brooks, M. (2009). *13 things that don't make sense: The most intriguing scientific mysteries of our time.* London: Profile Books.

Chalmers, D. (1996). *The conscious mind.* New York: Oxford University Press.

Cohen, B. (1985). *Revolution in science.* Cambridge, MA: Harvard University Press.

Dennett, D. (1991). *Consciousness explained.* Boston: Little and Brown.

Kurzweil, R. (1992). *The age of intelligent machines.* Cambridge, MA: MIT Press.

Matthews, G. (2000). *Neurobiology: Molecules, cells, and systems* (2nd ed.). Hoboken, NJ: Wiley.

Nicholls, J. (1981). Introduction: Perspectives on the cell biology of glia. *Journal of Experimental Biology, 95,* 3–5.

Oberheim, N., Takano, T., Han, X., He, W., Lin, J., Wang, F., et al. (2009). Uniquely hominid features of adult human astrocytes. *Journal of Neuroscience, 29*(10), 3276–3287.

Vul, E., Harris, C., Winkielman, P., and Pashler, H. (in press). Puzzlingly high correlations in fMRI studies of emotion, personality, and social cognition. *Perspectives in Psychological Science.*

MYSTERIOUS MINDS

Dressed for the Turquoise Curtain

CHAPTER 1

Quantum Theory, Neurobiology, and Parapsychology

William G. Roll and Bryan J. Williams

Parapsychology has been hampered by an assumption that it is impossible to explain occurrences, such as extrasensory perception (ESP, including telepathy and precognition) and psychokinesis (PK) collectively known as psi, in terms of mainstream scientific principles. This chapter takes the contrary position, namely that psi research data are quite consistent with the principles of both neurobiology and quantum physics.

Neurobiology and Psi

The brain generates streams of electric activity from its surface that can be detected by an electroencephalograph (EEG). There are five types of brain waves, distinguished by their association with different mental states and frequency in cycles per second, or hertz (Hz): gamma waves (30–80 Hz) appear when we process complex sensory information; beta waves (13–29 Hz) appear when we are alert and attentive; alpha waves (8–12 Hz) appear when we are relaxed and disengaged from thought as in meditation; theta waves (3.5–7.5 Hz) often appear in deeper meditative states, but more commonly when we are drowsy and falling asleep; and delta waves appear during deep sleep and have the slowest wave cycles (Cahn and Polich, 2006). We produce all five types in the course of a 24-hour day and, at the end of days, 0 Hz, the sign of death.

Psi Studies Involving Brain Waves

In her overview of accounts from highly successful ESP percipients, Rhea White (1964) found "a great deal of emphasis on achieving a state of deep mental and physical relaxation" (pp. 28–29). When experimenters turned to this issue, they did not rely on personal statements, but used an objective sign of wakeful relaxation, the presence of alpha waves. The first method, which looked for an ESP-alpha relationship, measured the amount of alpha in the EEGs of participants from the occipital lobe during ESP tests. Cadoret (1964) reported that research participants scored more "hits" (i.e., correct scores) in a clairvoyance study when slow-frequency brain waves (mostly in the alpha range) were present, as opposed to more rapid waves (unlike telepathy, there is no "sender" in clairvoyance). Honorton (1969) selected participants who did well in a practice clairvoyance test, and administered a formal test with EEG monitoring. They obtained higher ESP scores during large amounts of alpha as compared to small amounts.

Stanford and Stevenson (1972) conducted a telepathy test in which Stanford was the receiver; it resulted in a positive but nonsignificant relationship. Stanford and Palmer (1975) found that college students who were successful at describing a hidden picture by attempting clairvoyance showed more alpha than unsuccessful students. EEG monitoring of the psychic claimant Lalsingh Harribance revealed high alpha percentages when Harribance correctly guessed the gender of people in hidden photographs (Morris et al., 1972). Low alpha percentages resulted when he scored at chance.

To compare ESP with ordinary sense perception, Maher (1986) recorded EEG from the temporal and parietal lobes of participants as they attempted the two modes of perception (ordinary and extrasensory). More alpha was present during ESP than during sense perception. In contrast, Stanford and Lovin (1970) found lower rates of alpha were associated with precognition with a group of college students. However, this result was not repeated in a second study (Stanford, 1971). Four studies that failed to identify a relationship between ESP and alpha waves were inconclusive, showing no evidence of ESP (American Society for Psychical Research, 1959; Morris and Cohen, 1969; Venturino, 1978; Wallwork, 1952).

In summary, if we exclude the work where evidence of ESP was lacking, six studies show a positive relationship between alpha and telepathy/clairvoyance, while one shows a negative relationship with precognition. Results in experiments in psychology and ESP may depend on the experimenter, the so-called experimenter effect. To determine if the alpha results could be due to the experimenter effect, we combined the three studies where Stanford was an experimenter. The outcome is that five different experimenters contributed to the finding of an ESP-alpha connection, which argues against the experimenter effect. In light of White's (1964) observation regarding exceptional ESP percipients, there is evidence that a state of relaxed attention may be conducive to telepathy and clairvoyance.

To "still the body and mind," the percipients in White's (1964) survey used specific techniques, which were, in most cases, "incorporated in a kind of ritual" (pp. 28–29). Later, Honorton et al. (1971) had participants receive alpha feedback training before a clairvoyance card test. Their clairvoyance performance was positively related to alpha production and also to participants' ratings of their mental state during training. However, Honorton and Carbone (1971) found a negative relationship between ESP and alpha with another group of participants who received training prior to the test.

Is alpha then positively or negatively related to ESP? A study by Lewis and Schmeidler (1971) suggests both. Initially, they found a positive relationship when their participants did not know that they were engaging in an ESP test (the test was covertly embedded in their training), and then found a negative relationship when participants knew they were being tested for ESP. A possible solution to this quandary comes from Rao and Feola's (1973) ESP test of a male participant who had previously received extensive alpha training. The participant showed higher ESP scores when asked to produce alpha than when asked to suppress alpha. The solution then may be to limit this type of research to participants already proficient in manipulating their alpha. Another study, by Venturino (1978), found no relationship between alpha training and ESP, but the study also showed no evidence for ESP and is therefore inconclusive.

In summary, two alpha training studies showed a positive relationship between alpha and ESP, a third showed a negative relationship, a fourth showed both, and a fifth was inconclusive. In short, it is unknown whether or not alpha feedback enhances ESP.

Another way to look for an ESP-alpha connection is to determine whether there are changes in the frequency of alpha waves during ESP tests. Most of the studies that used this method were conducted by Stanford and his associates, who generally found that increases in alpha frequency, from the time participants began to relax to the time they reported their impression of the ESP target, were associated with higher ESP scores (Stanford, 1971; Stanford and Lovin, 1970; Stanford and Stanford, 1969; Stanford and Stevenson, 1972). Stanford (1971) surmised that the frequency increase might be due to the increased arousal and attentiveness required to make the ESP responses. The only other study (Venturino, 1978) that used this method was inconclusive because, in addition to finding no relation between ESP and alpha frequency, there was no evidence for ESP.

A third method is to ask if there are changes in the amplitude (i.e., the strength of alpha waves as shown by their height on the EEG record) during an ESP test. This method has been used in two studies. In the first, Alexander (2000) monitored the EEG of a female psychic claimant during a so-called remote viewing trial; alpha activity in the frontal and temporal regions on both sides of her brain showed higher amplitude during the remote viewing trial than during a control trial. In the second study, May (2001) recorded the EEGs of three so-called "remote viewers" while they attempted to view pictures in an adjacent room. Since brief alpha amplitude changes can occur in relation to planning body movement, cognitive processing, and sensory stimulation (Pfurtscheller and Aranibar, 1979; Sergent et al., 1987), May predicted that similar changes would occur in successful remote viewing. Although the research participants produced evidence for ESP, their EEGs showed no associated amplitude changes.

In summary, the positive relationship between ESP and alpha frequency rests largely on Stanford's studies, which raises the possibility that it was due to an experimenter effect. Last, in this regard, two studies examined ESP in relation to alpha amplitude; one study found amplitude increases, while the other found no changes, so nothing can be concluded from this slender outcome. In brief, there is little evidence that alpha frequency and amplitude are related to ESP.

High ESP scores may involve brain waves other than alpha. McDonough et al. (1994) recorded the EEGs of professional artists who served as "receivers" in a telepathy test and found that artists who correctly identified the target pictures showed more alpha and beta activity, while artists whose guesses were incorrect showed more delta and theta. In a precognition test disguised as a card game, McDonough et al. (2000) found that 20 gamblers showed a preponderance of 40 Hz gamma waves when viewing cards that would later be selected (i.e., precognitive targets), but not when viewing nontarget cards. During her EEG study of the psychic claimant, Alexander (2000) observed beta waves in the frontal and temporal regions of her left hemisphere during the remote viewing trial, indicating that her left hemisphere was more cognitively active. Compared to a database of EEGs from normal adults, her pretest resting EEG also showed more beta activity, suggesting her mind was more active, even while resting, than the minds of nonpsychics.

In examining anecdotal ESP accounts from supposed psychics, Healy (1986) found indications of theta waves, which normally appear when one is falling asleep, a condition characterized by hypnagogic (i.e., presleep) images. If psychic claimants produce theta during ESP, this could mean that they have evoked a hypnagogic state, which facilitates mental imagery. Persinger developed the "Octopus" device to enhance theta waves; eight solenoids are placed around the head, which apply a series of 1 microtesla magnetic pulses to the brain to increase theta wave production (Richards et al., 2002). While the EEG of a telepathic receiver was monitored, a "sender" in another room was stimulated with the Octopus device. When the sender's brain was stimulated by the pulses, the receiver's EEG showed theta in the frontal and occipital lobes. In another study, Persinger et al. (2003) found that the psychic claimant, Ingo Swann, showed an unusual theta wave pattern during a remote viewing task.

In summary, two studies point to an ESP-theta connection, while three others are interesting in their own right. In this regard, it seems a useful idea to adjust tests for potential ESP ability to fit participants whose professions may be relevant to ESP (e.g., picture targets were used with artists, while a PK card game test was tailored for gamblers). The finding that a psychic claimant showed beta in her left frontal and temporal lobes, both during remote viewing and when resting, indicated a more active mind and brain than is seen with nonclaimants; hence, differences in brain structure and functioning may distinguish psychic claimants from other people (Persinger et al., 2003).

Using Event-Related Potentials

When people discuss an ESP experience, they describe a conscious recollection. However, ESP often bypasses conscious awareness. For instance, you may have a "gut feeling" that something is about to happen, but not know why you had the feeling unless the event occurs. If your body responds to future events without awareness, the signal may have been conveyed by your autonomic nervous system (ANS). To explore this possibility, parapsychologists have examined the unconscious electrical activity of the brain. In addition to registering the five brain waves, an EEG can register neuroelectric changes in voltage known as event-related potentials (ERPs; Kolb and Whishaw, 1990).

ERPs usually occur in response to sensory stimulation, such as when your arm is touched, your fingertip is pricked, or a light is flashed in your eyes. The resulting voltage change appears within several thousandths of a second afterwards, and can be positive or negative in polarity. ERPs appear in the cortical region that processes the sensory stimulus. For example, an ERP appears in the somatosensory cortex of the parietal lobe when your arm or fingers are touched, while a light flash produces an ERP in the primary visual cortex of the occipital lobe. EEG voltage signals with frequencies below 2 Hz are called slow cortical potentials (SCPs). One type of SCP, known as contingent negative variation (CNV) for its negative voltage polarity, occurs in the frontal lobe, and is involved in anticipation, expectation, and preparation for bodily movement (Walter et al., 1964).

Four studies by Warren, Don, and McDonough explored the possible role of ERPs in putative precognition. In each study, participants' EEGs were recorded while they participated in a computer-based task called ESPerciser™ (invented by Honorton, 1987). In this task, the computer screen flashes images of one of the four playing cards (spade, heart, club, or diamond) to the participant. Each flash allows the EEG to record an ERP for each image. Then, the four images are displayed together on the screen, and the participant is asked to guess which one the computer selected as the ESP target. After making their choices, the participants are shown the actual targets as feedback.

The ESPerciser™ can test clairvoyance as well as precognition. In a clairvoyance test, the computer selects the target *before* participants make their choices. In a precognition test, the computer selects the target *afterward*. In their first two studies, Warren et al. (1992, 1996) examined the EEG of psychic claimant Malcolm Bessent, who had previously succeeded on the ESPerciser™ (Honorton, 1987). Although Bessent's ESP scores in both studies were insignificant, his EEG showed a voltage difference between the ERPs recorded when he was looking at cards selected as targets and the ERPs recorded for nontarget cards. Compared to nontarget ERPs, the target ERPs had a greater negative voltage. In other words, Bessent's brain seemed to distinguish between targets and nontargets before he knew what cards were which (recall that the ERPs were recorded *before* he made his choice and was given feedback).

In the other two studies (Don et al., 1998; McDonough et al., 2002), the researchers recruited gamblers as participants. Not only did this allow them to see if gamblers succeeded on the precognition test (which they thought was a standard gambling task), but it also enabled them to see if the gamblers' brains displayed precognitive ERPs. Like Bessent, the gamblers scored at chance, but they too showed ERP voltage differences for target and nontarget cards.

Radin (1997) coined the term "presentiment" for unconscious precognitive responses by the ANS. To examine presentiment, McCraty et al. (2004) recorded participants' ERPs as they viewed pictures of emotional (violent and erotic) and neutral scenes (landscapes, fruit, trees, animals, and household items). In the four to six seconds *prior* to viewing an emotional picture, the participants displayed ERPs that were more negative in voltage than ERPs for neutral pictures. Two studies explored the role of SCPs in presentiment. In the first, Bierman and van Ditzhuijzen (2006) recorded participants' EEGs during a slot machine task. As with casino slots, three outcomes were possible: three different fruits, two identical fruits and one different, and three identical fruits. The third is termed a "winner," with about 12.5 percent chance of occurring, while the others are "losses." One second before receiving a "win," the participants showed a higher SCP than before a "loss," suggesting their brains were anticipating a win before they knew they had won.

In the second study, Radin and Lobach (2006) examined presentiment responses to an impending light flash. SCPs were recorded from participants while they were stimulated with light-emitting diodes fitted in a pair of opaque glasses. One second before a light flash, females showed a higher SCP than before the no-flash condition; in contrast, males showed a lower but insignificant SCP. Two studies also explored a CNV role in precognition. In the first, Levin and Kennedy (1975) recorded CNVs from participants watching a display that flashed either a red or a green light. Upon seeing the green light, the participants pressed a button as quickly as they could. The participants showed a higher CNV before the green light than before the red light, suggesting their brains were anticipating the green light and readying their bodies to respond with a button press. However, Hartwell (1978) attempted to repeat the result, but did not succeed.

In summary, five studies examined the relationship between ERPs and precognition. All showed voltage differences that suggest participants' brains distinguished between targets and nontargets. Again taking account of possible experimenter effect, three studies found a relationship between ERP and precognition, which suggests that the brains of participants distinguished between targets and nontargets on the basis of voltage. Two studies with different experimenters found SCP to be linked to presentiment, and two studies looked at CNV and precognition of which one was significant. Six of seven studies that measure brain voltage indicated that the brains of participants responded to future events without the owners of the brains being aware of this process. Because ERP, SCP, and CNV reflect normal brain functions, their association with precognition indicates that this may be a normal brain function.

Studies of Emotionally Connected Pairs

It takes two to tango and the same is true for telepathy experiments: there is always a so-called "sender" and a "receiver" in telepathy, which does not imply what (if anything) might be sent or received. Studies of reported telepathy from everyday life by

Sannwald (1963), Stevenson (1970), Persinger (1974), and Feather and Schmicker (2005) conclude that telepathic experiences occur primarily between pairs who are connected genetically or emotionally, while telepathy between strangers is less frequent. Experiments by Stuart (1946), Rice and Townsend (1962), Broughton and Alexander (1997), and Alexander and Broughton (2001) concluded that the same relationship is found in telepathy experiments. To determine if the brains of connected pairs are correlated, EEGs have been used. In a typical EEG-telepathy test, the two participants are in different rooms. In one room, the sender is seated in front of a monitor screen while the EEG is recorded; meanwhile, the receiver, who is attached to another EEG, relaxes in the other room. At various times, a bright flash from the screen stimulates the sender, producing a voltage change on the EEG. After the experiment, the EEGs of the sender and receiver are compared. If their brains are correlated, the receiver's EEG should show a corresponding voltage change during the sender's stimulation periods.

Two studies examined genetically related pairs. Duane and Behrendt (1965) tested 14 pairs of identical twins. To elicit alpha activity, the sending twins opened and closed their eyes in a lighted room. Meanwhile, the receiving twins sat quietly in a lit room with eyes open. Visual comparison of the EEG records showed similar alpha in two pairs of twins. In the other genetically related pair study, Persinger et al. (2003) tested four pairs of siblings. To stimulate the sender, the Octopus, known to generate theta waves, was used. When this happened, the receiver showed theta waves in the frontal and occipital lobes.

Four studies tested emotionally bonded pairs. In the first, Wackermann et al. (2003) had pairs spend 20 minutes together before testing to strengthen their empathic bond. During the sender's stimulation, the receiver showed voltage changes that were not seen in control receivers whose sender was either not stimulated, or there was no designated sender. In the second study, Standish et al. (2004) found significant correlations between emotionally connected pairs. In the third study, Radin (2004) also observed voltage changes between emotionally connected pairs. And, in the fourth study, where Kittenis et al. (2004) created brain maps from the EEGs of each emotionally connected pair, the maps revealed that as the sender's brain became electrically active during the stimulation, the receiver's occipital-parietal region was also activated.

In summary, six EEG correlation studies, conducted by different experimenters, showed correlations between the brains of connected pairs. Two were genetically related pairs, and four were emotionally bonded. One study found a theta-ESP correlation; another reported an alpha-ESP correlation, while the four others found EEG voltage changes in the brains of the receivers when the senders' brains were stimulated. These experiments are consistent with reports of telepathy experiences from everyday life and with other telepathy experiments, both types showing that telepathy may be relatively common between pairs who are genetically or emotionally connected.

Functional Magnetic Resonance Imaging

Functional magnetic resonance imaging (fMRI) has enabled neuroscientists to better monitor brain activity for medical and biological purposes. Unlike the common magnetic resonance image, which is static, an fMRI provides ongoing impressions of neural activity. Many fMRI studies commonly use a technique called blood oxygenation level dependent (BOLD) hemodynamic response, which measures the amount of oxygen in the brain from cerebral blood flow. Following the hypothesis that brain regions with the most oxygen-rich blood are the most active, BOLD make it possible to estimate the level of neural activity in a particular region during a specific behavior, thereby indicating a functional correlate of the behavior (Buxton, 2001).

Bierman and Scholte (2002) were the first to use BOLD fMRI to explore presentiment responses in the brain. They had participants view sequences of emotional (violent and erotic) and neutral (landscapes) pictures while undergoing fMRI scanning. Compared to neutral pictures, females showed higher BOLD activity in the visual cortex four seconds before seeing emotional pictures. Males' responses were quicker, showing higher BOLD in the visual cortex three seconds before viewing the emotional pictures, but only the erotic ones. When Bierman's brain was scanned, he too showed higher BOLD three seconds before seeing erotic pictures. The participants' brains evidently reacted to emotional pictures before they were consciously observed. Two additional experiments used BOLD fMRI to explore brain correlations between bonded pairs. In the first, by Standish et al. (2003), a male-female pair spent 10 minutes meditating together before participating in the experiment, in which they alternated as sender and receiver. While the receiver relaxed in the fMRI scanner, the sender viewed a flashing display in the control room. When the receiver was a female, her fMRI scan showed activation in her visual cortex when the male sender was stimulated. However, no activation was seen in the male's brain when he was the receiver.

In the second experiment, Richards et al. (2005) had another male-female pair, who had shown EEG correlations (in Standish et al., 2004) undergo fMRI scanning in the same manner as the first. While she was the receiver, the female's fMRI scan showed a decrease in visual cortex activity during stimulation periods. The male showed visual cortex activation during his first fMRI, but no change during his second. Last, we omit a study by Moulton and Kosslyn (2008) because they dismissed what they considered their main positive finding as an artifact, and we also omit a study by Venkatasubramanian et al. (2008) because of methodological flaws.

In summary, there are five fMRI studies of ESP, of which we omit two because of shortcomings. Of the remaining three, one suggests the visual cortex may reflect presentiment responses. The other two expand on brain correlations between bonded pairs. Both revealed changes in a receiver's visual cortex when a sender was stimulated but, strangely enough, one study found reduced cortical activity while the other found increased activity. These studies are also consistent with the EEG research discussed and provide additional evidence that the brains of emotionally connected people may be correlated.

Studies Involving the Cortical Hemispheres

Like the double face of the Roman god Janus, the brain's two cortical hemispheres look alike, but have different functions. To enable them to work in unison, they are bridged by a large neural bundle called the corpus callosum. Evidence for their different functions initially came from Sperry (1968), who had the corpus callosum of epileptic patients surgically cut to prevent seizures in one hemisphere from reaching the other. Based on observations of his "split-brain" patients, Sperry (1974) wrote:

> Each hemisphere has its own private sensations, perceptions, thoughts, and ideas, all of which are cut off from the corresponding experiences in the opposite hemisphere. Each left and right hemisphere has its own private chain of memories and learning experiences that are inaccessible to recall by the other hemisphere. In many respects, each disconnected hemisphere appears to have a separate "mind of its own." (p. 7)

Consistent with the facts that Broca's area in the left frontal lobe and Wernicke's area in the left temporal lobe are specialized for language, the left hemisphere is proficient at remembering words (Funnell et al., 2001) and processing written words (McAuliffe and Knowlton, 2001). The left hemisphere may also be specialized for controlling limb movement on both sides of the body (Rogers et al., 2004). Patients with left brain damage may suffer apraxia, the inability to perform skilled hand and finger movements (Carlson, 1992). Similarly, some patients have difficulty controlling the muscles of their mouths, thereby affecting their speech (Carlson, 1992). Other studies show that in tasks requiring hand movement, touch, or gesturing, the left hemisphere is more active than the right (Rogers et al., 2004).

In short, the left hemisphere represents our verbal, active, and analytical side (Springer and Deutsch, 1993). Sperry (1982) also noted that the right hemisphere is superior in performing nonverbal, nonarithmetical, and nonsequential tasks, such as "the reading of faces, copying of designs . . . the discrimination and recall of nondescript factual and visual shapes, spatial transpositions and transformations . . . and perceiving whole forms from a collection of parts" (pp. 57–58). Hence, the right hemisphere is adept at visual-spatial processing (Vogel et al., 2003). The right cortical hemisphere may also be adept at identifying objects. People tend to respond faster to objects shown in their left field of vision rather than their right (McAuliffe and Knowlton, 2001), and they tend to recall them better (Laeng et al., 2007).

If ESP is a brain function, the question arises if it is a function of both hemispheres or only of one? Broughton (1975) called attention to an observation by Myers (1885) that the scrawled automatic writing of mediums resembles communication attempts by patients whose right hemisphere has taken over because of damage to the left. Ehrenwald (1975, 1977) similarly compared telepathic receivers' drawings to the drawings of patients suffering from agnosia, the inability to attach meaning to sensory impressions due to left parietal and occipital lobe damage (Kolb and Whishaw, 1990). Ehrenwald (1977) wrote:

> The telepathic subject, like the patient suffering from agnosia, uses his *right*, rather than the dominant *left*, hemisphere for the central processing and organization of his impressions. The brain-injured patient has to fall back on the groping attempts of the "other side" of his brain to make up for the existing deficit on the left side. In turn, the telepathic percipient's productions carry all the hallmarks of the same difficulty in the organization and comprehension of his target material. That is, his responses likewise point to the part played in their origin by the right hemisphere. (p. 725, italics in original)

To get a more decisive answer, parapsychologists have examined ESP in relation to the cognitive abilities and the EEG activities of the cortex's two hemispheres. Braud (1975) pointed out that a right hemisphere mind-set is more in line with psychic claimants' descriptions of their mental state during ESP than the mind-set of the left, and considers it part of a "psi-conducive syndrome" (p. 142). He conducted a test in which one group of participants listened to an audiotape emphasizing a left hemisphere mind-set, while another group listened to a right hemisphere tape. A difference between the two groups was observed in the telepathy test that followed, with the left group displaying psi missing (Braud and Braud, 1975), scoring significantly more misses than hits.

Targ (1994, 2004) noticed that when remote viewers tried to rationally analyze a distant scene, their viewing quality diminished. Schwartz (2007), who tested the writer Michael Crichton and the psychic claimant Judith Orloff for remote viewing, found they used the free-flowing style of the right hemisphere, but switched to the analytical mode of the left when interpreting their impressions afterward. If the left hemisphere holds ESP captive, as it were, perhaps it will loosen its grip if distracted. Broughton (1976, 1977) explored this in two studies where participants made separate ESP responses with their left and right hands while either counting back from a thousand by threes or reading aloud from legal reports. He found a tendency for better ESP scores when participants used their left hands (controlled by the right hemisphere) and distracted the left hemisphere with reading.

About the same time, Maher and Schmeidler (1977) conducted a study to see how each hemisphere might influence ESP. To test the influence of the left hemisphere, they had participants reach into an opaque bag with their right hands and pull out one of 25 clear plastic cubes. Target cubes contained paper slips with the word "clover," while decoy cubes contained slips with "wrong." As they did so, the participants used their left hands to trace a pattern to engage the right hemisphere's visual-spatial abilities, and thus distract it from the choices made by the left hemisphere. To test the right hemisphere's influence, the participants again selected cubes from the bag, but now they used their left hands, and the target cubes contained actual clover leaves while the decoys had bits of plastic. During their selections, the participants solved syllogisms to distract the left hemisphere. Contrary to Broughton's findings, the participants were more successful when using their right hands and distracting the right hemisphere with pattern tracing. However, Maher et al. (1979) attempted to reproduce the finding, but did not succeed.

Broughton's and Maher et al.'s findings may be confounded by issues surrounding the tasks used to distract the left and right hemispheres. To have participants make ESP responses without speaking, Broughton (1976) requested them to lift one of five wooden geometric shapes with their hands, with each shape corresponding to an ESP card symbol. Maher and Schmeidler (1978) pointed out that handling the shapes might have engaged the right hemisphere because of its ability to identify objects. Broughton (1978) pointed out that Maher and Schmeidler's (1977, 1978) distraction of the right hemisphere through pattern tracing may have engaged the left hemisphere because of the hand skill needed for tracing.

Similarly, Alexander and Broughton (2001) examined participants' tendencies for right or left hemispheric dominance by having them take a battery of neuropsychological tests designed to measure the hemispheres' abilities. Right hemisphere dominant participants were found to score insignificantly fewer hits in a subsequent telepathy test than left dominant subjects.

Some studies examined hemispheric mentation in relation to belief in ESP. Roig and Neaman (1992) found that college students showing a preference for right hemispheric thinking had a stronger "belief" in ESP. Brugger et al. (1993) found that ESP "believers" showed better left eye accuracy for distinguishing words from nonsense syllables in a list than "nonbelievers." When the researchers examined the participants' EEGs, they found more beta waves in the right brains of believers than in nonbelievers (Pizzagalli et al., 2000).

Two studies (Schulter and Papousek, 2008; Sumich et al., 2008) attempted to replicate or extend Brugger et al.'s (1993) and Pizzagalli et al.'s (2000) findings that related to hemispheric correlates of belief. While the latter was about *belief in ESP*, the former studies were about *belief in the "paranormal,"* in which the authors included UFOs and astrology. Since the two studies are not exclusive to ESP, we have not included them.

In summary, in addition to four studies with insignificant results, two studies that explored ESP and hemispheric cognitive abilities showed opposite results. Three studies indicate that ESP believers tend to prefer right brain to left brain mentation. The reasoning for this finding ranges from the opinion that belief in ESP is a sign of psychopathology, to the opinion that belief in ESP may result from actual ESP experiences. All these studies need to be read with the understanding that hemispheric specialization is reversed in many left-handed people, and that hemispheric specialization is muted for speakers of Japanese and similar languages (e.g., Springer and Deutsch, 1993).

Maher (1986) examined how the two hemispheres process emotional material received through normal vision and through ESP. She first recorded participants' EEGs as they attempted to receive ESP impressions about two films playing in a distant, empty room. One film depicted interviews with people about love, and its intimate and empathic nature was expected to elicit strong emotion. The other film was more emotionally neutral, showing views of city buildings. Following the ESP test, Maher asked the participants to watch the films, again recording their EEGs. Males showed more right hemisphere activity during the love film, which is consistent with the view that the right brain is involved in emotion. In contrast, females showed more right hemisphere activity during the city film. Maher speculated that this unexpected reversal could be because "females, as a group, may be more analytical than males when evaluating or responding to emotional disclosures made by others" (p. 246). Maher then found that males and females processed the films the same way by ESP as they did when viewing them. That is, males again showed more right hemisphere activity while trying to perceive the love film by ESP, whereas females showed more right hemisphere activity while trying to perceive the city film. This finding suggests that vision and ESP utilize the same brain processes.

Maher's study was partly based on the premise that the right hemisphere is more highly specialized for emotion. Although several experiments support this view (Adolphs et al., 1996; Borod et al., 1998, 2001; Campbell, 1982; Heller et al., 1998), not all data have pointed in this direction (Murphy et al., 2003). Part of the reason may be a confound stemming from hemispheric differences between male and female brains (Cahill, 2006). Don et al. (1990) recorded multifrequency (delta, theta, alpha, beta) EEG data from psychic claimant Mel Doerr during psychometry readings (i.e., attempting to describe an unknown person while holding an object belonging to him or her). Although his ESP scores were at chance, Doerr showed significantly more EEG activity in his right hemisphere when correctly guessing the gender of the owner of the psychometric object. In contrast, there was more left hemispheric activity during incorrect guesses. In a test where McDonough et al. (1996) recorded multifrequency EEG data from McDonough himself during an ESPerciser™ task, he showed more alpha in his left hemisphere during correct guesses as compared to his right.

Using functional near-infrared spectroscopy, Kokubo et al. (2005) measured the amount of participants' cerebral blood flow as they attempted to describe pictures on a concealed computer screen. They found blood flow changes in the participants' right temporal lobes during ESP, and these changes tended to coincide with accurate impressions of the target. In summary, EEG measurements of hemispheric activity during ESP have produced mixed results. Two studies suggest ESP is processed by the left or both hemispheres, while two other studies suggest ESP is mostly handled by the right hemisphere.

The Role of Memory

A person's history is encompassed by a four-dimensional map of space and time, which is accessed by long-term memory. The hippocampus in the temporal lobe appears to be the main organ responsible for retrieval of memory, and electrical stimulation of the hippocampus can evoke hallucinatory flashbacks of places or events from the past (Bancaud et al., 1994). People with hippocampal damage may suffer from severe amnesia and be unable to form new long-term memories

(Schneider and Tarshis, 1995). Attached to the front of the hippocampus is the amygdala, the organ responsible for assigning emotion, and for regulating and expressing instinctive emotional reactions. Electrical stimulation of the amygdala can induce sudden feelings of fear (Gloor et al., 1982). Conversely, humans and animals whose amygdala has been damaged or removed may show reduced fear to threatening stimuli (Phelps and LeDoux, 2005). The amygdala's ability to regulate these reactions may derive in part from its modulating influence on the hypothalamus and the attached pineal gland (Schneider and Tarshis, 1995). The hippocampus and amygdala are part of the limbic system, located in the middle of the temporal lobe.

Penfield (1959) discovered that electrical stimulation of the temporal lobe (which he called "the interpretive cortex") evoked hallucinations in some neurosurgical patients relating to people and events in their past. The stimulation may have activated a neural circuit to the limbic structures, including the hippocampus. On the basis of Penfield's discovery, Roll (1966) suggested,

> If memory traces are a part of the ESP reception system and if the interpretive cortex specializes in the retrieval of memory traces, it is possible that it also plays a part in the ESP process. The interpretive cortex in that case would function as an "ESP cortex," having a similar relation to ESP stimuli as the visual cortex and optic nerve have to light rays. (p. 516)

Neppe (1983) also proposed that the functional area for possible ESP "could be the temporal lobe of the brain . . . because the temporal lobe is *the* great integrator of polymodal perceptual input" (p. 2, his emphasis). The hypothesis that ESP, unlike the ordinary senses, has no sensory mode of its own is consistent with these observations. Vision results in visual images, hearing in sounds, and so on for the other senses, but putative ESP has no sensory expression mode of its own and must borrow from other senses. In particular, ESP would have to rely on implicit memory, which is also the case in sense perception. To perceive and identify an object, the brain must call forth memories for similar objects perceived in the past. Irwin (1979) illustrated the use of implicit memory for ESP using an imaginary experience:

> Suppose that by ESP you learn of the death of your friend John in a car accident some distance away. Now, John has never died before, so there cannot have been a (single) trace in memory corresponding to John's death in his car. However . . . each discrete piece of information is already contained in memory at the time of the experience: there is stored information about John, about death, and so on. (p. 87)

The ESP response connects these traces to the experience that John has died in a car accident. Familiar sensory experiences do the same; if we had directly witnessed the car crash, the implicit memories of "John," "car," and so on would be activated in our minds so that we would immediately comprehend what we were seeing. The possibility that ESP uses the modalities of the other senses resolves the paradox that a person may be aware of the mental images evoked in the ESP experience, and yet be unaware of the source of the images, a form of source amnesia.

Abramowski (1914) gave a succinct description of telepathy when he described it as a process of cryptomnesia: that is, of hidden memory. Saltmarsh (1929) concluded from his work with the medium Mrs. Warren Elliott that she used her "subliminal memory" for her ESP responses. In discussing telepathy, Warcollier (1938) suggested that,

> The images which appear to the mind of the percipient under the form of hallucinations, dreams or more or less well-formed images, spring exclusively from his own mind, from his own conscious or subconscious memory. *There is no carrying of the visual impression from the agent to the percipient,* any more than there is actual carrying of a letter of the alphabet from the sending apparatus of a telegraph office to the receiving office. The transmission of the message consists in making the same letter *appear,* but it already *exists* at the receiving apparatus, along with all the others, before the transmission took place. (p. 133, his emphases)

Experiments have also provided evidence that long-term implicit memory may be part of the ESP response (see Palmer, 2006; Roll, 1966, 1975; Stanford, 2006). The possibility that memories may be building blocks for the ESP response is underscored by indications that people who do well in ESP also have good memories. While studying the medium Leonora Piper, William James (1889–1890) noticed that she displayed an exceptionally proficient memory for past sessions when in trance, while her waking memory was ordinary. Osty (1923) found that "good metagnomic subjects [i.e., psychic claimants] whose faculty is exercised in the waking state have exceptional memories" (p. 78). Rhine (1954) remarked that people experiencing precognition often marveled at the fact that the precognitive experience was "just like 'remembering' the future" (p. 121).

Several case studies indicate that reports of ESP experiences in everyday life are primarily about death and crisis (Feather and Schmicker, 2005; Persinger, 1974; Sannwald, 1963; Stevenson, 1970). Similarly, sense perception seems to unconsciously affect attention and memory to benefit one's well-being (Dolan, 2002). If you encounter a threat, the limbic system forms a long-lasting emotional memory so that you will respond appropriately if you face a similar threat. Brain imaging indicates that the amygdala is active during emotionally guided behavior, a role that disappears if it is damaged or removed (Phelps and LeDoux, 2005). Broughton (2006) suggested that the emotional system works in a similar way in ostensible ESP by influencing the selection of implicit memories for the ESP response. In this way, emotion would determine which images make it into consciousness. Similarly, the emotional system would influence unconscious ESP responses to emotional stimuli, as in presentiment. Broughton suggested that the involvement of the emotional system would be consistent with the spontaneous and largely uncontrollable nature of ESP.

Dolan (2002) pointed out that emotions "are less susceptible to our intentions than other psychological states insofar as they are often triggered, in the words of [William] James, 'in advance of, and often in direct opposition of our deliberate reason concerning them' " (p. 1191). Broughton (2006) added,

> Indeed, it seems the very nature of the emotional system's operation as a survival response system and decision-making system is that it is *unconscious and independent of our intentions*. That is precisely the type of system by which psi information may best serve survival-related needs. (p. 268, his emphasis)

Observations of the Temporal Lobe

The suggestion that the temporal lobe may play a role in ESP is supported by studies that found a relationship in the general population between the frequency of psi experiences and signs of temporal lobe sensitivity (Neppe, 1983; Persinger, 1984; Persinger and Makarec, 1987; Persinger and Valliant, 1985). The hippocampus has the lowest seizure threshold of any brain area (MacLean, 1970; Persinger, 1974), which means that it can be activated by electrical stimulation. In particular, people with complex partial seizure (CPS) may have temporal lobes that are electrically unstable due to small structural malformations that lead to minor dysfunction, and they may consequently exhibit small, sporadic discharges across the temporal and limbic regions. When this happens, the person may suddenly experience memory-like hallucinations, feelings of unreality or apprehension, sudden depression, or tingling sensations (Vignal et al., 2007). The origin of the malformations causing CPS can include congenital birth defects, mild head injuries, hypothermia, viral infection, and hypoxia (insufficient oxygen in brain tissue).

The increased electrical sensitivity of the temporal lobe may not be limited to CPS patients and extreme populations; several studies suggest that the general population is distributed along a continuum of temporal lobe sensitivity (Makarec and Persinger, 1990; Persinger and Makarec, 1987, 1993; Persinger and Richards, 1994; Roberts et al., 1990). People who claim frequent ESP experiences may be found at the upper end of this continuum. We should note that reported "ESP experiences" are not necessarily evidence of ESP and that the data discussed in this section are experiential not experimental.

Neppe (1983) found that members of a South African psychical research society who related several psi experiences to him showed more temporal lobe sensitivity than members who reported few or none. Persinger and his colleagues surveyed six groups of college students (a total of 414), and found that the frequency of ESP experiences among the students was related to higher temporal lobe sensitivity (Persinger, 1984; Persinger and Makarec, 1987; Persinger and Valliant, 1985). Palmer and Neppe (2003, 2004) reported a similar relation among patients at a neuropsychiatric treatment center.

Psychic claimants and mediums may belong to the upper end of the continuum, as well. A group of British researchers gave clinical interviews and neuropsychological tests to 17 psychic claimants "in training," noting that 11 showed temporal lobe dysfunction in their right hemispheres (Fenwick et al., 1985). Similarly, Persinger and Fisher (1990) found that women who regularly participated in a psychical study group showed elevated signs of CPS and reported more psi experiences than other women. Alexander (2000) noted that a psychic claimant scored high on a questionnaire partly designed to measure temporal lobe sensitivity. Some mediums have also shown increased temporal lobe sensitivity, whether on their EEG (Nelson, 1970) or through a questionnaire designed to measure CPS signs (Reinsel, 2003).

In summary, there are numerous apparent connections between ESP research data and the findings of neurobiology, including brain waves and other neuroelectric changes, neuroanatomy such as hemispheric differentiation and temporal lobe sensitivity, as well as memory processes. This does not mean that ESP can be reduced to neurobiology, but, rather, suggests that the two disciplines are quite compatible in a variety of ways. The claim that parapsychological data are contrary to mainstream science does not hold up under scrutiny, at least with respect to neurobiology.

Quantum Theory and Psi

Mainstream science has evolved considerably and is no longer based on classical physics, which opens up a variety of approaches to understanding psi from a present-day view of science. The famous thought experiment of Einstein, Podolsky, and Rosen (EPR; 1935), shows how quantum effects are produced. Briefly stated, EPR proposes that when a fundamental particle is split into X and Y, the two parts will remain correlated regardless of how far apart they are from each other. Before X or Y is measured on any detectors, each of the split particles in the system represents both X and Y with equal probability, a condition known as "quantum superposition." If part X is sent to detector 1, which is being observed by experimenter 1, and part Y is sent to detector 2, which is not connected to detector 1 in any way, the experimenter at detector 2 will of necessity observe Y for the other part. When experimenter 1 measures X on detector 1, the system is no longer in superposition, but has "collapsed" to X1 Y2. Objects that are in superposition have no definite location and cannot be measured, but when one is measured, the other is also determined, regardless of separation by time and space.

Einstein and his colleagues designed EPR, not as an illustration of how two particles are correlated across space without any signal passing from one to the other, but on the contrary to demonstrate the absurdity of the idea. Einstein believed that if detector 2 shows Y, it should be irrelevant if detector 1 showed X. The idea that detector 1 and experimenter 1 could affect detector 2 and experimenter 2, across space without any signal from 1 to 2, Einstein (1949) called "spooky action at a distance." Einstein was convinced that reality is independent of human observation, an assumption that is basic to classical physics and also to Westerners' common sense.

However, a mathematical restatement of the predictions of the EPR experiment by Bell (1964) showed that if Einstein and his colleagues were right, then the statistical predictions of quantum theory would be negated. The issue could not be addressed by another thought experiment, but required actual testing. Experiments by Aspect et al. (1981, 1982a, 1982b) confirmed the predictions of quantum theory and negated Einstein's local theory. This provided empirical evidence that "quantum entities that have interacted with each other remain mutually entangled" (Polkinghorne, 2002, p. 80). Since that time, quantum entanglement and with it EPR have been verified using multiple particles (Häffner et al., 2005; Pan et al., 2000; Sackett et al., 2000) and distances of several kilometers (Marcikic et al., 2004; Tittel et al., 1998). More importantly for our purpose, quantum superposition and entanglement have been experimentally extended to large-scale objects (Friedman et al., 2000; Julsgaard et al., 2001).

Something else needs to be said about EPR. The correlated pairs are conjugate or opposed, in that X and Y represent opposite spins of an electron; if the spin of X is clockwise, then the spin of Y has to be counterclockwise. Other conjugate pairs are position and momentum, and energy and time. "Inherent limitation on the simultaneous specification of such conjugate properties" (Jahn and Dunne, 1987, p. 211) leads to the Heisenberg principle of uncertainty. Going back to EPR, if the spins of the two electrons were the same, the two would be indistinguishable and represent the principle of indistinguishability. This principle in turn leads to the principle of exclusion, according to which two interacting particles cannot exist in the same state. These principles are not merely theoretical, but are seen in actual chemical reactions (Jahn and Dunne, 1987).

Vedral (2008) stated, "In less than a century, researchers have moved from distrusting entanglement because of its 'spooky action at a distance' to starting to regard it as an essential property of the macroscopic world" (p. 1004). If "spooky" is equated with psi, this is in fact what is empirically seen. [Nobel laureate] Josephson and Pallikari-Viras (1991) acknowledged the experimental evidence in quantum physics for instantaneous action at a distance, but argued that "the existence of such remote influences or connections is suggested more directly by experiments on phenomena such as telepathy (the direct connection of one mind with another) and PK (the direct influence of mind on matter)" (p. 199). From this perspective, quantum physics bridges parapsychology with mainline physical science. Quantum physics represents a revolution in epistemology no less than in physics because it is about *how* we know, not just *what* we know. Henry Stapp (2001) observed:

> A faraway system can instantly change when we learn something about a nearby system. ... If certain properties of two systems are known to be strongly correlated, then finding out about one system can tell us something about the other. For example, if we know that two particles start from some known point at the same time, and then move away from that point at the same speeds, but in opposite directions, then finding one of these particles at a certain point allows us to "know" where the other particle lies at that same instant: it must lie at the same distance from the starting point as the observed particle, but in the opposite direction. In this simple case, we do not think that the act of

observing one particle *causes* the other particle to *be* where it is. We realize that it is only our knowledge of the faraway system that has changed. This analogy allows us resolve … any mystery about an instantaneous faraway effect of a nearby act: if something faraway can be altered by a nearby act then it *must* be our knowledge. (His emphases, p. 1468)

Similarly, Stapp (2001) quoted Werner Heisenberg (1958):

The conception of the objective reality of the elementary particles has thus evaporated not into the cloud of some obscure new reality concept, but into the transparent clarity of a mathematics that represents no longer the behaviour of the particle but rather our knowledge of this behaviour. These findings have profound implications for understanding psi. (p. 1467)

The observations of Stapp and Heisenberg make it easier to understand quantum physics and its relationship to parapsychology.

On the basis of the fact that the velocity of light is measured the same in all directions regardless of the velocity of the measuring device, Costa de Beauregard (1998) stated, "An unexpected consequence, with far-reaching implications resulted: matter is extended in time no less than in space. Retrocognitive and precognitive flashes could then cross the border line of consciousness" (p. 316). Costa de Beauregard then mentioned PK via entropy and negentropy, and cited Lewis (1930): "A gain in entropy means loss of information, nothing more (p. 318)." In other words, physical entropy is missing information or "incomplete knowledge and control" at the microscopic level. Costa de Beauregard (1998) continued, "Reciprocal to the normal $N \rightarrow I$ transition there is the paranormal $I \rightarrow N$ one" (p. 318), where N stands for negentropy, I for information, and *paranormal* for PK. He then distinguished between internal and external PK, stating internal PK "is advocated by [Nobel laureate] Eccles (1986) as explaining voluntary motion" (p. 318) and external PK is implied by [Nobel laureate] Eugene Wigner on the basis of "his own symmetry arguments that 'reciprocal' to the action of matter upon mind, there must exist a 'direct action of mind upon matter'" (p. 318).

In summary, quantum theory is not concerned about reality as much as about information. The seemingly paradoxical fact that distant objects and events are related according to quantum theory is resolved because information about a near system provides information about a similar distant system. In this way, two individuals, who are distant from each other, may be connected, as in telepathy; and a person may be connected with a physical object as in PK. Because matter is extended in both time and space, retrocognition (anomalous knowledge of past events) and precognition (anomalous knowledge of future events) may be explained in terms of physics; and because PK restores the missing information and control of entropy, reciprocal to the familiar negentropy to information transition, there has to be a psychokinetic transformation of information to negentropy. If we bring in the proposal that volition is due to PK, there would be an internal type of PK in addition to the familiar external type. External PK follows from the principle of symmetry that reciprocal to the action of matter upon mind, there has to be action of mind upon matter.

Recurrent Spontaneous Psychokinesis

According to our interpretation of quantum physics, large-scale objects no less than subatomic particles should follow the rules of quantum theory. Unlike ESP, where things are correlated at a distance without transmission of energy, the movement of large-scale objects entails expenditure of energy, and the farther or faster an object moves (at least under ordinary conditions) the more energy it spends. In contrast to familiar moving things, such as automobiles and airplanes that have internal sources of energy, the inanimate object of recurrent spontaneous psychokinesis (RSPK, better known as "poltergeist" phenomena) may be impelled by energy from their source. They seem to behave like stones thrown from a volcano that fly certain distances depending on the energy that impelled them and on their weight. The weights of RSPK that move through the air have not been measured, but they usually appear to be a few ounces, such as cups and glasses, that someone could easily toss about. The theory of conscious or unconscious throwing is the most likely explanation of flying objects because the incidents usually occur when a certain person is present, but in 116 cases of RSPK reported 1,612–1,977 individuals considered reputable (at least by their peers) witnessed and described one or more incidents that appeared genuine (Roll, 1977/1986).

For several cases, the witnesses included Roll (Roll, 1968; Roll and Pratt, 1971; Roll, 1972/2004, Ch. 11; Roll et al., 1973; 1974; Roll, 1993; Roll and Storey, 2004, Ch. 17). Although some of the cases are not immune to the machinations of clever hoaxsters, in other cases the hoaxing hypothesis seems difficult to sustain. In three of the cases, Roll and a coinvestigator were present when they observed the center of the incidents, the so-called RSPK agent, at the same time as objects moved in areas where no one other than the investigators were present (Roll and Pratt, 1971; Roll, 1972/2004, Ch. 11; Roll, 1993; Roll and Storey, 2004, Ch. 17). In most of the 116 cases, someone was identified as the focus of the incidents, and therefore seemed to be their "agent" or "source." Assuming a physical energy, the number of occurrences should decrease with increased distance from this source. In six cases that involved Roll, in which the location of the agent was known when an object moved, the distance between the agent and the starting point of the object was measured (i.e., by tape measure and subsequently divided into objects that moved when they were 1–5 feet, 6–10 feet, 11–15 feet, etc., from the agent). In these six cases, the number of object movements decreased with increased distance from the agent. Assuming a physical energy, the decreases may have been due to the inverse square function, the exponential decay function, or both. The inverse square function describes the dispersal of energy, such as light, from a point source into space, while the exponential decay function describes the attenuation of light by the medium through which it travels, such as air or water.

Because both functions may apply to RSPK, Roll and Joines (2001) construed a formula that combines the two functions and applied it to the three cases for which the evidence for RSPK seemed compelling: data from two cases fit exactly the same equation with the same constants, while the data from the third (Roll and Joines, 2001) fit the equation with different constants.

Anomalous Light Phenomena

Light is converted to heat, that is, kinetic energy, when it travels through air and water, and thereby conforms both to the inverse square and to the exponential decay function. Because RSPK represents kinetic energy, the energy could be light, but this would have to be in the invisible spectrum and its source would have to be the agent. There have been three published studies of anomalous light emitted by people. In 1962 strong flashes of light were apparently produced at night by a 19-year-old girl, Frances Howell, and investigated by Roll and the local police (Roll, 1972/2004). Two police officers who watched Howell when the lights came on could find no normal source. Roll, who watched the house from outside, saw no one shine a light into the house. Because no ordinary source could be found for the lights and because Howell was always near when they happened, they seemed to be due to PK.

The other light studies are experimental. In an unpublished study in the 1970s, Joines and Roll discovered that a supposed psychic healer, Karen Getsla, built up an electrical charge on her body and emitted photons from her hands when she brought them near to a photomultiplier tube and concentrated on "sending healing energy." This resulted in a wave with a wavelength peak of 385 nanometers, which dropped off to progressively lower values. Since the visible spectrum consists of wavelengths between 700 and 400 nanometers (red to violet), 385 nanometers is in the violet to ultraviolet range. This is close to visible, and there were occasions when a faint light seemed to emanate from Getsla in the darkened room.

Baumann et al. (2005) examined a young man who twice produced large spikes on the photomultiplier, the first of 205,535 counts per half-second, the second of 42,411 counts, with the baseline being less than 20 counts. Each count corresponds to 4–5 photons of ultraviolet light at 385 nanometers, the same frequency Joines and Roll measured from Getsla. Each spike was accompanied by a negative voltage surge of more than −1.0 volts from an electrode on the man's upper left arm, which caused the computer program to freeze. The study then had to be terminated because the effort resulted in health problems for the man (p. 221). Neither Getsla nor the young man was known to cause object movements, but the fact that they transmitted ultraviolet light could indicate that RSPK agents do something similar.

Assuming RSPK agents belong to the rare breed of people who may be able to generate light, the question remains, how can light make objects move? According to Blanchard et al. (1959), the state of an object, including its location, is determined

by four quantum numbers, one of which refers to the spin of an electron. In principle, any of the numbers may be changed by a signal from an agent, but changing the
direction of electron spin requires a very small amount of signal energy for an interaction to occur. If it does occur, the object becomes unstable and may immediately
move to another location where it is again stable. This change may be induced by
an applied magnetic field. RSPK is associated with two types of electromagnetism,
one originating in space, the other in the agent. It has been found that the onset of
RSPK is apparently associated with above-average geomagnetic activity (Gearhart
and Persinger, 1986; Roll and Gearhart, 1974). Such activity can cause seizures in
epileptic rats (Michon and Persinger, 1997; Persinger, 1996), and seizures have been
more common during increased geomagnetism (Rajaram and Mitra, 1981). The
RSPK of Tina Resch began in the midst of three days of increased geomagnetic activity, a so-called geomagnetic storm (Persinger and Roll, 1993). A cursory look at the
subsequent RSPK did not indicate a connection with geomagnetic activity; such
activity may only start the RSPK engine, after which it may run by emotional tension. In this context, it is relevant that this individual had a major confrontation with
her father that coincided with the geomagnetic storm. While the storm subsided, the
emotional tension within the family continued and may have led to a continuation of
the RSPK. The neuronal discharges that seemed to bring on RSPK appear to be
electromagnetic and may thereby provide signals to objects, as discussed by Blanchard et al. (1959) and congruent with the anomalous neuroelectric impulses that
were detected in Resch's brain stem (Roll and Storey, 2004, Ch. 19).

Based on the familiar rule that negentropy leads to information, there might be a
reciprocal rule that information leads to negentropy, that is to PK, which would then
be an expected phenomenon, according to quantum theory, rather than an anomaly.
There is a second consequence of quantum theory for PK. Because matter is
extended in time as well as space, this entails retroactive PK and pre-PK. In RSPK
cases from Indianapolis (Roll, 1970), Miami (Roll and Pratt, 1971), and elsewhere
(Roll, 1972/2004), there were reports of occurrences when the agent was absent.

In addition, fundamental particles behave both like waves and like particles. If the
same is true for the large-scale objects of RSPK, this may explain some features of
their movement. RSPK may conform to the inverse square and exponential decay
functions that ordinarily apply to waves and not to material objects. While light
waves on earth may move thousands of miles, RSPK objects seem to travel only several feet before they fall to the ground. The objects do not move at the speed of
waves, but they are rapid.

Four Dimensional Space-Time?

RSPK objects sometimes seem to penetrate matter. Grottendieck (1906) claimed
that stones fell from the roof of his bedroom in Sumatra. He climbed up

and examined [the roof from which] the stones were flying. They came right through the
"Kadjang," but there were no holes in the kadjang. This kadjang is [a building material]

that cannot be penetrated (not even with a needle) without making a hole. Each kadjang is one single leaf of about 2 by 3 feet in size. It is a specialty of the neighborhood of Palembang. It is very tough and offers a strong resistance to penetration. (pp. 262–263)

One investigator visited a home where RSPK was said to occur and was told that objects disappeared and were then seen falling to the ground outside the house. The investigator put a bottle of perfume and a bottle of tablets on the kitchen table, asked the occupants to go outside, closed the windows and doors, and also went outside: "After a short time, the perfume bottle appeared in the air outside the house, and a bit later on, the bottle of tablets appeared in the air at the height of the roof and fell to the ground in a zigzag manner" (Bender, 1969, p. 96). In 18 of 105 cases of moving objects in Roll's (1977/1986) survey, some of the objects were said to move through walls or other obstacles. If material objects exist in four-dimensional space-time, such incidents become less mysterious.

A defining characteristic of RSPK is that objects do not seem to move when watched. If the object happens to be close to the agent and if the observer is looking at the agent, the object may be seen the moment after it takes off. Things always or nearly always happen when the agent is in the company of others, especially when he or she is being observed, but observation of the object is another matter. If the observer looks at an object that has previously moved, it will stay in place until the observer looks away, when it again may move. Filming or video recording an active area also seems to stop the occurrences until the camera is turned off (Roll and Pratt, 1971; Roll and Storey, 2004). However, audio recording has no perceptible effect, as the crashing sounds from objects hitting the floor around one participant were recorded on Roll's tape recorder (Roll and Storey, 2004).

The explanation for this phenomenon (if trickery can be excluded) may be the so-called quantum Zeno effect. Ourjoumtsev (2008) wrote, "Before picking up the phone and calling a technician to fix a faulty microwave oven, there are always a few simple things one should check . . . . So far, 'stop looking at it' has not been part of the checklist" (p. 880). He referred to an experiment by Bernu et al. (2008) where the buildup of a microwave field inside a resonating cavity was inhibited by measuring, and thereby observing, the number of photons in the field. Josephson (personal communication, 2008) suggested that the quantum Zeno effect may account for the observer effect in RSPK.

Conclusion

Psi has been problematic for mainstream science because of the absence of physical stimuli between the people and objects involved, and the uncertain way in which the brain handles ostensible psi. These two problems may be overcome by considering psi in the light of quantum theory and neurobiology. Quantum theory demonstrates correlations between distant objects that resemble ESP connections. It asserts that the physical world we perceive is largely determined by the conscious observer, a notion also congruent with ESP and that may also account for PK. Studies with both normal and psychic claimants suggest psi is associated with well-known neurobiological processes, especially with brain waves in the alpha and theta range. On the other hand, there is little if any evidence that ESP is facilitated by alpha feedback, frequency, or amplitude.

An especially interesting finding from studies of people who claim no psychic ability is that precognition (including presentience) may be associated with brain voltage as shown by ERP, SCP, and CNV. Because ERP, SCP, and CNV reflect normal brain functions, their seeming association with precognitive occurrences indicates that precognition may likewise be a normal brain function. There are indications that ESP may be associated with the right brain hemisphere of ordinary people, but there is little if any experimental confirmation of this. Frequent ESP experiences among the general population may also be associated with increased temporal lobe sensitivity.

There appear to be two kinds of psychokinesis, micro-PK, which is usually inferred from the nonrandom behavior of random event generators (REGs), and macro-PK, which is directly observed. Micro-PK, in turn, may be internal or external. Internal micro-PK may underlie voluntary behavior within the body, while external micro-PK appears as voluntary behavior that occurs outside the body. Several studies with simultaneous EEG recording found micro-PK to be associated with alpha wave activity, while several other studies that explored attempts at voluntary control over brain waves suggest such attempts may have a PK component.

In the type of macro-PK known as RSPK, objects seem to follow rules that govern the attenuation of light waves (inverse square and exponential decay), and the distance they travel is much shorter. Material objects usually obey the classical Newtonian laws, but objects affected by RSPK seem to follow the rule of quantum theory that things are both matter-like and wave-like. Some individuals seem to emit light. If the same is true for RSPK, a light signal from the agent may affect one of the four quantum numbers that keep an object in place, causing it to be unstable and move to another location where it becomes stable. There are other features of RSPK that seem to follow quantum theory, such as the quantum Zeno effect that prevents an object in direct view from moving.

Pratt (1974) wrote, "acceptance of the findings of parapsychology by other scientists will not occur until a theory is available that 'makes sense' of psi" (p. 134). Combining quantum theory and neurobiology with parapsychology may provide such a theory. Rhine (1962) stated, "When psi capacities transcend space or time . . . they are revealing fundamental properties of the human mind as a whole" (p. 153), a view with which many quantum physicists would agree. As d'Espagnat (1979) stated, "The doctrine that the world is made up of objects whose existence is independent of human consciousness turns out to be in conflict with quantum mechanics and with facts established by experiment" (p. 158).

Acknowledgments

B. J. W. gratefully acknowledges support from the Parapsychology Foundation. Both authors express their gratitude to Cheryl Alexander, Ph.D., and Ruth Reinsel, Ph.D., for providing them with copies of their research papers.

References

Abramowski, E. (1914). *Le subsconscient normal*. Paris: Librarie Felix Alcan.

Adolphs, R., Damasio, H., Tranel, D., and Damasio, A. R. (1996). Cortical systems for the recognition of emotion in facial expressions. *Journal of Neuroscience, 16*, 7678–7687.

Alexander, C. H. (2000). Neurophysiological and psychological assessment of an individual experiencing anomalous mental phenomena: A second case study. *Proceedings of Presented Papers: The Parapsychological Association 43rd Annual Convention*, 2–13.

Alexander, C. H., and Broughton, R. S. (2001). Cerebral hemisphere dominance and ESP performance in the autoganzfeld. *Journal of Parapsychology, 65*, 397–416.

American Society for Psychical Research, Research Committee. (1959). Report of the research committee for 1958. *Journal of the American Society for Psychical Research, 53*, 69–71.

Aspect, A., Graingier, P., and Roger, G. (1981). Experimental tests of realistic local theories via Bell's theorem. *Physical Review Letters, 47*, 460–463.

Aspect, A., Grangier, P., and Roger, G. (1982a). Experimental realization of Einstein-Podolsky-Rosen-Bohm *gedankenexperiment*: A new violation of Bell's inequalities. *Physical Review Letters, 49*, 91–94.

Aspect, A., Grangier, P., and Roger, G. (1982b). Experimental tests of Bell's inequalities using time-varying analyzers. *Physical Review Letters, 49*, 1804–1807.

Bancaud, J., Brunet-Bourgin, F., Chauvel, P., and Halgren, E. (1994). Anatomical origin of déjà vu and vivid 'memories' in human temporal lobe epilepsy. *Brain, 117*, 71–90.

Baumann, S., Joines, W. T., Kim, J., and Zile (2005). Energy emissions from an exceptional subject. *Proceedings of Presented Papers: The Parapsychological Association 48th Annual Convention*, 219–223.

Bell, J. S. (1964). On the Einstein-Podolsky-Rosen paradox. *Physics, 1*, 195–200.

Bender, H. (1969). New developments in poltergeist research: Presidential address. *Proceedings of the Parapsychological Association, 6*, 81–102.

Bernu, J., Deléglise, S., Sayrin, C., Kuhr, S., Dotsenko, I., Brune, M., Raimond, J. M., and Haroche, S. (2008). Freezing coherent field growth in a cavity by the quantum Zeno effect. *Physical Review Letters, 101*, 180402-1–180402-4.

Bierman, D. J., and Scholte, H. S. (2002). Anomalous anticipatory brain activation preceding exposure of emotional and neutral pictures. *Proceedings of Presented Papers: The Parapsychological Association 43rd Annual Convention*, 25–36.

Bierman, D. J., and van Ditzhuijzen, J. (2006). Anomalous slow cortical components in a slot-machine task. *Proceedings of Presented Papers: The Parapsychological Association 49th Annual Convention*, 5–19.

Blanchard, C. H., Burnett, C. R., Stoner, R., and Weber, R. L. (1959). *Introduction to modern physics*. New York: Prentice-Hall.

Borod, J. C., Cicero, B. A., Obler, L. K., Welkowitz, J., Erhan, H. M., Santschi, C., Grunwald, I. S., Agosti, R. M., and Whalen, J. R. (1998). Right hemisphere emotional perception: Evidence across multiple channels. *Neuropsychology, 12*, 446–458.

Borod, J. C., Zgaljardic, D., Tabert, M. H., and Koff, E. (2001). Asymmetries of emotional perception and expression in normal adults. In G. Gainotti (Ed.), *Handbook of Neuropsychology* (Vol. 5, 2nd ed., pp. 181–205). Amsterdam: Elsevier.

Braud, W. G. (1975). Psi-conducive states. *Journal of Communication, 25,* 142–152.

Braud, W. G., and Braud, L. W. (1975). The psi conducive syndrome: Free response GESP performance following evocation of "left-hemispheric" vs. "right-hemispheric" functioning. In J. D. Morris, W. G. Roll, and R. L. Morris (Eds.), *Research in Parapsychology 1974* (pp. 17–20). Metuchen, NJ: Scarecrow Press.

Broughton, R. S. (1975). Psi and the two halves of the brain. *Journal of the Society for Psychical Research, 48,* 133–147.

Broughton, R. S. (1976). Possible brain hemisphere laterality effects on ESP performance. *Journal of the Society for Psychical Research, 48,* 384–399.

Broughton, R. S. (1977). Brain hemisphere differences in psi-influenced reaction time. In J. D. Morris, W. G. Roll, and R. L. Morris (Eds.) *Research in Parapsychology 1976* (pp. 86–88). Metuchen, NJ: Scarecrow Press.

Broughton, R. S. (1978). Comments on "Cerebral Lateralization Effects in ESP Processing." *Journal of the American Society for Psychical Research, 72,* 384–389.

Broughton, R. S. (2006). Memory, emotion and the receptive psi process. *Journal of Parapsychology, 70,* 255–274.

Broughton, R. S., and Alexander, C. H. (1997). Autoganzfeld II: An attempted replication of the PRL autoganzfeld research. *Journal of Parapsychology, 61,* 209–226.

Brugger, P., Gamma, A., Muri, R., Schäfer, M., and Taylor, K. I. (1993). Functional hemispheric asymmetry and belief in ESP: Towards a "neuropsychology of belief." *Perceptual and Motor Skills, 77,* 1299–1308.

Buxton, R. B. (2001). *Introduction to Functional Magnetic Resonance Imaging: Principles and techniques.* New York: Cambridge University Press.

Cadoret, R. J. (1964). An exploratory experiment: Continuous EEG recording during clairvoyant card tests [Abstract]. *Journal of Parapsychology, 28,* 226.

Cahill, L. (2006). Why sex matters for neuroscience. *Nature Reviews Neuroscience, 7,* 477–484.

Cahn, B. R., and Polich, J. (2006). Meditation states and traits: EEG, ERP, and neuroimaging studies. *Psychological Bulletin, 132,* 180–211.

Campbell, R. (1982). The lateralisation of emotion: A critical review. *International Journal of Psychology, 17,* 211–229.

Carlson, N. R. (1992). *Foundations of physiological psychology* (2nd ed.). Boston: Allyn and Bacon.

Costa de Beauregard, O. (1998). The paranormal is not excluded from physics. *Journal of Scientific Exploration, 12,* 315–320.

d'Espagnat, B. (1979). The quantum theory and reality. *Scientific American, 241,* 158–181.

Dolan, R. J. (2002). Emotion, cognition, and behavior. *Science, 298,* 1191–1194.

Don, N. S., McDonough, B. E., and Warren, C. A. (1990). EEG effects associated with psi-hitting and psi-missing in a token-object task. In L. A. Henkel and J. Palmer (Eds.), *Research in parapsychology 1989* (pp. 53–57). Metuchen, NJ: Scarecrow Press.

Don, N. S., McDonough, B. E., and Warren, C. A. (1998). Event-related brain potential (ERP) indicators of unconscious psi: A replication using subjects unselected for psi. *Journal of Parapsychology, 62,* 127–145.

Duane, T. D., and Behrendt, T. (1965). Extrasensory electroencephalographic induction between identical twins. *Science, 150,* 367.

Eccles, J. C. (1986). Do mental events cause neural events analogously to the probability fields of quantum mechanics? *Proceedings of the Royal Society of London B, 227,* 411–428.

Ehrenwald, J. (1975). Cerebral localization and the psi syndrome. *Journal of Nervous and Mental Disease, 161,* 393–398.

Ehrenwald, J. (1977). Psi phenomena and brain research. In B. B. Wolman (Ed.), *Handbook of Parapsychology* (pp. 716–729). New York: Van Nostrand Reinhold.

Einstein, A. (1949). In P. A. Schilpp (Ed.), *Albert Einstein: Philosopher-scientist.* Evanston, IL: The Library of Living Philosophers.

Einstein, A., Podolsky, B., and Rosen, N. (1935). Can quantum-mechanical description of physical reality be considered complete? *Physical Review, 47,* 777–780.

Feather, S. R., and Schmicker, M. (2005). *The gift: ESP, the extraordinary experiences of ordinary people.* New York: St. Martin's Press.

Fenwick, P., Galliano, S., Coate, M. A., Rippere, V., and Brown, D. (1985). 'Psychic sensitivity', mystical experience, head injury and brain pathology. *British Journal of Medical Psychology, 58,* 35–44.

Friedman, J. R., Patel, V., Chen, W., Tolpygo, S. K., and Lukens, J. E. (2000). Quantum superposition of distinct macroscopic states. *Nature, 406,* 43–46.

Funnell, M. G., Corballis, P. M., and Gazzaniga, M. S. (2001). Hemispheric processing asymmetries: Implications for memory. *Brain and Cognition, 46,* 135–139.

Gearhart, L., and Persinger, M. A. (1986). Geophysical variables and behavior: XXXIII. Onsets of historical and contemporary poltergeist episodes occurred with sudden increases in geomagnetic activity. *Perceptual and Motor Skills, 62,* 463–466.

Gloor, P., Olivier, A., Quesney, L. F., Andermann, F., and Horowitz, S. (1982). The role of the limbic system in experiential phenomena of temporal lobe epilepsy. *Annals of Neurology, 12,* 128–144.

Grottendieck, W. G. (1906). A poltergeist case. *Journal of the Society for Psychical Research, 12,* 260–266.

Häffner, H., Hänsel, W., Roos, C. F., Benhelm, J., Chek-al-kar, D., Chwalla, M., Körber, T., Rapol, U. D., Riebe, M., Schmidt, P. O., Becher, C., Gühne, O., Dür, W., and Blatt, R. (2005). Scalable multiparticle entanglement of trapped ions. *Nature, 438,* 643–646.

Hartwell, J. W. (1978). Contingent negative variation as an index of precognitive information. *European Journal of Parapsychology, 2,* 83–103.

Healy, J. (1986). Hippocampal kindling, theta resonance, and psi. *Journal of the Society for Psychical Research, 53,* 352–368.

Heisenberg, W. (1958). The representation of nature in contemporary physics. *Daedalus, 87,* 95–108.

Heller, W., Nitschke, J. B., and Miller, G. A. (1998). Lateralization in emotion and emotional disorders. *Current Directions in Psychological Science, 7,* 26–32.

Honorton, C. (1969). Relationship between EEG alpha activity and ESP card-guessing performance. *Journal of the American Society for Psychical Research, 63,* 365–374.

Honorton, C. (1987). Precognition and real-time ESP performance in a computer task with an exceptional subject. *Journal of Parapsychology, 51,* 291–321.

Honorton, C., and Carbone, M. (1971). A preliminary study of feedback augmented EEG alpha activity and ESP card-guessing performance. *Journal of the American Society for Psychical Research, 65,* 66–74.

Honorton, C., Davidson, R., and Bindler, P. (1971). Feedback-augmented EEG alpha, shifts in subjective state, and ESP card-guessing performance. *Journal of the American Society for Psychical Research, 65*, 308–323.

Irwin, H. J. (1979). *Psi and the mind: An information processing approach.* Metuchen, NJ: Scarecrow Press.

Jahn, R. G., and Dunne, B. J. (1987). *Margins of reality: The role of consciousness in the physical world.* New York: Harcourt Brace Jovanovich.

James, W. (1889–1890). A record of observations of certain phenomena of trance. *Proceedings of the Society for Psychical Research, 6*, 443–457.

Josephson, B. D., and Pallikari-Viras, F. (1991). Biological utilization of quantum nonlocality. *Foundations of Physics, 21*, 197–207.

Julsgaard, B., Kozhekin, A., and Polzik, E. S. (2001). Experimental long-lived entanglement of two macroscopic objects. *Nature, 413*, 400–403.

Kittenis, M., Caryl, P. G., and Stevens, P. (2004). Distant psychophysiological interaction effects between related and unrelated participants. *Proceedings of Presented Papers: The Parapsychological Association 47th Annual Convention*, 67–76.

Kokubo, H., Yamamoto, M., and Wantanabe, T. (2005). Impression and spontaneous blood flow change at the temporal lobe while guessing for a hidden figure. *Journal of International Society of Life Information Science, 23*, 306–309.

Kolb, B., and Whishaw, I. Q. (1990). *Fundamentals of human neuropsychology* (3rd ed.). New York: W. H. Freeman.

Laeng, B., Øvervoll, M., and Steinsvik, O. O. (2007). Remembering 1500 pictures: The right hemisphere remembers better than the left. *Brain and Cognition, 63*, 136–144.

Levin, J., and Kennedy, J. (1975). The relationship of slow cortical potentials to psi information in man [Abstract]. *Journal of Parapsychology, 39*, 25–26.

Lewis, L., and Schmeidler, G. R. (1971). Alpha relations with non-intentional and purposeful ESP after feedback. *Journal of the American Society for Psychical Research, 65*, 455–467.

MacLean, P. D. (1970). The limbic brain in relation to the psychoses. In P. Black (Ed.), *Physiological correlates of emotion* (pp. 129–146). New York: Academic Press.

Maher, M. (1986). Correlated hemispheric asymmetry in the sensory and ESP processing of 'emotional' and 'nonemotional' stimuli. *European Journal of Parapsychology, 6*, 217–257.

Maher, M., Peratsakis, D., and Schmeidler, G. R. (1979). Cerebral lateralization effects in ESP processing: An attempted replication. *Journal of the American Society for Psychical Research, 73*, 167–177.

Maher, M., and Schmeidler, G. R. (1977). Cerebral lateralization effects in ESP processing. *Journal of the American Society for Psychical Research, 71*, 261–271.

Maher, M., and Schmeidler, G. R. (1978). Correspondence: The authors reply to Mr. Broughton. *Journal of the American Society for Psychical Research, 72*, 389–392.

Makarec, K., and Persinger, M. A. (1990). Electroencephalographic validation of a temporal lobe signs inventory in a normal population. *Journal of Research in Personality, 24*, 323–327.

Marcikic, I., de Riedmatten, H., Tittel, W., Zbinden, H., Legré, M., and Gisin, N. (2004). Distribution of time-bin entangled qubits over 50 km of optical fiber. *Physical Review Letters, 93*, 180502–180503.

May, E. (2001). ESP and the brain: Current status. *3^0 Simpósio da Fundação Bial: Aquém e Além do Cérebro* [3rd Symposium of the Bial Foundation: Behind and Beyond the Brain] (pp. 321–352). Porto, Portugal: Fundação Bial.

McAuliffe, S. P., and Knowlton, B. (2001). Hemispheric differences in object identification. *Brain and Cognition, 45*, 119–128.

McCraty, R., Atkinson, M., and Bradley, R. T. (2004). Electrophysiological evidence of intuition: Part 2. A system-wide process? *Journal of Alternative and Complementary Medicine, 10*, 325–336.

McDonough, B. E., Don, N. S., and Warren, C. A. (1994). EEG in a ganzfeld psi task. *Proceedings of Presented Papers: The Parapsychological Association 37th Annual Convention*, 273–283.

McDonough, B. E., Don, N. S., and Warren, C. A. (1996). Mind, brain, and behavior: A preliminary study of their interrelationships during performance on a psi task. In E. W. Cook (Ed.), *Research in parapsychology 1992* (pp. 12–16). Lanham, MD: Scarecrow Press.

McDonough, B. E., Don, N. S., and Warren, C. A. (2000). Gamma band ("40 Hz") EEG and unconscious target detection in a psi task [Abstract]. *Journal of Parapsychology, 64*, 247.

McDonough, B. E., Don, N. S., and Warren, C. A. (2002). Differential event-related potentials to targets and decoys in a guessing task. *Journal of Scientific Exploration, 16*, 187–206.

Michon, A. L., and Persinger, M. A. (1997). Experimental simulation of the effects of increased geomagnetic activity upon nocturnal seizures in epileptic rats. *Neuroscience Letters, 224*, 53–56.

Morris, R. L., and Cohen, D. (1969). A preliminary experiment on the relationship among ESP, alpha rhythm and calling patterns. *Proceedings of the Parapsychological Association, 6*, 22–23.

Morris, R. L., Roll, W. G., Klein, J., and Wheeler, G. (1972). EEG patterns and ESP results in forced-choice experiments with Lalsingh Harribance. *Journal of the American Society for Psychical Research, 66*, 253–268.

Moulton, S. T., and Kosslyn, S. M. (2008). Using neuroimaging to resolve the psi debate. *Journal of Cognitive Neuroscience, 20*, 182–192.

Murphy, F. C., Nimmo-Smith, I., and Lawrence, A. D. (2003). Functional neuroanatomy of emotions: A meta-analysis. *Cognitive, Affective, & Behavioral Neuroscience, 3*, 207–233.

Myers, F. W. H. (1885). Automatic writing. *Proceedings of the Society for Psychical Research, 8*, 1–63.

Nelson, G. K. (1970). Preliminary study of the electroencephalograms of mediums. *Parapsychologia, 4*, 30–35.

Neppe, V. M. (1983). Temporal lobe symptomatology in subjective paranormal experiences. *Journal of the American Society for Psychical Research, 77*, 1–28.

Osty, E. (1923). *Supernormal faculties in man.* London: Methuen.

Ourjoumtsev, A. (2008). Don't look now. *Nature, 456*, 880–881.

Palmer, J. (2006). Memory and ESP: A review of the experimental literature. *6° Simpósio da Fundação Bial: Aquém e Além do Cérebro* [6th Symposium of the Bial Foundation: Behind and Beyond the Brain] (pp. 121–147). Porto, Portugal: Fundação Bial.

Palmer, J., and Neppe, V. M. (2003). A controlled analysis of subjective paranormal experiences in temporal lobe dysfunction in a neuropsychiatric population. *Journal of Parapsychology, 67*, 75–97.

Palmer, J., and Neppe, V. M. (2004). Exploratory analyses of refined predictors of subjective ESP experiences and temporal lobe dysfunction in a neuropsychiatric population. *European Journal of Parapsychology, 19*, 44–65.

Pan, J.-W., Bouwmeester, D., Daniell, M., Weinfurter, H., and Zeilinger, A. (2000). Experimental test of quantum nonlocality in three-photon Greenberger-Horne-Zeilinger entanglement. *Nature, 403*, 515–518.

Penfield, W. (1959). The interpretive cortex. *Science, 129*, 1719–1725.

Persinger, M. A. (1974). *The paranormal* (Vols. 1 and 2). New York: M.S.S. Information Corporation.

Persinger, M. A. (1984). Propensity to report paranormal experiences is correlated with temporal lobe signs. *Perceptual and Motor Skills, 59*, 583–586.

Persinger, M. A. (1996). Enhancement of limbic seizures by nocturnal application of experimental magnetic fields that simulate the magnitude and the morphology of increases in geomagnetic activity. *International Journal of Neuroscience, 86*, 271–280.

Persinger, M. A. (2006). Private communication to Roll on November 26.

Persinger, M. A., and Fisher, S. D. (1990). Elevated, specific temporal lobe signs in a population engaged in psychic studies. *Perceptual and Motor Skills, 71*, 817–818.

Persinger, M. A., Koren, S. A., and Tsang, E. W. (2003). Enhanced power within a specific band of theta activity in one person while another receives circumcerebral pulsed magnetic fields: A mechanism for cognitive influence at a distance? *Perceptual and Motor Skills, 97*, 877–894.

Persinger, M. A., and Makarec, K. (1987). Temporal lobe epileptic signs and correlative behaviors displayed by normal populations. *Journal of General Psychology, 114*, 179–195.

Persinger, M. A., and Makarec, K. (1993). Complex partial epileptic-signs as a continuum from normals to epileptics: Normative data and clinical populations. *Journal of Clinical Psychology, 49*, 33–45.

Persinger, M. A., and Richards, P. M. (1994). Quantitative electroencephalographic validation of left and right temporal signs and indicators in normal people. *Perceptual and Motor Skills, 79*, 1571–1578.

Persinger, M. A., and Roll, W. G. (1993). Potential neurofunctional correlates of the Tina Resch 1984 poltergeist episode. *Proceedings of Presented Papers: The Parapsychological Association 36th Annual Convention*, 483–491.

Persinger, M. A., and Valliant, P. M. (1985). Temporal lobe signs and reports of subjective paranormal experiences in a normal population: A replication. *Perceptual and Motor Skills, 60*, 903–909.

Pfurtscheller, G., and Aranibar, A. (1979). Evaluation of event-related desynchronization (ERD) preceding and following self-paced movement. *Electroencephalography and Clinical Neurophysiology, 46*, 138–146.

Phelps, E. A., and LeDoux, J. E. (2005). Contributions of the amygdala to emotion processing: From animal models to human behavior. *Neuron, 48*, 175–187.

Pizzagalli, D., Lehmann, D., Gianotti, L., Koenig, T., Tanaka, H., Wackermann, J., and Brugger, P. (2000). Brain electric correlates of strong belief in paranormal phenomena: Intracerebral EEG source and regional omega complexity analyses. *Psychiatry Research: Neuroimaging, 100*, 139–154.

Polkinghorne, J. (2002). *Quantum theory: A very short introduction*. New York: Oxford University Press.

Pratt, J. G. (1974). Some notes for the future Einstein of parapsychology. *Journal of the American Society for Psychical Research, 68*, 133–155.

Radin, D. I. (1997). Unconscious perception of future emotions: An experiment in presentiment. *Journal of Scientific Exploration, 11*, 163–180.

Radin, D. I. (2004). Event-related electroencephalographic correlations between isolated human subjects. *Journal of Alternative and Complementary Medicine, 10,* 315–323.

Radin, D., and Lobach, E. (2006). Presentiment in the brain. *Proceedings of Presented Papers: The Parapsychological Association 49th Annual Convention,* 164–175.

Rajaram, M., and Mitra, S. (1981). Correlations between convulsive seizures and geomagnetic activity. *Neuroscience Letters, 24,* 187–191.

Rao, K. R., and Feola, J. (1973). Alpha rhythm and ESP in a free-response situation. In W. G. Roll, R. L. Morris, and J. D. Morris (Eds.), *Research in parapsychology 1972* (pp. 141–144). Metuchen, NJ: Scarecrow Press.

Reinsel, R. (2003). Dissociation and mental health in mediums and sensitives: A pilot survey. *Proceedings of Presented Papers: The Parapsychological Association 46th Annual Convention,* 200–221.

Rhine, J. B. (1962). *The reach of the mind.* New York: William Sloane.

Rhine, L. E. (1954). Frequency of types of experience in spontaneous precognition. *Journal of Parapsychology, 18,* 93–123.

Rice, G. E., and Townsend, J. (1962). Agent-percipient relationship and GESP performance. *Journal of Parapsychology, 26,* 211–217.

Richards, M. A., Koren, S. A., and Persinger, M. A. (2002). Circumcerebral application of weak complex magnetic fields with derivatives and changes in electroencephalographic power spectra within the theta range: Implications for consciousness. *Perceptual and Motor Skills, 95,* 671–686.

Richards, T. L., Kozak, L., Johnson, L. C., and Standish, L. J. (2005). Replicable functional magnetic resonance imaging evidence of correlated brain signals between physically and sensory isolated subjects. *Journal of Alternative and Complementary Medicine, 11,* 955–963.

Roberts, R. J., Varney, N. R., Hulbert, J. R., Paulson, J. S., Springer, J., Sheperd, J., Swan, C., Legrand, J., Harvey, J., and Steuben, M. (1990). The neuropathology of everyday life: The frequency of partial seizure symptoms among normals. *Neuropsychology, 4,* 65–85.

Rogers, B. P., Carew, J. D., and Meyerand, M. E. (2004). Hemispheric asymmetry in supplementary motor area connectivity during unilateral finger movements. *NeuroImage, 22,* 855–859.

Roig, M., and Neaman, M. A. W. (1992). Hemisphericity style and belief in ESP. *Psychological Reports, 71,* 995–1000.

Roll, W. G. (1966). ESP and memory. *International Journal of Neuropsychiatry, 2,* 505–521.

Roll, W. G. (1968). Some physical and psychological aspects of a series of poltergeist phenomena. *Journal of the American Society for Psychical Research, 62,* 263–308.

Roll, W. G. (1970). Poltergeist phenomena and interpersonal relations. *Journal of the American Society for Psychical Research, 64,* 66–99.

Roll, W. G. (1972/2004). *The poltergeist.* New York: Nelson Doubleday.

Roll, W. G. (1975). *Theory and experiment in psychical research.* New York: Arno Press.

Roll, W. G. (1977). Poltergeists. In B. B. Wolman (Ed.), *Handbook of parapsychology* (pp. 382–413). New York: Van Nostrand Reinhold.

Roll, W. G. (1993). The question of RSPK versus fraud in the case of Tina Resch. *Proceedings of Presented Papers: The Parapsychological Association 36th Annual Convention,* 456–482.

Roll, W. G., Burdick, D., and Joines, W. T. (1974). The rotating beam theory and the Olive Hill poltergeist. In W. G. Roll, R. L. Morris, and J. D. Morris (Eds.), *Research in parapsychology 1973* (pp. 64–67). Metuchen, NJ: Scarecrow Press.

Roll, W. G., and Gearhart, L. (1974). Geomagnetic perturbations and RSPK. In W. G. Roll, R. L. Morris, and J. D. Morris (Eds.), *Research in parapsychology 1973* (pp. 44–46). Metuchen, NJ: Scarecrow Press.

Roll, W. G., and Joines, W. T. (2001). RSPK and consciousness. *Proceedings of Presented Papers: The Parapsychological Association 44th Annual Convention*, 267–284.

Roll, W. G., Morris, R. L., Damgaard, J. A., Klein, J., and Roll, M. (1973). Free verbal response experiments with Lalsingh Harribance. *Journal of the American Society for Psychical Research, 67*, 197–207.

Roll, W. G., and Pratt, J. G. (1971). The Miami disturbances. *Journal of the American Society for Psychical Research, 65*, 409–454.

Roll, W. G., and Storey, V. (2004). *Unleashed—of poltergeists and murder: The curious story of Tina Resch.* New York: Paraview Pocket Books.

Sackett, C. A., Kielpinski, D., King, B. E., Langer, C., Meyer, V., Myatt, C. J., Rowe, M., Turchette, Q. A., Itano, W. M., Wineland, D. J., and Monroe, C. (2000). Experimental entanglement of four particles. *Nature, 404*, 256–259.

Saltmarsh, H. F. (1929). A report on the investigation of some sittings with Mrs. Warren Elliott. *Proceedings of the Society for Psychical Research, 39*, 47–184.

Sannwald, G. (1963). On the psychology of spontaneous paranormal phenomena. *International Journal of Parapsychology, 5*, 274–292.

Schneider, A. M., and Tarshis, B. (1995). *Elements of physiological psychology.* New York: McGraw-Hill.

Schulter, G., and Papousek, I. (2008). Believing in paranormal phenomena: Relations to asymmetry of body and brain. *Cortex, 44*, 1326–1335.

Schwartz, S. A. (2007). *Opening to the infinite: The art and science of nonlocal awareness.* Buda, TX: Nemoseen Media.

Sergent, J., Geuze, R., and Van Winsum, W. (1987). Event-related desynchronization and P300. *Psychophysiology, 24*, 272–277.

Sperry, R. W. (1968). Hemispheric disconnection and unity in conscious experiences. *American Psychologist, 23*, 723–733.

Sperry, R. W. (1974). Lateral specialization in the surgically separated hemispheres. In F. O. Schmitt and F. G. Worden (Eds.), *The neurosciences third study program* (pp. 5–19). Cambridge, MA: MIT Press.

Sperry, R. W. (1982). *Science and moral priority: Merging mind, brain, and human values.* New York: Columbia University Press.

Springer, S. P., and Deutsch, G. (1993). *Left brain, right brain* (4th ed.). San Francisco: W. H. Freeman.

Standish, L. J., Johnson, L. C., Kozak, L., and Richards, T. (2003). Evidence of correlated functional magnetic resonance imaging signals between distant human brains. *Alternative Therapies in Health and Medicine, 9*, 122–125, 128.

Standish, L. J., Kozak, L., Johnson, L. C., and Richards, T. (2004). Electroencephalographic evidence of correlated event-related signals between the brains of spatially and sensory isolated human subjects. *Journal of Alternative and Complementary Medicine, 10*, 307–314.

Stanford, R. G. (1971). EEG alpha activity and ESP performance: A replicative study. *Journal of the American Society for Psychical Research, 65*, 144–154.

Stanford, R. (2006). Making sense of the "extrasensory": Modeling receptive psi using memory-related concepts. *6⁰ Simpósio da Fundação Bial: Aquém e Além do Cérebro* [Behind and Beyond the Brain] (pp. 169–197). Porto, Portugal: Fundação Bial.

Stanford, R. G., and Lovin, C. (1970). EEG alpha activity and ESP performance. *Journal of the American Society for Psychical Research*, *64*, 375–384.

Stanford, R. G., and Palmer, J. (1975). Free-response ESP performance and occipital alpha rhythms. *Journal of the American Society for Psychical Research*, *69*, 235–243.

Stanford, R. G., and Stanford, B. E. (1969). Shifts in EEG alpha rhythm as related to calling patterns and ESP run-score variance. *Journal of Parapsychology*, *33*, 39–47.

Stanford, R. G., and Stevenson, I. (1972). EEG correlates of free response GESP in an individual subject. *Journal of the American Society for Psychical Research*, *66*, 357–368.

Stapp, H. P. (2001). Quantum theory and the role of mind in nature. *Foundations of Physics*, *31*, 1465–1499.

Stevenson, I. (1970). *Telepathic impressions: A review and report of thirty-five new cases.* Charlottesville: University Press of Virginia.

Stuart, C. E. (1946). GESP experiments with the free response method. *Journal of Parapsychology*, *10*, 21–35.

Sumich, A., Kumari, V., Gordon, E., Tunstall, N., and Brammer, M. (2008). Event-related potential correlates of paranormal ideation and unusual experiences. *Cortex*, *44*, 1342–1352.

Targ, R. (1994). Remote viewing replication: Evaluated by concept analysis. *Journal of Parapsychology*, *58*, 271–284.

Targ, R. (2004). *Limitless mind: A guide to remote viewing and transformation of consciousness.* Novato, CA: New World Library.

Tittel, W., Brendel, J., Zbinden, H., and Gisin, N. (1998). Violation of Bell inequalities by photons more than 10 km apart. *Physical Review Letters*, *81*, 3563–3567.

Vedral, V. (2008). Quantifying entanglement in macroscopic systems. *Nature*, *453*, 1004–1007.

Venkatasubramanian, G., Jayakumar, P. N., Nagendra, H. R., Nagaraja, D. D. R., and Gangadhar, B. N. (2008). Investigating paranormal phenomena: Functional brain imaging of telepathy. *International Journal of Yoga*, *1*, 66–71.

Venturino, M. (1978). An investigation of the relationship between EEG alpha activity and ESP performance. *Journal of the American Society for Psychical Research*, *72*, 141–152.

Vignal, J.-P., Maillard, L., McGonigal, A., and Chauvel, P. (2007). The dreamy state: Hallucinations of autobiographic memory evoked by temporal lobe stimulations and seizures. *Brain*, *130*, 88–99.

Vogel, J. J., Bowers, C. A., and Vogel, D. S. (2003). Cerebral lateralization of spatial abilities: A meta-analysis. *Brain and Cognition*, *52*, 197–204.

Wackermann, J., Seiter, C., Keibel, H., and Walach, H. (2003). Correlations between brain electrical activities of two spatially separated human subjects. *Neuroscience Letters*, *336*, 60–64.

Wallwork, S. C. (1952). ESP experiments with simultaneous electro-encephalographic recordings. *Journal of the Society for Psychical Research*, *36*, 697–701.

Walter, W. G., Cooper, R., Aldridge, V. J., McCallum, W. C., and Winter, A. L. (1964). Contingent negative variation: An electric sign of sensori-motor association and expectancy in the human brain. *Nature*, *203*, 380–384.

Warcollier, R. (1938). *Experimental telepathy* (J. B. Gridley, Trans.). Boston, MA: Boston Society for Psychical Research.

Warren, C. A., McDonough, B. E., and Don, N. S. (1992). Event-related brain potential changes in a psi task. *Journal of Parapsychology*, *56*, 1–30.

Warren, C. A., McDonough, B. E., and Don, N. S. (1996). Partial replication of single subject event-related potential effects in a psi task. In E. W. Cook (Ed.), *Research in parapsychology 1992* (pp. 17–21). Lanham, MD: Scarecrow Press.

White, R. A. (1964). A comparison of old and new methods of response to targets in ESP experiments. *Journal of the American Society for Psychical Research, 58*, 21–56.

The Dreamer

CHAPTER 2

The Parapsychologist's Lament

James E. Alcock

Why, parapsychologists ask, does parapsychology continue to be rebuffed by mainstream science? Given that many parapsychologists are highly trained in psychology or physics or other mainstream domains, given that they belong to professional parapsychological organizations and publish in refereed parapsychological journals, and given that they have accumulated an extensive research corpus over the past century, what is the justification for this continuing rejection? If the data are as persuasive as they believe, it is natural to conclude that this rejection must reflect either ignorance of their work or dogmatic refusal to take it seriously because of its implications. The official Web site of the Society for Psychical Research (n.d.) makes this explicit: "Opposition to psychical research is often against its implications and not the quality of the evidence. The evidence of psychical research, if accepted, challenges the fundamental assumptions about how the world works generally accepted by the scientific community." Over the years, it has been argued that skeptical scientists reject the reality of paranormal phenomena because of personal anxiety (e.g., Eisenbud, 1946; Irwin, 1989; LeShan, 1966; Wren-Lewis, 1974) or because of an unconscious fear of their own psychic powers (Tart, 1982, 1984). Parker (2003) has suggested that skeptical psychologists fear the "unwanted implications" that scientific acceptance of paranormal phenomena would have for psychology itself, and Carter (2006) has attributed some of the motivation to anxiety about competition for scarce research funds.

Such attributions distract parapsychologists from the real message that the rejection carries and keep them from coming to terms with the actual barrier to their acceptance in the "Hallways of Science": It is not the dogmatism or emotional weakness of scientists; it is the weakness of the data. I have never met a scientist who has expressed anxiety about the possibility of paranormal phenomena, but I have met many who have initially shown interest in parapsychological claims, only to have this interest dissipate after a close look at the data or after carrying out their own experiments (e.g., Jeffers, 2003). Indeed, there have been a number of occasions over the past century when leading psychologists and other scientists have shown particular openness to parapsychological claims, but this interest has evaporated each time because of the lack of satisfactory evidence (Alcock, 1987).

Parapsychologists need to understand why mainstream scientists fail to be impressed by their work. I have written a number of times (e.g., Alcock, 1981, 1986, 1987, 1989, 2003) about problems in parapsychological research, and I shall summarize these—a baker's dozen reasons for continuing skepticism.

Ambiguous Definition of Subject Matter

What is the subject matter of parapsychology? I doubt that one could find consensus amongst parapsychologists as to what phenomena fall within its proper realm. While some would limit the field to such putative phenomena as telepathy, clairvoyance, remote viewing, psychokinesis (PK), psychic healing, and precognition (a listing that appears on the Web page of the Parapsychological Association), others would include trance channelers, apparitions, survival after death, dowsing, and poltergeists (as on the Web page of the American Society for Psychical Research), and paranormal healing, mediums, near-death and out-of-the-body experiences, and postmortem survival (as on the Web page of Britain's Society for Psychical Research). Even the most bizarre notions are tolerated, and there seems to be no "horizon of the ridiculous" beyond which claims can be ignored, at least for the time being. Moreover, to my knowledge, there are no phenomena that parapsychologists have ever deemed unlikely to exist, despite their long history of investigation.

Thus, careful attempts to produce ESP in the laboratory are published alongside studies of the psychic abilities of cockroaches (Schmidt, 1979) and even brine shrimp! PK operating forwards and backwards in time is granted the same respect as "simple" telepathy. Recent issues of the *Journal of Parapsychology* have included such topics as a "healer's" effects on the growth of lettuce seeds (Roney-Dougal and Solfvin, 2003), a laboratory study of the *I Ching* (e.g., "the significant sheep-goat effect does suggest that I Ching usage does involve some kind of paranormal process," Storm, 2006, p. 139), and methodology for research into mediumistic communication (Beischel, 2007), something that was a major focus during the Spiritualist craze a century ago. Inherent in this generosity with regard to what is appropriate subject matter is a lack of focus on what might be considered key phenomena within the field.

Negative Definition of Constructs

Beyond the difficulty of delineating the limits of its subject matter, parapsychology is the only field that claims to be scientific and yet deals exclusively with phenomena that are negatively defined. What is extrasensory perception (ESP)? It is perception that supposedly occurs when all "normal" sensory communication can be ruled out. PK? This supposedly occurs when an individual can produce effects on the physical environment without the application of any known force. Definitions of parapsychological phenomena tell us not what the phenomena are, but only what they are not.

Because of the total reliance on negative definitions, the demonstration of para-psychological effects must be accompanied by the assurance that no normal processes were in operation that could account for the data. Of course, the researcher may not always be aware of all normal processes that might be at play. Since the assumption must be made that all normal explanations have been ruled out, such claims demand much more scrutiny than generally needs to be applied in other areas of scientific research. This puts the focus on the possibility of design errors, methodological flaws, statistical oversights, overinterpretation of data, and even at times, fraud. It would be unwise for scientists to do otherwise, and I therefore disagree with those parapsychologists who criticize scientist-critics for spending much more time looking for faults in parapsychological methodology than they do when vetting other areas of research where data gathering is guided by a solid foundation of established findings and by well-developed theory.

Misleading Concept of Anomaly

Anomalies in observation—inconsistencies between theory and observation—are a major driving force in scientific discovery, and philosophers of science have written at length about how such anomalies have promoted major changes in scientific understanding. It is therefore not surprising that parapsychologists should like to consider their data as constituting scientific anomalies. However, to apply this term to parapsychological data is misleading.

In mainstream science, an anomaly refers to something that both is reliably observable and contradicts the current scientific theory. For example, while the pre-cession of Mercury can be observed reliably even by amateur astronomers, it is at variance with what Newtonian mechanics would predict; it was an anomaly. Einstein made sense of it all, which contributed greatly to the acceptance of his theory of rel-ativity and led to a paradigm shift in physics.

However, when parapsychologists speak of "anomalies," something altogether dif-ferent is involved. First of all, there is no coherent, well-articulated theory against which particular observations stand in contrast and, second, there is no body of reli-able observations that would demand revision of any such theory.

Incidentally, one wonders why, if parapsychological phenomena are genuine, they do not present as genuine anomalies in the very delicate experiments conducted in modern physics. Despite physicists' differing predictions, expectations, moods, desires, and personalities, their data do not show any such anomaly that would sug-gest that the mind of the experimenter has affected the outcome of an experiment.

Lack of Replicability

In mainstream science, inability to replicate an experiment throws results of the experiment into extreme doubt. However, despite frequent claims to the contrary, parapsychologists have not yet produced a single successful experiment that neutral scientists can reproduce for themselves. To their credit, a few parapsychologists acknowledge this problem. For example, Watt and Irwin, in Chapter 3 of this volume, conclude that, "parapsychologists are not yet able to specify the testing conditions that would allow other researchers, skeptics included, to be able to demonstrate for themselves reasonably reliable evidence in support of the ESP hypothesis." Parker writes in a similar vein with respect to PK:

> Clearly PK cannot be considered in any sense proven on such shaky data as this . . . . Ironically, given the purpose of the retreat to laboratory testing was with the aim of providing incontrovertible proof of PK, the most impressive accounts still come from studies of phenomena outside the laboratory—so called macro scale PK . . . carried out with specially selected individuals or groups. (see Chapter 4)

Multiplication of Entities

Pluralitas non est ponenda sine neccesitate or "plurality should not be posited without necessity"; these words are attributed to the medieval English philosopher and Franciscan monk William of Ockham (ca. 1285–1349), and "Ockham's razor" describes the recommended practice of using no more explanatory concepts than are absolutely necessary to explain an apparent phenomenon. Parapsychological practice stands in stark contrast to that principle for not only are vague, negatively defined explanatory concepts invoked to account for departures from chance in probability experiments, but other ad hoc constructs are used to explain away both inconsistencies in the data and the absence of significant findings.

For example, the so-called *psi-experimenter effect* is invoked when different parapsychologists have obtained dissimilar results after carrying out the same experiment, particularly if one researcher obtained an apparent parapsychological effect, while the other did not. This "effect," which is just a descriptive label, is then taken to reflect a quality of paranormal processes. In mainstream science, such an outcome would indicate only that there are methodological problems that need to be rooted out. Similarly, the *psi-missing effect* and the *decline effect* supposedly account for why participants in an experiment obtain significantly poorer results than were anticipated, and the *sheep-goat effect* is noted when motivated believers appear more likely than nonbelievers to produce significant results in a psi experiment. The use of such arbitrary constructs to explain away failed predictions and inconsistencies in the data raises a red flag to any competent scientist.

Unfalsifiability

Ad hoc constructs such as those listed above make it impossible to falsify any parapsychological claims. For example, when others cannot replicate a parapsychologist's results, this is taken as another manifestation of the psi-experimenter effect. Scientists have learned through long and hard experience that effects that are observable only by the motivated few, thereby making the claim impossible to falsify, are unlikely to be worthy of any further study.

Unpredictability

Prediction is a keystone of science. Even when scientists have difficulty understanding the nature of a phenomenon, being able to predict its effects and under what conditions they will occur gives them confidence that the phenomenon is genuine. Thus, even though scientific understanding of the nature of gravity is far from complete, the effects of gravity can be easily measured by anyone; they occur in an orderly and predictable fashion for any researcher.

Parapsychological effects appear unpredictably; that is why replication is so elusive. However, not only can parapsychologists not tell us when such effects are likely to occur, but because such effects are apparently impervious to distance and time, and to blockage by any material barrier, they cannot even describe conditions under which they will *not* occur. In recognition of this, Parker (2003) concluded that this "appears to be an intractable problem in parapsychology. Until we can predict such outcomes ahead of time, the establishment of lawful relationships still evades us" (p. 127).

Lack of Progress

Over the past century, as new tools have been developed in biology, psychology, physics, and other scientific fields, many of these have been adapted for use in parapsychology. Yet, while normal science is characterized by the development of more sophisticated methodology and equipment that allows for more sensitive measurements, which in turn leads to the refinement of theory and the gradual accumulation of more and more reliable knowledge, such is not the case in parapsychology. Despite the employ of new methodologies and sophisticated statistical analyses, effect sizes have not grown; no well-articulated theory supported by data has emerged; and psychic phenomena, if they actually exist, remain as mysterious as ever. Some parapsychologists have devoted much of their professional lives to the pursuit of psi, but despite the efforts of people such as Edmund Gurney, F. W. H. Myers, Henry and Eleanor Sidgwick, J. B. and Louisa Rhine, Charles Honorton, and many others, the scientific case for psi is no stronger now than it was a century ago. This lack of progress distinguishes parapsychology from mainstream scientific endeavors.

Methodological Weaknesses

At the heart of the dispute between parapsychologists and their critics is the adequacy of methodology. As noted earlier, because psi is defined only negatively, the importance of ruling out methodological flaws and statistical inadequacies is of utmost importance in parapsychological experiments. Parapsychological studies that are free of obvious methodological flaws are relatively few and far between.

Certainly, a few leading parapsychologists recognize this problem. However, some argue that a critic who discovers a methodological problem must go on to show that the problem could account for the observed effect. Such an argument would be preposterous in mainstream science and it is just as preposterous here. The onus is on the researcher to "do it right" by eliminating the problem and running the experiment again. Of course, given the notorious problem of replicability, one can perhaps understand a researcher's reluctance to follow that path.

Reliance on Statistical Decision Making

Modern parapsychological research depends to a very large extent on the power of sophisticated statistical analysis to reveal tiny, but statistically significant, departures from chance that would otherwise likely go unnoticed. There is nothing wrong with that in principle. What is wrong, however, is that such a departure is then considered to be evidence in support of the psi hypothesis. In the absence of both well-articulated theory and a body of other established research findings, there is no basis for linking the observed deviation to any particular hypothesis. Statistical significance can never tell us anything about what caused the departure. It could be due to any number of things—perhaps psi, perhaps methodological flaws, fraud, or statistical error. If one had prayed for a successful outcome, it would just as well support the hypothesis that God exists.

Problem of Theory

Virtually no one in astronomy disputes the existence of black holes, even though they have not been directly observed. Astronomers have come to believe in their existence because they were predicted by a well-articulated theory that was in turn supported by a body of reliable observations unrelated to black holes. On the basis of theory, other observations have been made that indirectly point to their existence.

Parapsychology is devoid of any well-articulated theory that could provide such guidance. That is not to say that it is without theory at all, for a host of theories have been proposed, including a Conformance Behavior Model (Stanford, 1990), Decision Augmentation Theory (May, Utts, and Spottiswoode, 1995), a quantum mechanical theory (Walker, 1984), the Thermal Fluctuation Model (Mattuck, 1982), and Statistical Balancing Theory (Pallikari, 2003). Yet, none of these theories serves to advance parapsychology, for they represent ad hoc efforts to explain something that is only assumed to exist. The notion of black holes emerged from a general theory in physics that had already proved its adequacy with regard to other well-understood phenomena; it did not begin with the belief in black holes and an attempt to construct a theory around the belief.

Disinterest in Competing, Normal Hypotheses

There is no doubt that most people have some very strange experiences in their lives and, lacking any normal explanation, they conclude that these experiences are paranormal. While experiences of "telepathy," "precognition," and many other supposed psi phenomena can be produced by the normal brain from time to time (Alcock, 1981), there is an obvious disinclination within parapsychology to explore such nonparanormal explanations.

Failure to Jibe with Other Areas of Science

There is nothing in modern biochemistry that contradicts the basic principles of physics, nor is there anything in genetics that stands in opposition to chemistry. Astronomy does not contradict geology and the basic principles of biology are consistent with those of the other sciences. In other words, while there may be debates and disputes at the leading edges of scientific discovery, the different domains of science harmonize with one another.

However, such is not the case with parapsychology; its claims stand in defiance of the modern scientific worldview. That by itself does not mean that parapsychology is in error, but as the eminent neuropsychologist Donald Hebb (personal communication, cited in Alcock, 1981) pointed out, if the claims of parapsychology prove to be true, then physics, biology, and neuroscience are horribly wrong in some fundamental respects. That might be, but the evidence supporting the modern scientific overview is in most respects overwhelming, and most scientists will demand strong evidence indeed from parapsychologists to persuade them of the reality of psychic phenomena. Moreover, mainstream science has not found any need to invoke the concept of psi for, as noted earlier, supposed psi anomalies do not present themselves in the course of mainstream scientific work.

Here we have 13 reasons to remain skeptical. The message is simple: provide replicable data and scientists will listen. Discounting skepticism by attributing it to dogmatism, fear, or other such motives is an egregious error; it is attacking the messenger because one does not like the message.

Obviously, few parapsychologists share this skepticism, and the hope that has sustained parapsychologists across the past century still flows in abundance. Hope triumphs over experience. Since one cannot prove that psychic phenomena do *not* exist, the search will continue for a long time to come, and one wonders what it would take for parapsychologists, if there is no psi, to accept that conclusion.

To paraphrase Tennyson: people may come and people may go, but (the search for) psi goes on forever. Now, neurobiology with its exciting new tools and methods offers renewed inspiration for parapsychologists, just as in the past did psychophysics, meta-analysis, perceptual Ganzfelds, and the murky world of quantum mechanics. Watt and Irwin (Chapter 3) suggest that improved cooperation between parapsychologists and neuroscientists will assist progress in understanding the "new neurobiology of ESP." However, before becoming overly enthused by the promise of a neurobiological approach, one should heed the Hyman Categorical Imperative: "Before setting out to explain something, first make sure that you have something to explain" (Ray Hyman, personal communication). There can be no "neurobiology of ESP and PK" until first one can be sure that there is ESP and PK. Dressing it up in fancy new scientific garb only leaves us with the flip side of the "Emperor's new clothes" and, in this case, we can see the attire, but is there really an Emperor inside?

References

Alcock, J. E. (1981). *Parapsychology: Science or magic?* Oxford: Pergamon Press.

Alcock, J. E. (1986). Parapsychology's past eight years: a lack-of-progress report. In K. Frazier (Ed.), *Science confronts the paranormal* (pp. 20–27). Buffalo, NY: Prometheus.

Alcock, J. E. (1987). Parapsychology: Science of the anomalous or search for the soul? *Behavioral and Brain Sciences, 10,* 553–565.

Alcock, J. E. (1989). Science and supernature. Buffalo, NY: Prometheus.

Alcock, J. E. (2003). Give the null hypothesis a chance. Reasons to remain doubtful about the existence of psi. In J. E. Alcock, J. Burns, and A. Freeman (Eds.), *Psi wars* (pp. 29–50). London: Imprint Academic.

Beischel, J. (2007). Contemporary methods used in laboratory-based mediumship research. *The Journal of Parapsychology, 71,* 37–69.

Carter, C. (2006). Review of E. L. Mayer's "Extraordinary knowing: Science, skepticism, and the inexplicable powers of the human mind." *The Journal of Parapsychology, 70,* 391–399.

Eisenbud, J. (1946). Telepathy and problems of psychoanalysis. *Psychoanalytic Quarterly, 15,* 32–87.

Irwin, H. J. (1989). On paranormal disbelief: The psychology of the sceptic. In G. K. Zollschan, J. F. Schumaker, and G. F. Walsh (Eds.), *Exploring the paranormal: Perspectives on belief and experience* (pp. 305–312). Bridgeport, Dorset, U.K.: Prism Press.

Jeffers, S. (2003). Physics and claims for anomalous effects related to consciousness. *Journal of Consciousness Studies, 10,* 135–152.

LeShan, L. (1966). Some psychological hypotheses on the non-acceptance of parapsychology as a science. *International Journal of Parapsychology, 8,* 367–385.

Mattuck, R. D. (1982). Some possible thermal quantum fluctuation models for psychokinetic influence on light. *Psychoenergetics, 4,* 211–225.

May, E. C, Utts, J. M., and Spottiswoode, S. J. P. (1995). Decision Augmentation Theory: Towards a model of anomalous phenomena. *The Journal of Parapsychology, 59,* 195–220.

Pallikari, F. (2003). Must the "magic" of psychokinesis hinder precise scientific measurement? *Journal of Consciousness Studies, 10,* 199–219.

Parker, A. (2003). We ask, does psi exist? But is this really the right question and do we really want an answer anyway? In J. E. Alcock, J. Burns, and A. Freeman (Eds.), *Psi wars* (pp. 111–134). London: Imprint Academic.

Roney-Dougal, S. M., and Solfvin, J. (2003). Field study of an enhancement effect on lettuce seeds: A replication study. *The Journal of Parapsychology, 67*, 279–298.

Schmidt, H. (1979). Search for psi fluctuations in a PK test with cockroaches. In W. G. Roll (Ed.), *Research in parapsychology 1977* (pp. 77–78). Metuchen, NJ: Scarecrow Press.

Society for Psychical Research. (n.d.). *Overview of psychical research: The achievements and the challenges*. Retrieved January 5, 2009, from http://www.spr.ac.uk/expcms/index.php?section=21.

Stanford, R. G. (1990). An experimentally testable model for spontaneous psi events. In S. Krippner (Ed.), *Advances in parapsychological research* (Vol. 6, pp. 54–167). Jefferson, NC: McFarland.

Storm, L. (2006). A parapsychological investigation of the *I Ching*: The relationship between psi, intuition, and time perspective. *The Journal of Parapsychology, 70*, 121–142.

Tart, C. T. (1982). The controversy about psi: Two psychological theories. *Journal of Parapsychology, 46*, 313–320.

Tart, C. T. (1984). Acknowledging and dealing with a fear of psi. *Journal of the American Society for Psychical Research, 78*, 133–143.

Walker, E. H. (1984). A review of criticisms of the quantum mechanical theory of psi phenomena. *The Journal of Parapsychology, 48*, 277–332.

Wren-Lewis, J. (1974). Resistance to the study of the paranormal. *Journal of Humanistic Psychology, 14*, 41–48.

The Sentinel

Processes Underlying the Phenomena of Mysterious Minds: Laboratory Evidence for ESP

Caroline A. Watt and Harvey J. Irwin

Mysterious experiences and physical events associated with psychic claimants, spiritualist mediums, shamans, and other extraordinary people have long intrigued the general public. At a more academic level, extensive documentation of these putative phenomena by anthropologists and sociologists has helped to contextualize them and thence to illuminate their cultural and subcultural significance. Although such research can be particularly instructive for an understanding of the impact of the phenomena on the lives of the experients (i.e., people who encounter them), a neurobiological appreciation of the phenomena requires scientists to explore more specifically their possible ontological reality. That is, could any of the mysterious phenomena actually be what they seem to be or, on the other hand, are they inevitably misperceptions, misinterpretations, deceptions, and phenomena otherwise attributable to far less mysterious psychological processes?

A preliminary step in addressing ontological issues here is to nominate fundamental explanatory processes that may underlie the phenomena. A psychic claimant, for example, may appear to give inexplicably accurate information about distant events; a medium or a shaman ostensibly may elicit information from a deceased spirit for the benefit of relatives and other sitters present at the performance; and other "psychically gifted" people or "sensitives" may have a vision about some remote circumstance and subsequently ascertain that the vision seemed unaccountably accurate. Scientific investigation of the ontological reality of each of these specific occurrences would nevertheless be an impractical and possibly futile research strategy, even if adequate control could be exercised during the observation of the incidents.

Despite the disparate social and cultural contexts in which the above experiences arise, it is evident that in essence they all appear to entail the acquisition of information about (spatially and/or temporally) remote events without the direct intervention of the conventional human senses such as sight, hearing, and so on. This *hypothetical* underlying process is often termed "extrasensory perception" (ESP), although such terms as "remote perception" are sometimes used. Thus, some of the mysterious experiences attributed to psychic claimants, mediums, and other extraordinary people could conceivably be based upon the hypothetical process of ESP. On this basis the properly scientific investigation of the ontological reality of psychic experiences might usefully progress in part from documentation of the anomalous experiences themselves to the critical scrutiny of the ESP hypothesis under appropriately controlled laboratory conditions. The focal question is no longer whether the revelations produced by the psychic in the fortune-telling booth are all an illusion but, rather, can experimental participants demonstrate knowledge about objects or events when any possibility of mundane sensory access and relevant logical inferences is procedurally excluded?

The aim of the present chapter is to survey the experimental study of the ESP hypothesis. Instances of so-called psi phenomena other than ESP that may underlie alleged psychic events are addressed in Chapter 4 of this volume. In addition, while the tone of the present review is duly critical, discussion of psi research from a more explicitly skeptical perspective is offered in Chapter 2 of this book. Space limitations mean that our review is necessarily abbreviated; however, we conclude with a more detailed section on studies addressing the ESP hypothesis from a neurobiological perspective.

Experimental ESP research can conveniently be reviewed in relation to two basic orientations. First, much of the initial research effort was devoted to the question of whether ESP can actually occur; work within this fundamental context is termed proof-oriented research. Second, other experimental studies have been more concerned with the properties of ESP or how the hypothesized process of ESP might work. Each of these two empirical objectives is addressed in turn.

Proof-Oriented Research on the ESP Hypothesis

As early as the seventeenth century, a few writers had suggested that psychic phenomena deserved critical scrutiny. Francis Bacon, for example, produced a cogent case in this regard (Bell, 1956). But it was not until the late nineteenth century that sustained and systematic attention began to be given to the issue. In the 1880s some academics and other interested people established groups with the focal objective of investigating psychic phenomena; the most prominent of these groups were the (British) Society for Psychical Research and the American Society for Psychical Research (Beloff, 1993; Inglis, 1977). The work of the members of these groups initially emphasized the documentation of relevant experiences or at best the observation of the performances of mediums and psychics under conditions that by today's standards would rarely have precluded sleight of hand and other forms of deception. Although a strong preference for tantalizing accounts of mysterious phenomena persisted in psychical research societies (and to some extent is evident even today), gradually there emerged an appreciation of the need for more rigorous investigation. Particularly in the first quarter of the twentieth century psychical researchers devised means to examine the ESP hypothesis under suitably controlled conditions. That is, investigators would select some target material, conceal it so as to make it sensorially inaccessible to the research participant, and then invite the participant to use his or her alleged psychic abilities to identify the material.

In some so-called free-response experiments (Sinclair, 1930/1962; Warcollier, 1938/1975) the range of potential targets was conceptually unlimited (e.g., drawings of objects chosen at random from a dictionary); at this time, however, the evidence educed from such experiments was essentially qualitative. In restricted choice experiments, on the other hand, the range of targets was known to the participant (e.g., when a deck of playing cards was used); this enabled the participant's performance to be quantified and, with contemporary advances in statistical probability theory, the accuracy of the performance could be compared objectively to that expected by random guessing or chance (Richet, 1888). During the first 50 years of psychical research a substantial number of simple card-guessing tests of the ESP hypothesis were undertaken (for a summary see Pratt, Rhine, Smith, Stuart, and Greenwood, 1940, Table 29), including occasional studies by skeptical experimenters (e.g., Coover, 1917/1975).

The large majority of these early restricted choice experiments were conducted as a single study by researchers who then made no further contribution to the issue. Without a sustained and coherent program of experimental research, the ESP hypothesis had scant discernable impact on mainstream academia. This situation was dramatically reversed with the work of J. B. Rhine (1934), who is generally regarded as the founder of modern experimental parapsychology. Rhine's fundamental contribution was to develop a standard experimental paradigm for investigating the ESP hypothesis. He devised a pack of ESP cards comprising five instances each of five simple geometric figures (square, circle, etc.) that were the targets for the experimental participant in each session. These targets had the advantage that they were not associated with strong preferences that could distort the randomness of participants' guesses as may well have been the case with playing cards as targets (in which aces, for example, may be favored as a choice on a given trial). Rhine also formulated standardized procedures for an ESP experiment. Finally, using the statistical expertise he had acquired during his previous botanical studies, Rhine developed formulae for the statistical evaluation of the performance of an individual participant or that of a group of participants over a substantial number of experimental sessions. Under this paradigm, Rhine (1934) was able to educe experimental ESP performances that were statistically significant to an impressive level. In addition, Rhine devised procedures designed to index precognition (extrasensory awareness of future events), telepathy (extrasensory awareness of another person's mentation), and clairvoyance (extrasensory awareness of objective events). At present, however, it seems safest to think of these terms as descriptors for different experimental procedures rather than as denoting discriminable "subtypes" of ESP.

Rhine's research came to the attention of the general public and instigated something of a craze for ESP cards. Many other academics nevertheless subjected his work to severe criticism. Small differences were noted in the obverse face of the ESP cards and suggested as a possible basis for a participant to learn the identity of such cards for subsequent tests. In some experiments the number of trials had not been specified in advance and thus left open the opportunity for an experimenter to terminate a study at a time when (purely by chance) the overall performance edged into statistical significance. These and other procedural limitations were openly acknowledged by Rhine and subsequently redressed by him. A professionally more damaging criticism came in the later charge by Hansel (1966) that the findings reported by Rhine could have been fraudulent. That is, it was argued that the experimenter, or the experimental participant, or both in collusion could have used fraudulent means to generate the significant data. Hansel outlined various scenarios under which this might have occurred. Some of these scenarios do seem rather fanciful, but the fact that they can be generated was sufficient for Hansel, and indeed many of his contemporaries, to conclude that the card-guessing ESP experiments by Rhine and his colleagues were methodologically unsound.

Since Rhine's pioneering work, successful ESP studies have been conducted with many groups of subjects by many experimenters in many laboratories in many countries (Bösch, 2004; Honorton and Ferrari, 1989; Milton, 1997). More recent tests also have routinely used computer-controlled experimental apparatus and more sophisticated devices for generating random series of targets. In addition, recent advances in statistical theory have served to counter the critics' claim of suppression of null findings in ESP experiments; thus, statistical indices of meta-analysis (Krippner et al., 1993) enable an estimation of the number of unreported null studies necessary to reduce the entire ESP database to chance level. As mentioned earlier, more recent ESP research has tended to emphasize free-response techniques; most notable among these are studies of extrasensory dreams in relation to target artworks (Sherwood and Roe, 2003; Ullman and Krippner, 1970) and extrasensory awareness of video clips under Ganzfeld or conditions of marked sensory restriction (Bem and Honorton, 1994). The free-response experiments are of particular note because, among other things, they avoid the theoretical possibility that extra-chance scores are merely a reflection of nonrandomness in both the target sequence and the set of responses. On these collective grounds it seems increasingly unlikely that the entire body of significant ESP test data can fairly be dismissed as an artifact of simple procedural flaws, crass methodological incompetence, or outright fraud. Indeed, the persistence of the dogmatic view among extreme counteradvocates that ESP research "must be" procedurally unsound has in turn raised questions about the objectivity and strategies of the so-called skeptical movement (Hansen, 1992; Hess, 1993).

At the same time it must be said that irrespective of years of procedural debates, proof-oriented ESP experiments have *not* succeeded in establishing the reality of ESP. Ultimately speaking, an ESP experiment is not a procedure that demonstrably taps the extrasensory process, but rather it is one that may merely yield a relatively weak trend for successful target identification that is beyond a level reasonably attributable to random guessing. The so-called ESP data certainly are consistent with the ESP hypothesis, but they are not conclusive for it, for the simple reason that it is possible to construct various alternative hypotheses that could equally accommodate the experimental findings. By way of illustration, perhaps the extrachance scores may be generated by some acausal process akin to Jung's (1955/1985) notion of synchronicity whereby a degree of concordance between a set of targets and a set of participants' guesses is achieved *without* any actual transference of information between targets and subjects (as is posited under the ESP hypothesis). Again, perhaps there is some unknown flaw in probability theory that renders inappropriate the comparison of an ESP score to a chance expectation. Or as Alcock (2003) more flippantly suggests, the statistically anomalous outcome may be simply an act of God. Whether or not such alternative accounts have independent empirical support is not of immediate concern in the present context; rather, the fact that such explanations of the ESP data can be devised means that these experiments, either individually or collectively, cannot be conclusive for the ESP hypothesis. For scientists to be persuaded of the reality of ESP, parapsychologists must also show empirically how this hypothesized process actually works. The focus of this chapter, and indeed that of more recent ESP research, therefore shifts to process-oriented investigation.

Process-Oriented Research on the ESP Hypothesis

In this section we review experimental work designed to identify the characteristics of the hypothetical ESP process. Such process-oriented research can in fact proceed independently of the laboratory demonstration of the ontological reality of ESP. That is, if ESP were demonstrated not to exist, the findings of process-oriented research would still attest to the nature of the phenomenon evidenced in ESP tests, whatever its identity. And if nothing else, the proof-oriented ESP research at least suggests there is some phenomenon here to be empirically explored. The following review cannot be fully comprehensive, but its emphasis is on findings that have been independently replicated or show clear consistency across cognate variables. Thus, we now address the characteristics and correlates of laboratory ESP performance; a survey of research on the correlates of putatively extrasensory experiences outside the laboratory is available elsewhere (Irwin and Watt, 2007).

Patterns in ESP Performance

Apart from the aggregate number of correct guesses or "hits" in an ESP test, researchers have given attention to patterns in the performance. This applies particularly in restricted choice experiments in which participants generate long sequences of guesses or "calls."

Psi Missing. In some ESP experiments performance has been found to fall significantly *below* chance. This effect, known as psi missing, does not represent a lack of the hypothesized extrasensory ability, because such a lack would be evidenced by statistically nonsignificant (chance) scores. Psi missing therefore seems to entail performance that is at odds with the participants' conscious intent; the subjects evidently are showing sensitivity to the targets (as shown by the statistical significance of the result), but for some reason they are making calls at odds with the targets' identity. Critics may be inclined to argue that results significantly below chance are merely the other tail of a distribution of test scores centered on chance, but this interpretation may be countered by the asymmetry between the reported incidence of psi missing and that of psi hitting. Further, the occurrence of psi missing has been found to correlate with negative attitudes or moods in the participants (e.g., Schmeidler and McConnell, 1958). With the increased use of free-response procedures in recent years, psi missing has received scant attention.

Position Effects and Decline Effects. Under an account of ESP performance in terms of random guessing, we would expect to see correct guesses haphazardly distributed throughout the test session. On the other hand, there are reports of higher rates of success at the beginning and the end of the set of calls (Rhine, 1969), and reports also of a "stringing together" or clustering of hits (Don, McDonough, and Warren, 1995). In addition, there may be a decline in the level of scoring across sessions (Rhine, 1969).

Displacement. In some ESP experiments a participant may show chance-level scores on the intended targets, but there is a significant level of correspondence between guesses and the target before (or the target following) the intended one. This might be interpreted as constituting a temporal or spatial displacement of the ESP process and has been found to correlate with negative attitudes or moods in the participants (Braud, 1987). Less interest has been shown in these so-called displacement effects in recent years, perhaps because they expose the researcher to a charge of "hypothesis saving": if a significant result is not obtained with the intended targets one might compare guesses against the preceding target, and then the following target, and then the targets for the previous participant, and so on. Alcock (2003) has been particularly critical of parapsychologists' "multiplication of entities" or appeal to these more obscure ESP scoring patterns to justify their inclination to rummage beyond the basic hypothesized correspondence between intended targets and calls.

In general, reported patterns in ESP performance may well be consistent with those associated with more orthodox signal-detection tasks. This may have some minor significance for a neurobiological model of ESP, but most of the patterns do not promise to reveal anything further about the nature of the hypothesized extrasensory process itself. A possible exception to this conclusion is the occurrence of clustering; given the broader theoretical implications of this phenomenon, an index of clustering might usefully be routinely cited in all reports of ESP tests, even if this phenomenon was not the focus of the investigation.

Target Variables in ESP Performance

Items used as targets in ESP experiments have included the standard ESP symbols, digits, letters, words, colors, simple line drawings, paintings, photographs, three-dimensional objects, distant environmental settings, video clips, and music. A few studies have examined the effect on ESP performance of specific aspects of the targets.

Physical Aspects. In the older card-guessing tests, simple physical characteristics such as size, number, distance, and distortedness either had no evident effect on performance or had an effect that was more readily interpreted in terms of the participants' expectations. In recent studies there have been indications that static targets (e.g., photographs) may be less effective than dynamic ones (e.g., video clips; Bem and Honorton, 1994). As Watt (1989) has suggested, dynamic targets may simply be more cognitively salient than static ones, and thus this trend does not help to distinguish ESP from conventional perceptual tasks. At the same time perhaps parapsychologists may have greater success in their ESP research if they use target material with greater ecological validity than is associated with relatively sterile geometrical symbols.

Psychological Aspects. Participants may prefer some types of targets over others because of their psychological associations. Some studies have observed higher scores on emotionally favored targets (e.g., friends' names versus strangers' names; Dean and Nash, 1967), although according to Delanoy (1989) the empirical support for this general view is meager. On the other hand, some negatively toned themes can be more evocative than emotionally positive ones. Perhaps for this reason many spontaneous extrasensory experiences relate to traumatic life events, such as the death of a loved one. Thus, by using video clips as ESP targets, Sherwood, Dalton, Steinkamp, and Watt (2000) obtained higher scores with emotionally negative targets than with positive or neutral video material. Further research is required to differentiate the effect of emotional evocativeness from that of emotional preference.

In summary, the diverse anecdotal justifications given by researchers for their choice of ESP targets presently tend to lack sufficient empirical grounding. Further research is needed to clarify these issues.

Participant Variables in ESP Performance

Although in most ESP experiments two participants are involved—the so-called agent or sender, and the recipient or receiver—regrettably little attention has been given to the role of the agent in ESP studies. In this section we therefore focus on the relationship between recipient characteristics and ESP performance.

Attitudes and Beliefs. The best-known work on the contribution of attitudes to ESP performance was conducted by Gertrude Schmeidler (1952; Schmeidler and McConnell, 1958). She divided ESP participants into two groups, the "sheep" comprising people who believed in the possibility of ESP and the "goats" who rejected that possibility. On pooling scores on ESP tests over a number of such groups, Schmeidler established a trend for these groups to score in the direction of their expectations. Thus, sheep tended to score above chance and goats significantly below chance level. This so-called "sheep-goat effect" is one of the most successfully replicated relationships in experimental ESP research (Lawrence, 1993; Palmer, 1977).

Mood. Carpenter (1991) conducted a series of studies investigating the relationship between mood and restricted-choice ESP performance. He found that ESP hitting was associated with the participant feeling strong-willed or assertive, detached or dreamy, and agreeable or outgoing; ESP missing was best predicted by a socially anxious mood. These findings are consistent with earlier research suggesting that a psi-conducive state is characterized by relaxation and a belief that success in the ESP task is possible. In addition, Carpenter has focused on free-response studies. He analyzed transcripts of over 600 Ganzfeld sessions looking at participants' experiences in these sessions. He found that hitting was predicted by neutral or positive physical or emotional experiences, whereas missing was associated with anxiety and unhappy adjustment to the situation (Carpenter, 2001, 2005). Earlier researchers also found that performance on projective tests of mood was associated with ESP performance (Humphrey, 1946a, 1946b). The available research therefore tends to suggest that mood does indeed influence ESP scores.

Personality. There has been considerable empirical interest in determining the personality correlates of ESP. The two principal variables in this regard are neuroticism and extraversion. On the evidence of a substantial number of studies, particularly those that have tested participants individually rather than in groups (reviewed by Palmer, 1978), it seems that ESP performance correlates negatively with neuroticism. This finding appears consistent with the research on mood described in the previous section. Related to neuroticism is defensiveness, and a number of studies have found a tendency for highly defensive participants to score relatively poorly at forced-choice ESP tasks (Haraldsson and Houtkooper, 1992; Haraldsson and Johnson, 1979; Watt, 1994; Watt and Morris, 1995). Also seemingly consistent with Carpenter's studies on ESP and mood, a number of studies have found a positive relationship between extraversion and ESP performance (Honorton, Ferrari, and Bem, 1998; Palmer, 1978, pp. 132–133; Palmer and Carpenter, 1998; Parra and Villanueva, 2003). These personality findings seem to be quite consistent in laboratory studies; however, their generalizability to spontaneous ESP experiences has not yet been established.

Physiological Variables. A number of studies have investigated EEG (brain electrical activity) correlates of ESP performance, and these are reviewed in the neurobiology section that concludes this chapter. However, probably the ESP procedures that have received the most empirical attention are those designed to bring about a state of reduced physiological arousal in the ESP recipient. These include hypnosis, meditation, progressive relaxation, dreaming, and drug intoxication. There is substantial evidence suggesting that each of the above states of consciousness is psi-conducive (Honorton, 1977; Luke and Friedman, Chapter 9), although that body of research is not without its methodological flaws (Schechter, 1984; Sherwood and Roe, 2003; Stanford and Stein, 1994). However, the procedure that has been most frequently used to induce a psi-conducive state of consciousness is the mild sensory isolation procedure known as the Ganzfeld. In this free-response procedure, the participant is immersed in unpatterned sensory stimulation, usually achieved using eyeshields and red light, the playing of "white noise" over headphones, and deep physical relaxation. After 30 minutes or so in this environment, the participants are asked to make a continuous verbal report of their experiences, including, for instance, visual imagery and emotions. At the same time as a participant reports his or her "mentation," the agent in a separate isolated room views the randomly chosen target (e.g., a two-minute video clip that is repeatedly played). The procedure tests whether the mentation contains more target-relevant material than material that is related to three other "decoy" targets, with the null hypothesis being that the participant can identify the actual target at levels no greater than chance expectation. If alternative sources of information about the target identity have been ruled out, and the observed rate of correct target identification is statistically greater than chance expectation, then it is inferred that this provides evidence in support of the ESP hypothesis.

In an early assessment of the Ganzfeld ESP literature by Honorton (1978), 23 of 42 experiments conducted in 10 different laboratories had yielded significant ESP performance under Ganzfeld conditions; this success rate of 55 percent was far beyond that expected by chance. Because the Ganzfeld effect loomed as a highly replicable phenomenon in parapsychology, it became the focus of intense critical debate (Honorton, 1985; Hyman, 1985), the result of which it is agreed there is an anomalous effect here to be explained, whether or not the underlying process is authentically extrasensory (Hyman and Honorton, 1986). Additionally, the debate instigated some methodological refinements to the ESP-Ganzfeld research (Dalton et al., 1996).

Despite these refinements some subsequent research has yielded data similar to the earlier work (Bem and Honorton, 1994; Honorton et al., 1990). A meta-analysis by Milton and Wiseman (1999) suggested that the more recent Ganzfeld studies had not elicited significant ESP performance. However, some researchers have suggested that the greater proportion of chance results in these more recent studies may be attributed to these studies being designed to explore ESP process variables, rather than being proof-oriented (e.g., Bem, Palmer, and Broughton, 2001).

Although some commentators (e.g., Wiseman, Smith, and Kornbrot, 1996) have remained skeptical of the quality of the experimental evidence for the Ganzfeld effect, the accumulated data have been cited as scientific testimony for the existence of psi (Bem and Honorton, 1994; Broughton, 1991). However, a review of the debate over Ganzfeld findings (Palmer, 2003) notes that there is considerable variability of results across experimenters, suggesting that work still needs to be done to establish the conditions needed to demonstrate a replicable effect (Milton, 1999).

In sum, there seems to be evidence from a number of converging lines of research that reduced physiological arousal is psi-conducive. Parapsychologists have investigated many other participant variables in ESP studies, including intelligence, creativity, proneness to dissociation and psychological absorption, gender, and age, and these are reviewed elsewhere (Irwin and Watt, 2007).

Neurobiology and ESP

The present chapter reviews controlled laboratory studies that are designed to empirically test the ESP hypothesis. A relatively small number of these studies have looked more explicitly at the neurobiology of ESP. Most of these have used electroencephalographic (EEG) measures, either looking at neural correlates of performance on ESP tasks or using the EEG itself as a dependent measure of ESP performance (much in the same way as electrodermal activity has been used as an indication of the physiological detection of remote observation, as reviewed by Schmidt, Schneider, Utts, and Walach, 2004). We review a selection of these studies and consider in some detail the handful of studies that have used functional magnetic resonance imaging (fMRI) as a dependent measure of ESP.

EEG Studies

It is perhaps appropriate given the context to remind readers that the development of human EEG can be traced directly to a striking occurrence of ostensible crisis telepathy experienced between German psychiatrist Hans Berger and his geographically distant sister during his year of military service in 1892 (Millett, 2001). Berger's conclusion that he and his sister had communicated by mental telepathy sparked his interest in psychophysics, and he spent the rest of his career searching for a method to detect the physiological correlates of the brain's mental activity. After years of struggling with inadequate technology, by 1927 he was making rudimentary EEG tracings from patients with skull defects (who had less intervening bone to obstruct measurements), and soon after he identified spontaneous oscillations in brain activity that he named alpha waves and beta waves. Berger's initial scientific reports were received with some skepticism, and it was felt that "the EEG was the result of some capricious electrical artifact" (Millett, 2001, p. 541). Eventually, however, Berger's work was replicated by other researchers, and in time many of his methods and terms became accepted and continue to be used in EEG research to this day.

Several studies have documented a relationship between the report of spontaneous extrasensory experiences and the presence of abnormalities in temporal lobe functions (Neppe, 1983; Palmer and Neppe, 2003; Persinger, 1984; Persinger and Makarec, 1987; Persinger and Valliant, 1985). However, the results of those laboratory-based studies that have sought EEG parameters as correlates of ESP activity paint an inconsistent picture. A high amount or density of alpha wave (8–13 Hz) activity during the ESP test may be a good predictor of performance, at least if the individual also reports having been in an altered state of consciousness at the time (Palmer, 1978). Alpha waves usually are associated with a relaxed, passive state of mind. In a single-subject design, McDonough, Warren, and Don (1989) found an association between "hits" in an ESP test and increased power in the delta (1–3 Hz) and theta (4–7 Hz) EEG bands, suggesting a facilitatory effect of low cortical arousal. In a subsequent study with a larger sample, however, the same researchers found a differential effect with psi hitting associated with stronger alpha and beta

(14–30 Hz) activity, and psi missing with delta and theta waves (McDonough, Don, and Warren, 1994). These investigators also have observed an association between gamma (30–70 Hz) activity and the mere presentation of a target symbol (McDonough, Don, and Warren, 2000), and in a forced-choice card-guessing design they found that a negative slow wave measured at 150–500 ms poststimulus was of marginally greater amplitude for target cards than for decoy cards ($p \le .05$; McDonough, Don, and Warren, 2002), although ESP task performance (overt guessing) was at chance. Evidently, the study of the relationship between ESP and EEG needs to take into account distinct stages of information processing.

In a slightly different line of research, a number of studies have used event-related EEG as a dependent measure of ESP,[*] with the event, such as photic flashes, occurring to a "sender" and the EEG being measured from the isolated recipient (e.g., Duane and Behrendt, 1965 [see critical commentary by Tart 1966]; Millar, 1979; Rebert and Turner, 1974; Tart, 1963). Perhaps the most systematic series of studies investigating the question of potential psychophysiological correlations between distant participants were published by Jacobo Grinberg-Zylberbaum (e.g., Grinberg-Zylberbaum et al., 1993, 1994). The Grinberg-Zylberbaum et al. (1994) study, which is probably the best known of the series, involved recording EEG from both participants of seven pairs, while one participant of each pair was photically stimulated at random intervals. In one testing condition, the subjects in each pair were brought to the separate testing rooms without having seen each other or knowing that the testing partner was in the other room. In the other condition, the participants were introduced to one another and were given instructions "to get to know and then feel one another in meditative silence for 20 minutes" prior to being separated for testing. From each photically stimulated participant, 100 EEG epochs related to the moments of photic stimulation were averaged and compared to the averaged activity of their nonstimulated partner. No correlation was found in the "nonconnected" condition, but significant correlations occurred in two of the pairs in the "connected" condition. Grinberg-Zylberbaum termed this effect a "transferred potential."

Although this is probably the most detailed of the publications of Grinberg-Zylberbaum et al., regrettably they do not present sufficient methodological detail to evaluate the exact procedure in this study, and only selected results are presented —and no overall statistical evaluation is made. The standards of Grinberg-Zylberbaum's methodology have also been criticized (e.g., McDonough, Don, and Warren, 2002; Wackermann, Seiter, Keibel, and Walach, 2003) and a follow-up study failed to replicate the effect (Sabell, Clarke, and Fenwick, 2001). Positive results have, however, been reported by subsequent conceptually similar studies (Radin, 2004; Standish, Kozak, Johnson, and Richards, 2004). In another similar study, Wackermann et al. (2003) found no transferred potential but did report significant fluctuations of the average EEG power in the nonstimulated participants at times of maximal visual evoked potentials in the stimulated participants. Confusing results were found in a replication by Wackermann, Muradás, and Pütz (2004): a negative deviation from chance expectation was found in the parts of the sessions in which the stimulated participant's monitor was covered by a piece of cardboard, and a positive deviation was found in the parts of the sessions in which the stimulated participant's monitor was uncovered, a pattern which the authors said they found difficult to interpret.

A similar confusing picture emerged from three event-related potential studies conducted by Kittenis. In his first study, significant differences were found in evoked-alpha global field power from nonstimulated participants in related pairs (with no effect being found for stranger pairs or for unpaired control participants) (Kittenis, Caryl, and Stevens, 2004). A subsequent replication study found the same effect; however, a third study using only related pairs failed to replicate the effect and Kittenis (2007) concluded that temporal characteristics of the changes in EEG activity observed in nonstimulated subjects did not support the interpretation of his overall findings in terms of event-related correlations in brain activity.

In sum, positive results are sometimes reported for EEG-ESP studies, but they appear to lack consistency or replicability. It is interesting to note that some of the EEG/ESP studies have been published in high impact journals, such as *Science*, *Neuroscience Letters*, and *Physics Essays*, perhaps reflecting mainstream interest in the theoretical and practical implications of these studies.

Neuroimaging Studies

Following a pilot study undertaken to establish the feasibility of using an EEG experimental design for an fMRI experiment (Standish, Johnson, Kozak, and Richards, 2003), a similar event-related protocol was adopted for a study that took both EEG and fMRI measures (here we will review only the fMRI part of the study). Richards, Kozak, Johnson, and Standish (2005), working with a selected participant pair who had shown consistent remote EEG correlations in a previous study (Standish et al., 2004), presented one member of the pair with checkerboard reversal ("flicker" = on or "static" = off) visual stimuli. Changes in fMRI brain activation were measured in the nonstimulated participants. The participants swapped roles so each was the stimulated participant twice and each was the nonstimulated partner twice.

Three of the four fMRI sessions gave evidence of differential activation in the occipital regions of the remote recipient. One session showed a decrease in activation, and this remote participant also showed a decrease in activation during the second session, suggesting a replication of the effect seen in the first session. The other remote participant showed no effect in the first session and an increase in activation in the second session. However, interpretation of these findings is difficult because the same nonrandom sequence (off, on, off, on, off, on) was used for each session, thereby introducing at least two potential artifacts: (1) There could be a coincidental match between a temporal drift in participants' physiology (e.g., increasing activation) and the target sequence; (2) After the participants were exposed to the stimulation sequence, they could deliberately or nonintentionally self-regulate when it came to their turn to be the nonstimulated partner. Richards et al. (2005) recommend replication with a larger sample size; we would also advocate improved methodology.

Achterberg et al. (2005) did have a larger sample size in an fMRI study using a slightly different procedure. Eleven pairs of participants were recruited, each pair consisting of a practitioner of "psychic healing" and a person to whom the healer felt closely connected. The healers were asked to attempt a distant connection with their partners, or during comparable control periods to direct their attention away from their partners, while the partners' brain activity was measured using fMRI. Significant differences in brain metabolic activity were reported, coinciding with the distant intentionality periods, though there seems to be a lack of detail in the statistical procedures used. The primary limitation of this study seems to be that the same randomized order of epochs was used for all participants, and also three other individuals knew this randomized order in addition to the healer (i.e., a nurse, a technician, and the experimenter). This violates a basic precaution in psi research that the condition order or target identity should be concealed to the maximum possible extent in order to avoid accidental or deliberate leakage of this information to the receiver, as well as to avoid bias in data handling or analysis. There could also be leakage about the condition order if healers communicated with future participants once the healers had themselves participated in the study. It is difficult to understand why, given the expense and difficulty of conducting fMRI studies, relatively simple methodological precautions such as adequate randomization and prevention of possible leakage of information about condition allocation were not implemented as a matter of routine. The studies above have all been published in alternative and complementary medicine journals, perhaps suggesting that this line of research is perceived as having potential practical and therapeutic applications.

A fourth fMRI study (Bierman and Scholte, 2002), which is conceptually different from the others in this section, since it used a precognitive rather than a telepathy design, reported evidence of greater anticipatory brain activation preceding participants' viewing of emotional stimuli compared to neutral stimuli. However, the authors described their study as exploratory and cautioned that their findings required replication with a more formalized procedure.

We close our review with a high-profile fMRI study published in *The Journal of Cognitive Neuroscience* by Harvard University researchers Moulton and Kosslyn (2008). The authors reasoned that any ESP-related brain activity would be clearly visible using fMRI methods when they contrasted "psi" epochs (where both the sender and the receiver saw the same target) with "nonpsi" epochs (where the sender and the receiver saw different targets). No difference in the receiver's fMRI activation was found between the two epoch types, leading the authors to conclude that "the current null results do not simply fail to support the psi hypothesis: They offer strong evidence against it" (p. 190). This conclusion was drawn despite Moulton and Kosslyn's earlier statement that "absence of proof is not proof of absence" (p. 183). The ESP method used in this study bears little resemblance to methods developed by parapsychologists, and the relevance of the study for the psi research literature could have been enhanced by adopting (and adapting) a method more similar to one already used by parapsychologists, and for which it was claimed to have previously shown some evidence in support of the ESP hypothesis. Finally, Moulton and

Kosslyn failed to note the existence of previous fMRI/ESP studies. Nevertheless, it is admirable for mainstream scientists to tackle the psi question and it would be exciting to see a future collaboration where their fMRI expertise was combined with parapsychologists' expertise in psi testing.

Conclusion

In this brief review, we have attempted to give an overview of the evolution of ESP testing methodology, the research questions asked, and the findings. We see a picture of gradually increasing methodological sophistication. We also see pockets of reasonably consistent findings, for instance in personality and attitudinal correlates of performance in ESP tasks, and in the apparent association between reduced physiological activity and ESP task performance. Nevertheless, parapsychologists are not yet able to specify the testing conditions that would allow other researchers, skeptics included, to be able to demonstrate for themselves reasonably reliable evidence in support of the ESP hypothesis. Those few studies that have explored ESP from a neurobiological perspective have mostly been proof-oriented in nature. The results of the EEG/ESP studies seem to lack consistency. Some of the fMRI studies have reported evidence of correlations in brain activity between distant individuals, but evaluation of these studies is hampered by methodological flaws. Parapsychologists could probably benefit from mainstream expertise in conducting psychophysiological research (Schmidt and Walach, 2000), and mainstream researchers could probably benefit from parapsychologists' expertise in devising methods to rule out possible artifacts. Progress in understanding the neurobiology of ESP could therefore be helped, in our opinion, by improved collaboration between parapsychologists and neuroscientists.

   * We are grateful to Dr. Marios Kittenis for his help in locating these event-related EEG/ESP studies.

References

Achterberg, J., Cooke, K., Richards, T., Standish, L., Kozak, L., and Lake, J. (2005). Evidence for correlations between distant intentionality and brain function in recipients: An fMRI analysis. *Journal of Alternative and Complementary Medicine, 11*, 965–971.

Alcock, J. (2003). Give the null hypothesis a chance: Reasons to remain doubtful about the existence of psi. *Journal of Consciousness Studies, 10*, 29–50.

Bell, M. (1956). A pioneer in parapsychology. *Hibbert Journal, 54*, 281–285.

Beloff, J. (1993). *Parapsychology: A short history.* London: Athlone Press.

Bem, D. J., and Honorton, C. (1994). Does psi exist? Replicable evidence for an anomalous process of information transfer. *Psychological Bulletin, 115*, 4–18.

Bem, D. J., Palmer, J., and Broughton, R. S. (2001). Updating the Ganzfeld database: A victim of its own success? *Journal of Parapsychology, 65*, 207–218.

Bierman, D. J., and Scholte, S. (2002). A FMRI brain imaging study of presentiment. *Journal of ISLIS, 20*, 380–389.

Bösch, H. (2004, August). *Reanalyzing a meta-analysis on extra-sensory perception dating from 1940, the first comprehensive meta-analysis in the history of science.* Paper presented at the 47th Annual Convention of the Parapsychological Association, Vienna, Austria.

Braud, W. (1987). Dealing with displacement. *Journal of the American Society for Psychical Research, 81,* 209–231.

Broughton, R. S. (1991). *Parapsychology: The controversial science.* New York: Ballantine Books.

Carpenter, J. C. (1991). Prediction of forced-choice ESP performance. Part III: Three attempts to retrieve coded information using mood reports and a repeated-guessing technique. *Journal of Parapsychology, 55,* 227–280.

Carpenter, J. C. (2001). A psychological analysis of Ganzfeld protocols. *Journal of Parapsychology, 65,* 358–359.

Carpenter, J. C. (2005, August). *Implicit measures of participants' experiences in the Ganzfeld: Confirmation of previous relationships in a new sample.* Paper presented at the 48th Annual Convention of the Parapsychological Association, Petaluma, CA.

Coover, J. E. (1975). *Experiments in psychical research at Leland Stanford Junior University.* New York: Arno Press. (Original work published 1917.)

Dalton, K. S., Morris, R. L., Delanoy, D. L., Radin, D. I., Taylor, R., and Wiseman, R. (1996). Security measures in an automated Ganzfeld system. *Journal of Parapsychology, 60,* 129–147.

Dean, E. D., and Nash, C. B. (1967). Coincident plethysmograph results under controlled conditions. *Journal of the Society for Psychical Research, 44,* 1–14.

Delanoy, D. L. (1989). Characteristics of successful free-response targets: Experimental findings and observations. In L. A. Henkel and R. E. Berger (Eds.), *Research in parapsychology 1988* (pp. 92–95). Metuchen, NJ: Scarecrow Press.

Don, N. S., McDonough, B. E., and Warren, C. A. (1995). Signal processing analysis of forced-choice ESP data: Evidence for psi as a wave of correlation. *Journal of Parapsychology, 59,* 357–380.

Duane, T. D., and Behrendt, T. (1965). Extrasensory electroencephalographic induction between identical twins. *Science, 150,* 367.

Grinberg-Zylberbaum, J., Delaflor, M., Attie, L., and Goswami, A. (1994). The Einstein-Podolsky-Rosen paradox in the brain: The transferred potential. *Physics Essays, 7,* 422–427.

Grinberg-Zylberbaum, J., Delaflor, M., Sanchez-Arellano, M. E., Guevara, M. A., and Perez, M. (1993). Human communication and the electrophysiological activity of the brain. *Subtle Energies, 3,* 25–43.

Hansel, C. E. M. (1966). *ESP: A scientific evaluation.* New York: Scribners.

Hansen, G. P. (1992). CSICOP and the skeptics: An overview. *Journal of the American Society for Psychical Research, 86,* 19–63.

Haraldsson, E., and Houtkooper, J. M. (1992). Effects of perceptual defensiveness, personality and belief on extrasensory perception tasks. *Personality and Individual Differences, 13,* 1085–1096.

Haraldsson, E., and Johnson, M. (1979). ESP and the Defense Mechanism Test (DMT). Icelandic study No. III. A case of experimenter effect? *European Journal of Parapsychology, 3,* 11–20.

Hess, D. J. (1993). *Science in the new age: The paranormal, its defenders and debunkers, and American culture.* Madison: University of Wisconsin Press.

Honorton, C. (1977). Psi and internal attention states. In B. B. Wolman (Ed.), *Handbook of parapsychology* (pp. 435–472). New York: Van Nostrand Reinhold.

Honorton, C. (1978). Psi and internal attention states: Information retrieval in the Ganzfeld. In B. Shapin and L. Coly (Eds.), *Psi and states of awareness* (pp. 79–90). New York: Parapsychology Foundation.

Honorton, C. (1985). Meta-analysis of psi Ganzfeld research: A response to Hyman. *Journal of Parapsychology, 49*, 51–91.

Honorton, C., Berger, R. E., Varvoglis, M. P., Quant, M., Derr, P., Hansen, G. P., Schechter, E., and Ferrari, D. C. (1990). Psi Ganzfeld experiments using an automated testing system: An update and comparison with a meta-analysis of earlier studies. In L. A. Henkel and J. Palmer (Eds.), *Research in parapsychology 1989* (pp. 25–32). Metuchen, NJ: Scarecrow Press.

Honorton, C., and Ferrari, D. C. (1989). "Future telling": A meta-analysis of forced-choice precognition experiments, 1935–1987. *Journal of Parapsychology, 53*, 281–308.

Honorton, C., Ferrari, D. C., and Bem, D. J. (1998). Extraversion and ESP performance: A meta-analysis and a new confirmation. *Journal of Parapsychology, 62*, 255–276.

Humphrey, B. M. (1946a). Success in ESP as related to form of response drawings: I. Clairvoyance experiments. *Journal of Parapsychology, 10*, 78–106.

Humphrey, B. M. (1946b). Success in ESP as related to form of response drawings: II. GESP experiments. *Journal of Parapsychology, 10*, 181–196.

Hyman, R. (1985). The Ganzfeld psi experiment: A critical appraisal. *Journal of Parapsychology, 49*, 3–49.

Hyman, R., and Honorton, C. (1986). A joint communiqué: The psi Ganzfeld controversy. *Journal of Parapsychology, 50*, 351–364.

Inglis, B. (1977). *Natural and supernatural: A history of the paranormal from earliest times to 1914.* London: Hodder & Stoughton.

Irwin, H. J., and Watt, C. A. (2007). *An introduction to parapsychology* (5th ed.). Jefferson, NC: McFarland.

Jung, C. G. (1985). *Synchronicity: An acausal connecting principle.* London: Routledge and Kegan Paul. (Original work published 1955.)

Kittenis, M. D. (2007). *Event-related EEG correlations between physically isolated participants.* Unpublished doctoral thesis, University of Edinburgh, Scotland.

Kittenis, M. D., Caryl, P. G. C., and Stevens, P. (2004, August). *Distant psychophysiological interaction effects between related and unrelated participants.* Paper presented at the 47th Annual Convention of the Parapsychological Association, Vienna, Austria.

Krippner, S., Braud, W., Child, I. L., Palmer, J., Rao, K. R., Schlitz, M., White, R. A., and Utts, J. (1993). Demonstration research and meta-analysis in parapsychology. *Journal of Parapsychology, 57*, 275–286.

Lawrence, T. R. (1993, August). *Gathering in the sheep and the goats . . . : A meta-analysis of forced-choice sheep-goat ESP studies, 1947–1993.* Paper presented at the 36th Annual Convention of the Parapsychological Association, Toronto, Canada.

McDonough, B. E., Don, N. S., and Warren, C. A. (1994, August). *EEG in a Ganzfeld psi task.* Paper presented at the 37th Annual Convention of the Parapsychological Association, Amsterdam, The Netherlands.

McDonough, B. E., Don, N. S., and Warren, C. A. (2000, August). *Gamma band ("40 Hz") EEG and unconscious target detection in a psi task.* Paper presented at the 43rd Annual Convention of the Parapsychological Association, Freiburg, Germany.

McDonough, B. E., Don, N. S., and Warren, C. A. (2002). Differential event-related potentials to targets and decoys in a guessing task. *Journal of Scientific Exploration, 16*, 187–206.

McDonough, B. E., Warren, C. A., and Don, N. S. (1989). EEG analysis of a fortuitous event observed during the psi testing of a selected subject. *Journal of Parapsychology, 53*, 181–201.

Millar, B. (1979). The "Lloyd effect." *European Journal of Parapsychology, 2*, 381–394.

Millett, D. (2001). Hans Berger: From psychic energy to EEG. *Perspectives in Biology and Medicine, 44*, 522–542.

Milton, J. (1997). Meta-analysis of free-response ESP studies without altered states of consciousness. *Journal of Parapsychology, 61*, 279–320.

Milton, J. (1999). Should Ganzfeld research continue to be crucial in the search for a replicable psi effect? Part I. Discussion paper and introduction to an electronic-mail discussion. *Journal of Parapsychology, 63*, 309–333.

Milton, J., and Wiseman, R. (1999). Does psi exist? Lack of replication of an anomalous process of information transfer. *Psychological Bulletin, 125*, 387–391.

Moulton, S. T., and Kosslyn, S. M. (2008). Using neuroimaging to resolve the psi debate. *Journal of Cognitive Neuroscience, 20*, 182–192.

Neppe, V. M. (1983). Temporal lobe symptomatology in subjective paranormal experiments. *Journal of the American Society for Psychical Research, 77*, 1–29.

Palmer, J. (1977). Attitudes and personality traits in experimental ESP research. In B. B. Wolman (Ed.), *Handbook of parapsychology* (pp. 175–201). New York: Van Nostrand Reinhold.

Palmer, J. (1978). Extrasensory perception: Research findings. In S. Krippner (Ed.), *Advances in parapsychological research, Vol. 2: Extrasensory perception* (pp. 59–243). New York: Plenum Press.

Palmer, J. (2003). ESP in the Ganzfeld: Analysis of a debate. *Journal of Consciousness Studies, 10*, 51–68.

Palmer, J., and Carpenter, J. C. (1998). Comments on the extraversion-ESP meta-analysis by Honorton, Ferrari, and Bem. *Journal of Parapsychology, 62*, 277–282.

Palmer, J., and Neppe, V. M. (2003). A controlled analysis of subjective paranormal experiences in temporal lobe dysfunction in a neuropsychiatric population. *Journal of Parapsychology, 67*, 75–98.

Parra, A., and Villanueva, J. (2003). Personality factors and ESP during Ganzfeld sessions. *Journal of the Society for Psychical Research, 67*, 26–36.

Persinger, M. A. (1984). Propensity to report paranormal experiences is correlated with temporal lobe signs. *Perceptual and Motor Skills, 59*, 583–586.

Persinger, M. A., and Makarec, K. (1987). Temporal lobe epileptic signs and correlative behaviors displayed by normal populations. *Journal of General Psychology, 114*, 179–195.

Persinger, M. A., and Valliant, P. M. (1985). Temporal lobe signs and reports of subjective paranormal experiences in a normal population: A replication. *Perceptual and Motor Skills, 60*, 903–909.

Pratt, J. G., Rhine, J. B., Smith, B. M., Stuart, C. E., and Greenwood, J. A. (1940). *Extrasensory perception after sixty years: A critical appraisal of the research in extrasensory perception.* New York: Holt.

Radin, D. I. (2004). Event-related electroencephalographic correlations between isolated human subjects. *Journal of Alternative and Complementary Medicine, 10*, 315–323.

Rebert, C. S., and Turner, A. (1974). EEG spectrum analysis techniques applied to the problem of psi phenomena. *Behavioral Neuropsychiatry, 6*, 18–24.

Rhine, J. B. (1934). *Extra-sensory perception.* Boston: Boston Society for Psychic Research.

Rhine, J. B. (1969). Position effects in psi test results. *Journal of Parapsychology, 33*, 136–157.

Richards, T. L., Kozak, L., Johnson, C., and Standish, L. J. (2005). Replicable functional magnetic resonance imaging evidence of correlated brain signals between physically and sensory isolated subjects. *Journal of Alternative and Complementary Medicine, 11*, 955–963.

Richet, C. (1888). Further experiments in hypnotic lucidity or clairvoyance. *Proceedings of the Society for Psychical Research, 6*, 66–83.

Sabell, A., Clarke, C., and Fenwick, P. (2001, August). *Inter-subject EEG correlations at a distance: The transferred potential*. Paper presented at the 44th Annual Convention of the Parapsychological Association, New York.

Schechter, E. I. (1984). Hypnotic induction vs. control conditions: Illustrating an approach to the evaluation of replicability in parapsychological data. *Journal of the American Society for Psychical Research, 78*, 1–27.

Schmeidler, G. R. (1952). Personal values and ESP scores. *Journal of Abnormal and Social Psychology, 47*, 757–761.

Schmeidler, G. R., and McConnell, R. A. (1958). *ESP and personality patterns*. New Haven, CT: Yale University Press.

Schmidt, S., Schneider, R., Utts, J., and Walach, H. (2004). Distant intentionality and the feeling of being stared at: Two meta-analyses. *British Journal of Psychology, 95*, 235–247.

Schmidt, S., and Walach, H. (2000). Electrodermal activity (EDA)—state of the art measurement and techniques for parapsychological purposes. *Journal of Parapsychology, 64*, 139–163.

Sherwood, S. J., Dalton, K., Steinkamp, F., and Watt, C. (2000). Dream clairvoyance Study II using dynamic video-clips: Investigation of consensus voting judging procedures and target emotionality. *Dreaming, 10*, 221–236.

Sherwood, S. J., and Roe, C. A. (2003). A review of dream ESP studies conducted since the Maimonides dream ESP programme. *Journal of Consciousness Studies, 10*, 85–109.

Sinclair, U. (1962). *Mental radio* (2nd ed.). Springfield, IL: Thomas. (Original work published 1930)

Standish, L. J., Johnson, L. C., Kozak, L., and Richards, T. (2003). Evidence of correlated functional MRI signals between distant human brains. *Alternative Therapies in Health and Medicine, 9*, 122–128.

Standish, L., Kozak, L., Johnson, L., and Richards, T. (2004). Electroencephalographic evidence of correlated event-related signals between the brains of spatially and sensorially isolated human subjects. *Journal of Alternative and Complementary Medicine, 10*, 307–314.

Stanford, R. G., and Stein, A. G. (1994). A meta-analysis of ESP studies contrasting hypnosis and a comparison condition. *Journal of Parapsychology, 58*, 235–269.

Tart, C. T. (1963). Physiological correlates of psi cognition. *International Journal of Parapsychology, 5*, 375–386.

Tart, C. T. (1966). More on extrasensory induction of brain waves. *Science, 151*, 28.

Ullman, M., and Krippner, S. (1970). Dream studies and telepathy. *Parapsychological Monographs, No. 12*. New York: Parapsychology Foundation.

Wackermann, J., Muradás, J. R. N., and Pütz, P. (2004, August). *Event-related correlations between brain electrical activities of separated human subjects: Preliminary results of a replication study*. Paper presented at the 47th Annual Convention of the Parapsychological Association, Vienna, Austria.

Wackermann, J., Seiter, C., Keibel, H., and Walach, H. (2003). Correlations between brain electrical activities of two spatially separated human subjects. *Neuroscience Letters, 336*, 60–64.

Warcollier, R. (1975). *Experimental telepathy.* New York: Arno Press. (Original work published 1938)

Watt, C. A. (1989). Characteristics of successful free-response targets: Theoretical considerations. In L. A. Henkel and R. E. Berger (Eds.), *Research in parapsychology 1988* (pp. 95–99). Metuchen, NJ: Scarecrow Press.

Watt, C. A. (1994). Meta-analysis of DMT-ESP studies and an experimental investigation of perceptual defense/vigilance and extrasensory perception. In E. W. Cook and D. L. Delanoy (Eds.), *Research in parapsychology 1991* (pp. 64–68). Metuchen, NJ: Scarecrow Press.

Watt, C. A., and Morris, R. L. (1995). The relationships among performance on a prototype indicator of perceptual defence/vigilance, personality, and extrasensory perception. *Personality and Individual Differences, 19,* 635–648.

Wiseman, R., Smith, M., and Kornbrot, D. (1996). Exploring possible sender-to-experimenter acoustic leakage in the PRL autoganzfeld experiments. *Journal of Parapsychology, 60,* 97–128.

The Model Maker

CHAPTER 4

The Mind-Body Problem and the Issue of Psychokinesis

Adrian Parker

Most normal human beings, whether or not they have ever consciously articulated it, have a theory of the mind as separate from the body. This implies that they believe other humans also possess minds with their own perspectives on life. With regard to the exact nature of the mind-body relationship, however, opinions become diverse and even emotionally loaded. These opinions may not only reflect unresolved philosophical issues but directly relate to how people regard their bodies, as well as their often strongly held religious and scientific beliefs.

For instance, if we choose to treat headaches with medication, then we are attributing a major role to protein receptors and cell membranes; in so doing, we could easily be subscribing to a *reductionistic materialistic* view where the mental experience is seen as a by-product of chemical reactions. This is, indeed, the approach that most neurobiologists would take. By contrast, if we choose to treat the pain with meditation, this might imply that we are partial to a view of pain being in the mind, a view that might imply that *idealism* is our philosophy. Most psychologists would likely subscribe to a third view in which mind and body are dual aspects of the same basic process; thus, by reducing stress with meditation, those mental processes involved in producing unwelcome symptoms will be largely inactivated.

There are other possibilities as well. The experience of anomalous phenomena such as out-of-body experiences or apparitions is often used to support *dualism*, harkening back to the philosophy of René Descartes claiming that we have a soul that can be separated from the body. Orthodox Christianity, however, mainly for historical reasons relating to its repression of pagan beliefs, seldom welcomes such phenomena as indicating the separateness of mind and body. At the same time, a minority of neurobiologists who are also Christians might accept such beliefs as that angels exist or Jesus could levitate, but not the phenomenon of psychokinesis (PK) itself, the power of the mind to exert an influence on distant physical surroundings.

One of the reasons for the skepticism amongst most neurobiologists regarding PK and related phenomena is not just that they appear to be irrational, but that accepting their validity would have profound and pervasive implications for their subject matter. Given that most neurobiologists are convinced materialists and reductionists, it is not surprising that claims for these phenomena are generally greeted in such circles with ridicule. Nevertheless, a few neurobiologists have shown an interest in parapsychology, and some even deviate radically from the materialistic philosophical standpoint. Among these are three Nobel Prize recipients—who were also well-known dualists. Sir Charles Sherrington (1857–1952), who was largely responsible for the knowledge of how the reflex arc works, was a clear dualist. Roger Sperry (1913–1994), who carried out pioneering work on split brains and initiated the work on functional differences in the hemispheres of the brain, while doubtful that mind and body were separable, believed that consciousness was a unique property in nature, one that had emerged during the course of evolution. And Sir John Eccles (1903–1997), who discovered how nerve impulses are passed from neuron to neuron at the synapses, believed that core consciousness was located in the dominant hemisphere (usually the left), with its locus of interaction uncovered through quantum processes governing the release of transmitter substances at the synapses.

Eccles's focus on the interaction between consciousness and quantum processes turns out to be a key feature in a modern development of this theory by the contemporary neurobiologist and anesthesiologist Stuart Hameroff and the mathematician Sir Roger Penrose (Hameroff, 2006). Instead of focusing on synapses, however, they believe that the site of interaction occurs in the microtubules, a part of the cell skeleton that appears to function like a "quantum computer." This notion is a rather fanciful way to describe the supposedly built-in function of the brain that turns out to resolve a long-standing paradox in quantum physics, the thought experiment of Schrödinger's cat. The life of this virtual cat depends on the outcome of a quantum process, since it is hypothetically enclosed in a situation the development of which determines whether or not poison is released into its cage; until the point of observation of this outcome, the cat is said to be in a paradoxical half-state, neither living nor dead. If similar quantum processes could be shown to occur in the brain, then the brain might be considered an organ that provides the precursors for conscious experience and, along with them, acts of observation that enable the outcomes of its numerous potential states to be realized. The big, as yet unanswered, question is, of course: Do quantum processes actually occur in the brain? (Some authorities argue that the brain is too warm for quantum effects to occur in it.) This question cannot be answered as yet, but this approach is a promising way of resolving the otherwise intractable mind-body problem.

The mind-body philosophy behind the Hameroff-Penrose type of view is not *idealism*, *dualism*, or *materialism*. Rather, it is *panpsychism*, meaning that consciousness can be seen as part of the natural world and not just as a function of the brain. This particular version of panpsychism conceives the precursors of consciousness as built into the fabric of the universe, while the brain enables these properties to be realized. According to this model, it is the unique property of neural matter to provide the means for producing consciousness as signaled by the generation of gamma frequencies through the resolution of quantum equations in the microtubules.

A panpsychism theory not only allows for phenomena such as PK; it may actually demand their existence. But leaving aside speculation, what is known and accepted in this field is that there are specific EEG frequencies associated with alertness and awareness within the so-called higher range of gamma frequency, namely, 80–90 Hz. It is this frequency range and, along with it, conscious awareness, that is eliminated by the action of general anesthetics. The details of how anesthesia actually works, which would obviously shed light on the mind-brain problem, are basically unknown. There are, however, some clues, a major one being that general anesthetics have a high solubility in lipids (hydrophobic fatty compounds). Since there are gap junctions rich in lipids containing microtubules (part of the cytoskeleton) that link individual nerve cells, it is these which could provide the necessary hydrophobic havens for receiving the anesthetics. Further support for the role of the microtubules in the reception of anesthetics comes from the nature of the tubulin protein, which has several transformational states due to its tridimensional form. It is possible that these changes are a way of coding information and that, when this coding occurs, it initiates the recruitment of other, even more distant sites in which a sequence of identical changes occurs by quantum processes known as *nonlocal entanglement*. Since, at the quantum level, information may be entangled irrespective of physical distance, this would occur in the manner of an orchestra suddenly becoming involved in playing a symphony, as it spreads consciousness to various parts of the brain.

A source of controversy in this area is the lip service that is often given to "explaining" the existence of psychic phenomena such as extrasensory perception (ESP) as a form of quantum entanglement exerting nonlocal effects. While such expressions as *entanglement* and *nonlocal effects* have a precise meaning in quantum physics in terms of a confluence in the behavior of paired nuclear particles, the above connotation is, by contrast, an imprecise speculation, because the leap cannot easily be made from a quantum level to that of ESP, which involves large-scale human interactions. Many theorists in this area argue that entanglement is a "micro-PK," or a quantum level form of PK; the effects of these entanglements or coincidences become what we call "extrasensory perception." But what, then, of macro PK—large-scale PK?

Dean Radin's (2006) otherwise lucid and well-argued book, *Entangled Minds: Experiences in Quantum Reality*, is largely mute on this point; in fact, Radin devotes less than one page to large-scale psychokinetic phenomena. Although he accepts a range of other puzzling phenomena, he expresses some skepticism about large-scale psychokinetic effects. So is there any solid evidence that these phenomena do exist? And if so, what do we know about the brain processes involved?

The Evidence for Psychokinesis

Like claims for its counterpart, ESP, the claims for PK attracted scientific attention during the heyday of spiritualism and mediumship. However, since many of them occurred in darkened séance rooms and can be reproduced by today's magicians, this type of evidence carries little weight, at least for those who have not witnessed such phenomena firsthand. Nevertheless, claims for PK are not new phenomena, but have always been part of folklore in the form of so-called "poltergeist" outbreaks. At the same time, this does not mean that they are a common occurrence. In Palmer's (1979) survey of psychic experiences, about 50 percent of the sample reported ESP-type experiences, but only 7 percent reported having "seen an object move without any apparent natural explanation." This represents, nevertheless, a frequency in excess of other aberrations of human functioning, such as epilepsy or hypnotic trance, so the obvious question arises: Given that PK leads to concrete and demonstrable effects, why was it not conclusively documented and demonstrated long ago? In attempts to answer this question, it is usually argued that the very nature of these phenomena—that they are a flagrant contradiction of our core belief systems about reality—actually presupposes limiting conditions on their validation (Batcheldor, 1984). The darkness during séances demanded by spiritualistic mediums is, of course, a good reason to view all such claims with suspicion, but it is just possible that these conditions create the degree of ambiguity necessary for the appearance of the phenomena. This is certainly the view taken by such critical and knowledgeable authorities as the magician George Hansen (2001) and the sociologist James McClenon (2001), both of whom have wide experience with trickery as well as with apparently verifiable phenomena.

While it is understandable that the efforts of the Victorian psychical researchers, even with the aid of their photographers, failed to produce even one case that today remains fully convincing, it is daunting that modern instrumentation and technology have not taken the debate further toward its resolution. The problem is that such advances in sophisticated documentation are hotly followed by equally sophisticated methods of fraud, as with the advent of the digital camera and computer technology that have led to a proliferation of ghost hunting sites, making subterfuge and silliness virtually limitless. Mentalists such as Derren Brown have confused the issue even more by using double bluffs, such as alluding that effects are due to subliminal perception or hypnotic suggestion, when in reality they are mainly due to the more reliable methods of editing and hidden instrumentation. Psychical research has for the most part not kept up with this digitalization of deception, so current attempts at controlling mediums are generally hopelessly outdated. Modern investigations of cases such as the Scole phenomena (Keen, Ellison, and Fontana, 1999) and the David Thompson séances (Keen, 2004) merely applied the best controls of a medium that, while appropriate a century ago, have not kept pace with the magician's store of devices, such as the deft use of light-emitting diodes and remote controls.

Faced with potentially deceptive participants, most modern parapsychologists have chosen to retreat to the apparent safety of the laboratory. However, this move requires making an enormous basic assumption—that individuals with the purported abilities to produce the effects are readily found (i.e., are normally distributed) among student or other volunteer populations. The decision having thus been made, the evidence that this is not the case (Millar, 1979) tends to be ignored and may be one reason why results are mostly marginal and highly dependent on the ambience of the laboratory. In a controversial field and in a cultural Zeitgeist that puts the emphasis on definitive results, the failure to produce large-scale effects to order means that the field becomes defined by its marginality. Science demands not only demonstrability of controversial phenomena, but also reliability in replicating the conditions for reproducing them.

The current results from laboratory research on PK are an example in point. An essential feature of modern PK experimentation involves testing whether or not the intention or the will of the participant can influence the outcome of random number generators by making them less random in prespecified directions. This form of experimentation was conducted at the Princeton Engineering Anomalies Research (PEAR) laboratory at Princeton University, which summarized in 1987 the laboratory's supposedly successful series of experiments of this type (Jahn, Dunne, and Nelson, 1987). The researchers reported a highly significant statistical effect over many millions of trials, but it was also a very marginal effect (of the order of one bit of information changed in approximately every 10,000 instances). Encouraged by the significance (rather than the marginality) of these results, the PEAR work became the center of the largest and most expensive collaborative study ever conducted in parapsychology, with a "consortium" of laboratories at Princeton, Freiberg, and Geissen (both of the latter in Germany). The results of this large-scale effort at replication failed to confirm either the effect size or the level of significance of the earlier studies (Jahn et al., 2000), even though the data for each center were in the direction of confirmation.

In 2006 a meta-analysis of all of the experimental data on PK that had used random number generators was conducted (Bösch, Steinkamp, and Boller, 2006). The analysis, based on 380 random number generation studies, found only a very small effect size, which its authors believed could, in principle, be accounted for by a publication bias, meaning that there may be a bias in research to report only significant studies.

On the other hand, some provocative trends in the data emerged from the three largest studies, which were between 100 and 1,000 times the size of the rest of the database and were linked to one laboratory. These larger studies actually showed a significant effect in the direction opposite to the participants' intentions. This out come suggests that concluding that PK probably did not exist was tantamount to saying that, because many patients were made worse by a drug and few were made better, the drug had no effect at all. Clearly, it could be important to look further at why such differences occurred.

One clue that emerged from the Bösch, Steinkamp, and Boller (2006) study was the significant negative correlation between study size and statistical significance, meaning that the smaller the study, the greater the effect that was found. To many counteradvocates, this meant that the small studies were unreliable, but this is a classical reasoning error in psychology, and most statisticians would likely argue for the opposite conclusion.

These statistically significant reversed findings on the larger studies (often called "psi-missing") are somewhat of an enigma in parapsychology and lead to skepticism in counteradvocates. Yet, if it turns out to be valid, psi-missing may be a uniquely important discovery in psi research. Similar findings are being reported in cognitive psychology concerning the studies of subliminal processes (Glaser and Kihlstrom, 2005), although as yet no plausible theory within this field can account for them. In addition, with the exception of the PEAR studies, the most successful results often came from work with selected "star participants," rather than from using massive indiscriminate testing.

It is almost a mantra in parapsychology that extraordinary phenomena require extraordinary evidence, but given this, they may need extraordinary theories as well. One such theory was developed by the German physicist and parapsychologist Walter Von Lucadou (1997); what makes it worth considering is that it is in line with what was mentioned earlier in terms of our beliefs imposing a limiting factor on PK. According to Von Lucadou, the achievement of complete and reliable paranormal effects is impossible, because such a state would upset the balance of the system of belief structures regulating the world of which we are a part. However, there appear to be some cases in psi research where a *completely correct* transfer of information (such as a word transmitted over a distance) has occurred; if these instances could be made to occur on a regular basis, this would, if not exactly upset the world order, at least invalidate this theory (Carpenter, 1975). Either the findings in parapsychology are illusory, due to an accumulation of varying sources of known and unknown errors, or they are due to a complexity of psychological factors, including those relating to beliefs, that make replications difficult (Etzold, 2006).

Where does this leave us? Clearly PK cannot be considered in any sense demonstrable or "proven" on such shaky data as these. It becomes ironic that, despite all the enormous efforts, the best supporting data appear to come from studies of phenomena outside the laboratory, such as with so-called macro-PK and through the testing of specially selected individuals or groups. The purpose of the retreat to laboratory studies was to enable incontrovertible evidence of PK to be found, but this has not occurred. Hence, in considering these claims, it should be mentioned that there is a crucial difference between the laboratory form of PK, so-called micro-PK, which tries to affect the outcome of random number generators, and macro-PK, which attempts to move entire objects. This difference does not only relate to the scale of the effect. As was mentioned earlier in the discussion of the panpsychism theory of Hameroff and Penrose, many advocates of micro-PK see it as the basis for understanding psi phenomena as a whole. For them, psi is the mediator of admittedly small but, over many trials, highly significant effects where the consciousness of the observer affects the outcome of random processes. Indeed, it is for this reason that these theories have become known as *observational theories*, since they refer to the interaction of conscious intention with otherwise random processes in the laboratory or even in nature, but still only at a micro level (Houtkooper, 2002). This is no doubt why the theorists in this area, who are mainly physicists, prefer to dismiss large-scale macro-PK phenomena as fraudulent or at best unresolved, because such effects cannot be easily accommodated by this theory. A different theory would be required to explain how the potential energy in matter is converted to kinetic energy. It is difficult to understand the actual mechanics of how this could produce intentional movements.

One area of testing that is intermediate between the study of large-scale effects (macro-PK) and the use of random number generators (micro-PK) concerns the use of small, moving objects, such as dice or ball bearings. Of course, even rolling dice can be regarded as entering a state of indeterminacy prior to their final stationary state and the act of observation, but this is not really within the sphere of what is usually considered to be *quantum* indeterminacy. A wholesale or meta-analysis of all the available research data from this area has been carried out, as described below.

For the meta-analysis, Radin and Ferrari (1991) included every dice-throwing PK study they could find that was carried out between 1935 and 1987. Their data included the results from 52 experimenters with 2,569 research participants making 2.6 million dice throws in a total of 148 experiments. The results showed a marginal, but nevertheless highly significant effect, with an overall hit rate of 51.2 percent with odds against chance of a billion to one compared to control studies, for which scores fell at the chance expectancy of 50 percent. Sifting out the studies that controlled for a bias of die face reduced the significance considerably, but even then the results were 5,000 to one against chance. Small, but highly significant, effect sizes in normal science are often valuable (such as in the anticoagulation effect of aspirin as a preventative remedy against heart disease). However, in controversial areas when there is a small effect, critics can always assume there is an "error some place," although it is hard in this case to conceive of an error that would have such a universal effect and at the same time is not present in control studies.

Returning to our earlier observation, the reason that the effect is so small may be quite simply that PK ability is not normally distributed in the population; even if it is, only a very few individuals will possess it to a marked degree. As a result, the high performance of these relatively few individuals could easily be lost in a large database. Indeed, the most successful PK studies come from two individuals: the

Norwegian electrical engineer Haakon Forwald and the German American physicist Helmut Schmidt, who were consistently and highly successful *both as participants and as experimenters*. Although criticized for this double role as researcher-participants, Forwald and Schmidt continued to succeed in the presence of other experimenters (Forwald and Pratt, 1958; Schmidt, 1993).

The database put together by Radin and Ferrari (1991) does reveal something more about the actual nature of the phenomena. The significance of the size of the PK effect appeared to increase with the number of dice used (up to a point of about 30 dice). It was as if PK were a force that could be directed at several dice at once. Laboratory experiments may not demonstrate PK, but they give us reason to look at the largely forgotten claims for large-scale psychokinetic phenomena such as poltergeist appearances and physical mediumship, where large objects ostensibly are moved by what seems to be a force. Needless to say, the implications here for a mind-body theory are provocative. If supported, PK data would suggest that the mind is associated with an actual force and that major aberrations in what we otherwise perceive as a stable reality can occur as a result of this force.

The issues concerning cases of physical mediumship are in some areas quite clear, while in others they seem to be intractable. What is clear, for instance, is that many outstanding feats of reported table levitation and so-called "materialization" were produced during poor conditions of human observation and that most of the claimed effects can be reproduced by professional magicians and illusionists. We now know much more about how belief can produce extensive and elaborate false perceptions and memories (Wilson and French, 2006). Because of this, the only cases that can carry any weight for the counteradvocate are those in which human testimony is supported by camera or video documentation. Even where there is documentation, the resulting controversy, such as that surrounding Uri Geller (Margolis, 1998), can become intractable. The videotapes of Geller being tested at the Stanford Research Institute during the 1970s are now, for the most part, available online for viewing (www.YouTube.com); they show Geller bending metallic objects without obvious evidence of fraudulent means, but never without his making physical contact with the objects. Whatever is concluded, without this form of preserved documentation to analyze, human testimony about what happened would naturally lose its impact with the passage of time. This is not to say that human testimony is worthless; indeed, if it were we could never use it in law courts. As it is, many findings in forensic psychology specify the conditions for accuracy and reliability (see Braude, 1997; Cornell and Gauld, 1979; Randall, 1982, for reviews of some of the more impressive poltergeist and physical medium cases).

One of the first attempts at providing such instrument-based documentation involved the Austrian medium Rudi Schneider, who was active from the 1920s until 1936 (Gregory, 1985). Even by today's standards, these investigations were sophisticated and enabled inexplicable movements to be documented by activating a camera and a flashlight. The resulting photographic records from such occasions generally failed to show anything suspicious that would account for the effects produced on objects in the room. Also unaccountable were occasions when instrumentation showed that the infra beam was being interrupted, while nothing was photographed in its path. It was precisely on such occasions that the most remarkable findings were obtained. The interruption of the beam was shown to be a result of its partial absorption, and this in turn was shown to follow the medium's pattern of breathing as he increased his breath rate upon entering what he experienced as a state of "spirit possession." Of course, it can be speculated that the increase in respiration rate might have occurred in the context of some form of fraudulent movement, but the graphic record of his breathing together with photographic evidence showed that this was not the case (Strutt, 1938). One conclusion is inescapable: either the PK effect was due to subtle fraudulent movements that somehow managed to evade the camera and instrumentation or, alternatively, PK is a force related to and correlated with unconscious mental effort to produce extraneous effects.

While photographic evidence strengthens the Schneider case, its absence or incompleteness faults some of the more modern "well documented" poltergeist cases, such as those of Rosenheim (Bender, 1974) and Enfield (Playfair, 1980). The same is true with regard to investigations of physical mediumship, such as the Scole case (Keen, Ellison, and Fontana, 1999). Even the results of the so-called Philip group in Canada during the 1970s, which recorded table-tilting experiments on camera (and which, like many others, is now available online at www.YouTube.com), are unconvincing, since the table appears to be lightweight and never is there a complete levitation. Such effects could easily be achieved by unconscious muscular movements of the kind shown to be involved in automatic writing.

A valiant attempt by the Danish photographer Sven Türck (1945) "to prove PK" by means of camera documentation occurred as early as the 1940s. Türck used three cameras operated by remote control to document what appeared to be *complete* table levitation. His intention was to simultaneously use his three cameras to obtain a complete view of the levitation that would make the sitters' positions and hands visible and would thereby exclude fraud as an explanation. Türck was even brave enough to get the photographs examined and certified as genuine by photographic experts. Sixty years later, Danish television managed to find one of the still-living participants in the séances who attested to the authenticity of the effects. So what do we conclude? The pictures are superficially impressive, but it could have been the case that they were taken after the table had been lifted by normal means and then intentionally released, so that at the point of photographing the table was dropping in midair rather than hovering or rising. A movie-camera recording that could have resolved this issue was also made by Türck, but following his death it was destroyed by his wife, who viewed the phenomena as diabolical.

A similar fate very nearly befell what appears to be another singularly impressive film recording, made by Charles Honorton (1993). It shows the alleged PK ability of one of Honorton's assistants at the Maimonides Dream Laboratory in Brooklyn,

Felicia Parise. Parise was inspired by the film recording of the Russian PK claimant Nina Kulagina, even though Kulagina's performance was not observed under rigidly controlled conditions. Because of political restrictions, Western visitors to Russia often resorted to observing her performance in hotel rooms and could not search her for hidden magnets or threads. Nevertheless, she did produce movements with nonmagnetic objects and even, on occasion, produced movement with objects that investigators had brought with them for this purpose (Keil et al., 1976).

After months of effort, Parise appeared to be able to produce similar effects. Even though this case concerned a research assistant in whom he had full confidence, Honorton was naturally cautious about drawing any conclusions concerning the authenticity of the phenomenon—at least until he had made the appropriate checks for magnets, threads, and other fraudulent means by which they might have been produced. After these possibilities were ruled out, he brought in a magician and filmed Parise's performance, following which he then persuaded her to demonstrate these ability to several of his colleagues. Like the cases of Nina Kulagina and Rudi Schneider, the production of the alleged phenomena appeared to demand a high physiological arousal in terms of breathing and heart rate, with the result that eventually Parise tired of being a research guinea pig and declined to carry out further experimentation.

According to Honorton's (1993) account, some of the PK effects occurred at a distance from her but, nevertheless, seemed related to her area of concentration and were not associated with her hand movements as in the case of Kulagina. For a period of time, only one copy of the Parise film was known to exist, and it appeared to have been, as often happens, irretrievably misplaced. After some searching, another copy was recently located in the Koestler Unit at Edinburgh University, Honorton's last place of work before his untimely death in 1992.

What is clear from this is that, if macro-PK ability actually exists, it is a rare phenomenon, and even rarer when it occurs at a conscious level, since it seems to require a physically demanding and constant state of arousal. There is, fortunately, some important research that gives further insights into why this may be so.

The Phenomenology of PK Performance

The most comprehensive and groundbreaking work on the rare individuals who claim to have PK ability was carried out by the physician/parapsychologist Pamela Heath (2000, 2003). Her participants were only eight in number, and all seemed to be talented adepts. Considering the rarity of this apparent ability and that, as an entry criterion to the study, Heath demanded a verification of the ability both by a reputable witness and by a research laboratory, finding so many adepts was a truly remarkable achievement. Since the focus of Heath's investigation was phenomenological, this meant asking nonleading and open-ended questions about the circumstances in which their experiences occurred. The report is even more remarkable in that, given the nature of subjective experiences, it reaches a clear consensus as to what the "core PK experience" is and how it may be produced. Heath was able to obtain a rather detailed and lengthy list of 17 agreed-upon characteristics. Paraphrasing all these and making coherent links between them entails, of course, some risk for simplification, but it is clear that the foremost of these concerned the induction of an altered state, possibly occurring as a result of emotional arousal. This PK-conducive state was further described as involving a suspension of one's critical ability and dissociation from one's ordinary sense of identity. It would seem that the resulting heightened awareness from this state could then be focused on the target material so as to reach a sense of "connectiveness" with it. A final part of the consensus description concerned the attainment of a physical state involving a sense of transcendental energy, a release of effort, and a trust in and openness to the experience so that the process could occur. Additionally, the process would be actively guided through intent and through visualization, and possibly aided by active hand movements. Heath found further confirmation for her definition of the core PK experience from descriptions contained in the older psychical research literature.

Several participants had their own personal explanations of how they produced the effects, such as carrying out certain rituals or linking themselves with discarnate entities, which Heath speculated might have simply served as a means of avoiding the burden of "owning" the ability. Conscious beliefs concerning PK were said not to be, in themselves, so critical; it was being open to the experience that was important.

Heath's criteria are important for two reasons. Even if the phenomena were of an illusionary nature, the described procedure could provide a recipe for studying how illusory effects might occur. On the other hand, if the effects were genuine, then we would have to ask what is happening in the brain to mediate them and what implications does this have for a theory of the mind-body relationship.

Psychokinesis and Neurobiology

The major effort aimed at connecting PK and neurobiology is to be found in the work of W. G. Roll and Michael Persinger (e.g., Roll and Persinger, 1998a, 1998b). Their goal was to relate PK in poltergeist cases to neural disturbances occurring in the context of epilepsy or epileptic-like episodes. Roll and his colleagues (e.g., Roll, 2003; Roll et al., 2002; Roll and Montagno, 1983; Roll and Pratt, 1971) have consistently assembled extensive case studies to support the theory that the PK agents in poltergeist cases usually are young, disturbed adolescents with a suspected neuropsychological dysfunction. Fifty-three percent of the agents in their sample were judged to have symptoms suggestive of epilepsy, in particular the form of epilepsy known as partial complex epilepsy involving the temporal lobe. Since there is also some evidence that PK and other anomalous experiences occur more often during sudden changes in geomagnetic and electromagnetic fields, Roll and his co-workers have made an ambitious attempt to develop a theory that brings together all these findings. In doing so, recurrent spontaneous psychokinesis (RSPK, the technical term for poltergeist cases) is thought to occur in the context of disturbed personal relationships, where there is a predisposition toward partial temporal lobe epilepsy and also, because of it, sensitivity to variations in geomagnetic fields. The theory proposes that the predisposition for epileptic episodes is exacerbated both by family conflicts and by changes in the ambient geomagnetic field. Such episodes, resulting as they might in a major neurological discharge, are supposed then—and this is the extreme part of the theory—to lead to a situation during which the brain converts the excess electromagnetic energy into kinetic energy in the form of effects on distant objects. Depending on family relationships, this can even become a means of expressing otherwise inhibited aggression.

Obviously, there is an enormous leap of reasoning toward the end of this hypothesized sequence, since there is no real understanding of how such an effect could occur over considerable distance, except perhaps by appealing to unknown quantum processes and nonlocal effects in the remote objects. Just how quantum decision-making processes can be applied to influencing remote objects is unclear; moreover, how such quantum effects, if they occur at all, can lead to the directional and intentional effects that typify RSPK reports is left unresolved.

There may even be reason to doubt the other part of the theory, which stands on the alleged epilepsy connection. Reaching a psychiatric diagnosis, especially when it is based on case records, can easily become a mirror reflecting personal biases to select and interpret ambiguous information as confirming the hypothesis being tested (Martinez-Taboas and Alvarado, 1984). In fact, the cases that had received an independent diagnosis of epilepsy amounted only to some 4 percent, a figure that is not substantially higher than the incidence of epilepsy amongst adolescents, usually given as around 1–2 percent.

In trying to understand further how PK might relate to brain processes, we have little to go on in terms of formal studies. A review of the literature by Williams and Roll (Chapter 1) concluded that PK scores on random event or random number generators tend to be associated with alpha wave activation. Psi-hitting was found to be mostly related to the activation of the right hemisphere, while psi-missing occurred in connection with the left hemisphere. Interesting as this is, it provides no deeper insight into the dynamics of the whole process. One of Roll's more long-term case studies (Roll, 1993; Roll and Storey, 2004) may yield some useful insights, and is based on the case of Tina Resch. Resch was an adopted teenager who fulfilled all the classical entry criteria for Roll's poltergeist cases involving suspected brain damage and associated suspected seizures.

The PK aspect was, however, controversial, involving claims and counterclaims between Roll and the magician James Randi. Roll, in his reports, assimilated photographic and witness evidence to support the conclusion that a genuine phenomenon was involved. Nevertheless, even though the case took place over several years, the photographic evidence is very meager and depends for its interpretation entirely on witness reliability and accuracy. The professional photographer involved commented on the difficulties involved in such documentation, observing that "trying to catch the phenomena on film was the most challenging assignment of [his] thirty years in the news business" (Roll and Storey, 2004, p. 82).

Resch went through extensive testing; the neuropsychological tests indicated two brain abnormalities, which might relate to RSPK: one occurred in the brain stem and one in the frontotemporal lobe. In commenting on the latter aspect, Roll and Persinger (1998b) noted:

> It may be significant that "autonoetic memory," memories as experiences of the *self*, is mediated by the right frontal lobe. Autonoetic consciousness is a unique attribute of the developed human brain and could explain why RSPK is not seen in animals or very young children. (p. 188)

Roll's colleague in this area, neuropsychologist Michael Persinger, has conducted further work on this "autonoetic consciousness" (Persinger and Makarec, 1993). When Persinger applied weak magnetic fields to the temporal lobes of normal volunteers, the participants commonly reported experiencing a sense of the presence of a "sentient being." In some cases Persinger found the procedure was potent enough to induce a religious-type experience. One hypothesis used to explain this is that the dominant hemisphere (usually the left) interprets a "sense of presence" from the increased awareness that results from the magnetic stimulation of the nondominant hemisphere (usually the right). Giving some further support to Roll's theory is the finding that many of the signs of complex partial epilepsy occur to some extent even in normal individuals; for them there is a strong relationship between experiencing a sense of presence and reporting parapsychological experiences. Moreover, there are supportive findings indicating that disturbances in the function of the temporal lobe occur more frequently in persons reporting parapsychological experiences (Neppe, 1983).

There is, however, a serious limitation to the above findings concerning claims for hemisphere activation producing a sense of presence, namely: the lack of adequate control groups that would permit evaluation of the effect of exposing participants to a procedure with the implicit expectancy of their experiencing something unusual. A dramatic confirmation of what can be produced by instilling expectancies in participants occurred when a Swedish research team used a *sham* magnetic field but otherwise followed the same procedure as did Persinger; they found that this group reported almost as many experiences of a sense of presence as those who were given actual magnetic stimulation of the temporal lobe (Granqvist et al., 2005).

In fact, there is good reason to view many findings in this larger area of neurobiology and neuroscience with some skepticism. In 2008, the neuroscience journal

Cortex published a special issue containing an array of articles claiming to relate para-psychological belief and experiences in the normal population to brain dysfunction. Since such beliefs and experiences are about as common as the denial of such experiences, it would surely be equally justifiable to reverse the rationale and carry out the same study, this time directed at finding abnormalities in the overskeptical group. The risk with neurologizing normal experiences is, of course, that of making neuroscience into the modern equivalent of psychoanalysis. Indeed, many of the findings reported in *Cortex* were statistically nonsignificant or were arrived at only after over-analyzing the data until significant results were bound to appear. For example, one study generalized directly from findings based on an extreme group of "believers," namely, those reporting extraterrestrial contact, to the psychological profile of all "believers" in so-called paranormal effects (French et al., 2008). Little attempt was made in any of the 10 reports to distinguish between those who claimed to be disturbed by paranormal experiences as part of their proneness to psychotic-like experiences (schizotypal personality) and those reporting paranormal experiences but experiencing balanced mental health. The editorial lamented "neuromythology" in this area, but then chose only to add more to it, on the ground that these contributions as a whole might open the door for wider use of the word "neuro" (Brugger and Mohr, 2008). One can only further lament that, had the enormous resources spent on these studies been given to researchers in parapsychology, some greater clarity as to the nature of the phenomena might have been reached.

Conclusion

In the absence of adequate research resources, what emerges from this analysis is a question: Is it reasonable to expect that a limited number of investigations can resolve all the doubts, contradictions, and uncertainties that bedevil this area? Intolerance for ambiguity seems to characterize much of the research in parapsychology; ironically, it is in terms of this precise characteristic that extreme advocates and extreme counteradvocates appear to share common ground (Lange and Houran, 2001). It seems foolhardy at this stage to set up absolute declarations in this area. More is to be gained by the human qualities of openness along with skepticism. If PK exists, then it seems clear from this review that the phenomenon occurs more in the form of a force rather than as a pure quantum effect. But could it be in some measure both? A possible answer may be found in a huge project (encouraged by the cosmic humor of the actor John Cleese who, as a benefactor of the Esalen Institute, supported it) that Edward and Emily Kelly and their co-workers undertook. This was an enormous scholarly work, titled *Irreducible Mind*, which brought together human knowledge about the mind and brain from all the relevant sciences: neurobiology, quantum physics, psychology, psychical research, and experimental parapsychology (Kelly et al., 2007). These authors concluded that the insights of

Frederic Myers and William James, whom they considered to be the two foremost classical thinkers in psychology, have now largely been validated by subsequent research, suggesting that it is, therefore, time to positively reevaluate their theories. Much of what Myers and James described is now becoming generally accepted—as, for example, their conclusion that considerable processing of information and emotion occurs outside of ordinary awareness. While the concept of the Freudian unconscious is thought by many writers to be obsolete, such terms as "the cognitive unconscious" and "the emotional unconscious" are now in vogue to describe a similar form of processing (Hassin, Uleman, and Barh, 2005).

When using these terms, contemporary psychologists actually owe more to Myers than to Freud, since it was Myers who introduced the concept of subliminal processes or information processing outside of awareness. Yet Myers viewed the mind as both a gold mine and a rubbish heap, citing many examples of a "higher supraliminal consciousness" and of a "co-consciousness." James had a similar view, at times doubting the existence of a stable core self and instead hypothesizing that the brain functions to filter a larger extended awareness of which our individual consciousness is part. It is when we occasionally gain a glimpse of the whole that we have a mystical experience. Evolution has reinforced the faculties necessary for survival, but there may remain vestigial ways of perceiving and experiencing. In arguing for this idea, both Myers and James were occupying a middle position, or perhaps even a third position, between dualism and panpsychism.

The treatise of the Kelly team (Kelly et al., 2007) had one further ambition, the formidable task of updating the theories of Myers and James with the findings of quantum physics. In so doing, they gave considerable importance to the work of the physicist Henry Stapp. Stapp regarded the passive processing of information in the brain, through what some psychologists call "bottom-up processes," as providing raw information, which leads to innumerable quantum states at the neurochemical level (Stapp, 2005). However, for one of these states to dominate and resolve into a perceptual experience, consciousness must provide an interpretation (or what some psychologists call "top-down processes"). Ordinarily, modern psychology sidesteps this issue by placing incoming information in what is called a "global workspace" or sometimes even "the theatre of the mind" (Baars, 1997), locating this space anatomically where most of the neurological action appears to be taking place, namely, in the rear of the forebrain (the diencephalon). According to conventional thinking, what we experience may be said to be produced by scene workers and actors, but it is a performance carried out by "philosophical zombies" without an audience; in other words, as Blackmore (2007) concludes, consciousness is simply an illusion.

The critical issue with which we are left is the following: Which portrayal of consciousness is correct? Many of the "rogue phenomena," which the Kelly team chooses to call PK, stigmata, and anomalous healing, seem—if genuine—to support the

Stapp scenario. According to Kelly et al., such effects would have to be brought about at the level of consciousness that we all require in order for learning to occur.

There are, of course, gaps in the theory. However, the Kelly team referred to another major psychologist and parapsychologist, William McDougall (1911–1961), whose work may fill in one of the gaps. It was McDougall who gave importance to consciousness in terms of expressing purpose, dispositions, and what he called the "Will," terms that until recently had become nearly taboo in cognitive psychology. From McDougall's point of view, it might be possible to regard PK as a rogue expression of consciousness—as perhaps the exertion of force or "Will"—in a quantum decision-making process. It is conceivable that such a theory could provide future grounds for reconciling what Heath (in her phenomenological approach) and Roll and Persinger (in their neurobiological approach) were describing. If so, the research reviewed here might make a deeper and more lasting contribution by showing both the importance and the complexity of intending to make something that is wished for actually happen. Certainly, any progress in parapsychology is contingent on progress in neurobiology and vice versa; if there are genuine phenomena at work here, then both disciplines are needed to solve the fundamental problem with which we began, namely, what consciousness is and how it relates to the body.

References

Baars, B. J. (1997). *In the theatre of consciousness: The workspace of the mind.* New York: Oxford University Press.

Batcheldor, K. J. (1984). Contributions to the theory of PK induction from sitter-group work. *Journal of the American Society for Psychical Research, 78,* 105–122.

Bender, H. (1974). Modern poltergeist research. In J. Beloff (Ed.), *New directions in parapsychological research* (pp. 122–143). London: Elek.

Blackmore, S. (2007). *Consciousness: An introduction.* London: Hodder & Stoughton.

Bösch, H., Steinkamp, F., and Boller, E. (2006). Examining psychokinesis: The interaction of human intention with random number generators—A meta-analysis. *Psychological Bulletin, 132,* 497–523.

Braude, S. (1997). *The limits of influence: Psychokinesis and the philosophy of science.* Lanham, MD: University Press of America.

Brugger, P., and Mohr, C. (2008). The paranormal mind: How the study of anomalous experiences and beliefs may inform cognitive neuroscience. *Cortex, 44*(10), 1291–1298.

Carpenter, J. (1975, January). *Toward the effective utilization of enhanced weak signal ESP effects.* Paper presented at the meeting of the American Association for the Advancement of Science, New York.

Cornell, A. D., and Gauld, A. (1979). *Poltergeists.* London: Routledge & Kegan Paul.

Etzold, E. (2006). Does psi exist and can we prove it? Belief and disbelief in psychokinesis research. *Journal of Parapsychology, 21,* 38–57.

Forwald, H. G., and Pratt, J. G. (1958). Confirmation of the PK placement effect. *Journal of Parapsychology, 22,* 1–19.

French, C., Santomaro, J., Hamilton, V., Fox. R., and Thalbourne, M. (2008). Psychological aspects of alien contact experience. *Cortex, 44*(10), 1387–1395.

Glaser, J., and Kihlstrom, J. F. (2005). Compensatory automaticity: Unconscious volition is not an oxymoron. In R. R. Hassin, J. S. Uleman, and J. A. Bargh (Eds.), *The new unconscious* (pp. 171–195). New York: Oxford University Press.

Granqvist, P., Fredrikson, M., Unge, P., Hagenfeldt, A., Valind, S., Larhammar, D., and Larsson, M. (2005). Sensed presence and mystical experiences are predicted by suggestibility, not by the application of transcranial weak complex magnetic fields. *Neuroscience Letter, 380*, 346–347.

Gregory, A. (1985). *The strange case of Rudi Schneider.* Metuchen, NJ: Scarecrow Press.

Hameroff, S. (2006). Consciousness, neurobiology, and quantum mechanics: The case for connection. In J. Tuszynsk (Ed.), *The emerging physics of consciousness* (pp. 194–253). Berlin: Springer-Verlag.

Hansen, G. P. (2001). *The trickster and the paranormal.* New York: Xlibris.

Hassin, R., Uleman, J., and Barh, J. (Ed.). (2005). *The new unconscious.* Oxford, U.K.: Oxford University Press.

Heath, P. R. (2000). The PK zone: A phenomenological study. *Iridis, 40*(6), 3–8.

Heath, P. R. (2003). What is psychokinesis? *Iridis, 46*(3), 1–5.

Honorton, C. (1993). "A moving experience." *Journal of the American Society for Psychical Research, 87*, 329–340.

Houtkooper, J. M. (2002). Arguing for an observational theory of paranormal phenomena. *Journal of Scientific Exploration, 16*, 171–185.

Jahn, R. G., Dunne, B. J., and Nelson, R. D. (1987). Engineering anomalies research. *Journal of Scientific Exploration, 1*(1), 21–50.

Jahn, R. G., Mischo, J., Vaitl, D., Dunne, B. J., Bradish, G. J., Dobyns, Y. H., et al. (2000). Mind/machine interaction consortium: PortREG replication experiments. *Journal of Scientific Exploration, 14*, 499–555.

Keen, M. (2004). Materializations at the David Thompson séance. *Journal of Religion and Psychical Research, 27*, 72–91.

Keen, M., Ellison, A., and Fontana, D. (1999). The Scole report. *Proceedings of the Society for Psychical Research, 58*(220), 150–542.

Keil, H. H. J., Herbert, B., Ullman, M., and Pratt, J. G. (1976). Directly observable PK effects: A survey and tentative interpretation of available findings from Nina Kulagina and other known related cases of recent date. *Proceedings of the Society for Psychical Research, 56*, 197–235.

Kelly, E. F., Kelly, E. W., Crabtree, A., Grosso, M., and Greyson, B. (2007). *Irreducible mind: Toward a psychology for the 21st century.* Lanham, MD: Rowman & Littlefield.

Lange, R., and Houran, J. (2001). Ambiguous stimuli brought to life: The psychological dynamics of hauntings and poltergeists. In R. Lange and J. Houran (Eds.), *Hauntings and poltergeists: Multidisciplinary perspectives* (pp. 280–306). Jefferson, NC: McFarland.

Margolis, J. (1998). *Uri Geller: Magician or mystic?* London: Orion.

Martinez-Taboas, A., and Alvarado, C. (1984). Poltergeist agents: A review of recent research trends and conceptualizations. *European Journal of Parapsychology, 4*, 99–110.

McClenon, J. (2001). The sociological investigation of haunting cases. In R. Lange and J. Houran (Eds.), *Hauntings and poltergeists: Multidisciplinary perspectives* (pp. 62–81). Jefferson, NC: McFarland.

McDougall, W. (1961). *Body and mind: A history and defense of animism*. Boston: Beacon. (Original work published 1911.)

Millar, B. (1979). The distribution of psi. *European Journal of Parapsychology, 3*, 78–110.

Neppe, V. M. (1983). Temporal lobe symptomatology in subjective paranormal experients. *Journal of the American Society for Psychical Research, 10*, 1–31.

Palmer, J. (1979). A community mail survey of psychic experiences. *Journal of the American Society for Psychical Research, 73*, 221–252.

Persinger, M. A., and Makarec, K. (1993). Complex partial epileptic signs as a continuum from normals to epileptics: Normative data and clinical populations. *Journal of Clinical Psychology, 49*, 33–45.

Playfair, G. L. (1980). *This house is haunted*. London: Sphere.

Radin, D. (2006). *Entangled minds: Extrasensory experiences in a quantum reality*. New York: Paraview.

Radin, D., and Ferrari, D. C. (1991). Effects of consciousness on the fall of dice: A meta-analysis. *Journal of Scientific Exploration, 5*, 61–84.

Randall, J. L. (1982). *Psychokinesis: A study of paranormal forces through the ages*. London: Souvenir.

Roll, W. G. (1993). The question of RSPK versus fraud in the case of Tina Resch. *Proceedings of Presented Papers: The Parapsychological Association 36th Annual Convention*, 456–482.

Roll, W. G. (2003). Poltergeists, electromagnetism, and consciousness. *Journal of Scientific Exploration, 17*, 75–86.

Roll, W. G., and Montagno, E. de A. (1983). Similarities between RSPK and psychomotor epilepsy. In W. G. Roll, J. Beloff, and R. A. White (Eds.), *Research in parapsychology 1982* (pp. 270–271). Metuchen, NJ: Scarecrow Press.

Roll, W. G., and Persinger, M. A. (1998a). Is ESP a form of perception? Contributions from a study of Sean Harribance. *Proceedings of Presented Papers: The Parapsychological Association 41st Annual Convention*, 199–209.

Roll, W. G., and Persinger, M. A. (1998b). Poltergeist and nonlocality: Energetic aspects of RSPK. *Proceedings of Presented Papers: The Parapsychological Association 41st Annual Convention*, 184–198.

Roll, W. G., Persinger, M. A., Webster, D. L., Tiller, S. G., and Cook, C. M. (2002). Neurobehavioral and neurometabolic (SPECT) correlates of paranormal information: Involvement of the right hemisphere and its sensitivity to weak complex magnetic fields. *International Journal of Neuroscience, 112*, 197–224.

Roll, W. G., and Pratt, J. G. (1971). The Miami disturbances. *Journal of the American Society for Psychical Research, 65*, 409–454.

Roll, W. G., and Storey, V. (2004). *Unleashed: Of poltergeists and murder. The curious story of Tina Resch*. New York: Paraview.

Schmidt, H. (1993). Observation of a psychokinetic effect under highly controlled conditions. *Journal of Parapsychology, 57*, 351–372.

Stapp, H. (2005). Quantum interactive dualism: An alternative to materialism. *Journal of Consciousness Studies, 12*, 43–58.

Strutt, J. R. (1938). The problem of physical phenomena in connection with psychical research. *Proceedings of the Society for Psychical Research, 44*, 152.

Türck, S. (1945). *Jeg var dus med aanderne* [I got personal with the spirits]. Copenhagen: Hasselbach.

Von Lucadou, W. (1997). Psi-Phänomene: neue Ergebnisse der Psychokinese-Forschung. [Psi-phenomena: New results of psychokinesis research]. Leipzig, Germany: Insel-Verlag.

Wilson, K., and French, C. C. (2006). The relationship between susceptibility to false memories, dissociativity, and paranormal belief and experience. *Personality and Individual Differences, 41*, 1493–1502.

The Monastery

CHAPTER 5

The Neurobiology of Trance and Mediumship in Brazil

Joan H. Hageman, Julio F. P. Peres, Alexander Moreira-Almeida, Leonardo Caixeta, Ian Wickramasekera II, and Stanley Krippner

Throughout most of the nineteenth and twentieth centuries, trance and mediumistic experiences were regarded as a manifestation of severe mental disorders by most members of the Western scientific community (Almeida, 2007; Moreira-Almeida, Almeida, and Lotufo Neto, 2005) and were usually described as rich in dissociative behavior, hallucinations, feelings of being controlled by an external power, depersonalization, personality shifts, and alleged posttrance amnesia. These phenomena were the subjects of numerous scientific studies around the turn of the twentieth century, but scientific interest subsequently declined. However, there has been renewed interest in dissociative and hallucinatory experiences in nonpathological samples, as there is evidence that these experiences often involve people not suffering from mental disorders (Cardeña et al., 1996; Krippner, 1997b; Martinez-Taboas, 1995; Moreira-Almeida, Lotufo Neto, and Greyson, 2007; Moreira-Almeida et al., 2008).

These experiences have been widespread in most societies throughout history and are part of the Greek, Roman, and Judeo-Christian roots of Western society, passed down through oracles, prophets, and shamans (Hastings, 1991). It is often difficult to differentiate the terms "medium" and "channeler" since both claim to refer to receiving information that supposedly does not originate from consensual reality (e.g., from living persons, media, their own memory). Mediums purportedly obtain this information from deceased persons, whereas channelers claim to obtain information from other spiritual entities (e.g., deities, nature spirits, inhabitants of other dimensions; e.g., Hastings, 1991; Klimo, 1998).

Although there are several possible definitional approaches to trance and mediumship, for the purposes of the present chapter we define trance as did Wulf (2000): "a state of profound absorption or lack of mental content during which the individual is experientially cut off from the outside world; it is frequently accompanied by vocal and motor automatisms, lack of responsive awareness, and amnesia" (p. 399). Mediumship is defined as an experience in which an individual (the medium) purports to be in communication with, or under the control of, the personality of a deceased person or other nonmaterial being (Moreira-Almeida, Lotufo Neto, and Cardeña, 2008). Frequently, mediumship takes place while the medium is in what Bourguignon (1976) refers to as a "possession trance" in which an alleged incorporeal agency takes possession of a medium's volition, speech, and bodily movements.

An interesting fact is that most of the world's population believes in life after death, including the possibility that trance and mediumship can bridge the two, reflecting certain basic assumptions about human nature and cognitive reference points (Peres et al., 2007a, 2007b). The availability of new neurobiological research tools has now opened doors to studying such topics in more sophisticated ways, which may help further understanding of the nature of human consciousness and its relationship with the brain.

This chapter reviews neurobiological studies on trance and mediumistic experiences with an emphasis on Brazilian samples, where these continue as a vibrant tradition. We also discuss some crucial methodological issues and the implications of current studies for the mind-brain relationship. Moreover, we report data from two parallel strands of our own investigations conducted in Brazil, namely by the team consisting of Joan H. Hageman, Ian Wickramasekera II, and Stanley Krippner (HWK) and the team of Julio F. P. Peres, Alexander Moreira-Almeida, and Leonardo Caixeta (PAC). The PAC team has studied the neurobiology of mediumship using electroencephalography (EEG) in a group of mediums during their trance state (Caixeta et al., 2009), while the HWK team has reported studies on two trance mediums using various neurobiological tools. Krippner was the only member of this team who participated in on-site investigations, and Hageman and her colleagues (Hageman, Krippner, and Wickramasekera II, 2009) also participated in psychophysiological studies of a channeler in the United States.

Trance and Mediumistic Investigation

Research on trance and mediumistic experiences has been seminal for understanding mind and its relationship with the body (Almeida and Lotufo Neto, 2004; Kelly et al., 2007). From the perspective of modern neuroscience, all behaviors and experiences have typically been related to the dynamic matrix of chemical and electromagnetic events within the human brain. However, resuming a rigorous, open-minded, and comprehensive investigation of trance and mediumship may provide important evidence and many insights capable of advancing an alternative understanding of mind-brain relationships. From this perspective, neurobiological studies hold potential as an important approach, as a point of view helping to solve the puzzle of these challenging human experiences. However, we must avoid an often naïve and overoptimistic approach in terms of the possibilities and interpretations of neurobiological investigations. In an attempt to avoid these problems, before presenting a summary of the available neurobiological findings on trance and mediumship, we shall very briefly point to certain methodological pitfalls that often occur when investigators analyze data from neurobiological studies on such experiences:

1. *Naïvely accepting materialist monism (mind as a brain product) as an obvious fact, and rejecting a fair consideration of other hypotheses for the mind-brain relationship.* Despite being a reasonable hypothesis, it is important to bear in mind that it is what Popper and Eccles (1977) called a "promissory materialism." It is a belief or a wager that science will, in the future, be able to show how brain fully explains mind. Although this hope may be fulfilled, we should not shun alternative explanations, such as those proposed by Henri Bergson, William James, and Frederic Myers, namely that the brain acts as a filter, rather than as the cause of mental manifestations (Chibeni and Moreira-Almeida, 2007; Kelly et al., 2007).
2. *Basing work on secondhand descriptions of original findings or writings.* This has led to many distortions that have been accepted as representing the thoughts or findings of important authors. Secondhand descriptions often produce, embellish, or disfigure inferences not supported by the original source. Some notorious examples are the widespread misrepresentation of Cartesian dualism as denying mind-body interaction (Duncan, 2000; Kirkebøen, 2001), impreciseness in reports of behavioral changes following the famous case of Phineas Gage's accident (Macmillan, 2000), and the reduction of spiritual experiences to a temporal lobe epileptic seizure (Kelly et al., 2007).
3. *Focusing only on one side of psychophysiological parallelism, i.e., changes in brain function modify mental states.* If we are to gain a better understanding of the mind-brain relationship, it is important to study the flip side (i.e., changes in the mind produce changes in the brain and body; e.g., Beauregard, 2007; Kelly et al., 2007).
4. *Assuming that experiences based on superficial similarities are identical.* This may lead to unwarranted inferences of causes and of physiological substrates. Some examples of this are taking mediumship as a manifestation of dissociative identity disorder (Moreira-Almeida et al., 2008), or assuming that a jet pilot's acceleration-induced hypoxia produces a near-death experience (Greyson, 2007).
5. *Identifying a brain region involved with some spiritual experience and concluding that this region is the ultimate cause of that experience.* Or, similarly, assuming that producing a certain experience by stimulating the brain shows that the brain is the final source of this experience. To be fair and rigorous, these findings do not imply that experience is merely a brain phenomenon, with no external reality. Although certain brain areas have been associated with hearing and even produce auditory experiences through brain stimulation, this obviously does not mean that there is no auditory experience based on an external source.
6. *Ignoring the complexity of the body and refusing to take a holistic perspective.* Our body has limited output pathways, so the same experience can have different etiologies (e.g., tachycardia can have a wide array of causes such as anxiety, heart failure, exercise, cocaine use). Therefore, finding the cause of an episode of tachycardia in one particular patient does not mean that we have found the cause of all tachycardia episodes for this patient, or for all human beings. This seems to often be the case for hallucinatory and similar experiences reported by mediums (Moreira-Almeida et al., 2007; Moreira-Almeida et al., 2008).

7. *Encountering problems in theoretical formulations.* One such limitation is the failure to propose a hypothesis that explains the whole range of phenomena involved in a certain kind of spiritual experience, which is to be expected of a good theory (Chibeni and Moreira-Almeida, 2007). Another aspect is that many hypotheses are too speculative, being based on hypothetical brain substances or activation, but lacking empirical support for such claims (Greyson, 2007). Finally, many hypotheses have been posed by authors who have failed to conduct in-depth and direct investigation of the people having the experience to be explained. Direct contact with a large number of research participants who have had the spiritual experience in question provides invaluable information to help formulate a hypothesis that might explain the whole experience and its implications for those experiencing it.

8. *Focusing studies on beginners or participants who have not had a full-blown spiritual experience.* Following William James, it is very important to concentrate our investigations on the most extreme forms of religious and spiritual experiences. The study of extreme cases has provided observations that have fostered scientific revolutions (Moreira-Almeida and Koenig, 2008).

Neurobiological Studies on Dissociation, Possession, and Trance

Having electrically stimulated the live brain to map cortical functions, Penfield (1978) postulated that neural networks alone would be incapable of producing consciousness, and he stated that the mind had a distinct existence from the brain, although closely related to it. He added that there was no place in the cerebral cortex where electric stimulation could cause a patient to make a decision. Neurofunctional findings in relation to psychotherapy, hypnosis, and the placebo effect, taken as a whole, can be interpreted to challenge the hypothesis that the mind is a by-product or epiphenomenon of the brain (Beauregard, 2007). Studies of cardiac-arrest survivors found that 11–20 percent of patients reported experiences that can be used to support the hypothesis that the mind can express itself independently of neural functioning.

Current conventional neuroscientific models involving neuronal processing and plasticity cannot account for certain observations related to human consciousness once these studies have demonstrated that, paradoxically, human consciousness may continue to function during cardiac arrest (Parnia, 2007). In line with these findings, some theories associate the brain with the role of mediating concepts such as "spirits" (i.e., noncorporeal minds or noncorporeal agencies) (Kelly et al., 2007). Thus, we should not be dogmatic in taking an a priori monist or dualist approach based on as-yet embryonic neurofunctional research.

For instance, the hasty proposal of "the God spot," which postulated a site in the brain as responsible for experience of the "divine," has been dismissed by recent neuroimaging studies (Beauregard and Paquette, 2006). Moreover, elucidating the neural circuits involved in subjective experiences such as prayer or mystical experience does not diminish or depreciate their significance or value.

Most studies in this field have focused on religious practices and their underlying neural circuitries. Because of the current nascent stage of this line of investigation, there are differences in methodology (measuring brain activity by topographical EEG, by cerebral blood flow, or by tracers of cerebral metabolism) and inconsistencies across studies. Nevertheless, findings tend to suggest higher activity of the frontal and prefrontal cortex during religious experiences (Azari et al., 2001; Beauregard and Paquette, 2006; Jevning et al., 1996; Newberg et al., 2001; Newberg et al., 2003; Newberg et al., 2006). Some similarities also include increased activity in the limbic system and decreased activity in the parietal lobes (Herzog et al., 1990; Lazar et al., 2000; Newberg et al., 2001).

The results indicate that mediumistic and trance experiences as well as intense mystical, religious, and spiritual experiences are distinct and mediated by several brain regions and systems. For instance, increased activity in the frontal cortex may reflect focused concentration during the altered states of consciousness (ASC) experiences elicited by meditation practices, while the correlation between the dorsolateral prefrontal cortex and the superior parietal lobe may reflect a nonordinary sense of space or time. Circuitries involved in sustaining reflexive evaluation of thought were found in religious experience (Azari et al., 2001; Beauregard and Paquette, 2006; Jevning et al., 1996; Newberg et al., 2001; Newberg et al., 2003; Newberg et al., 2006). The major findings are shown in Table 1.

Although spiritual, mystical, and religious experiences may be related to trance and mediumship manifestations, the actions of the main neurotransmitters during these practices remain poorly investigated and understood. Nevertheless, it has been proposed that higher activity of the dopaminergic system (DRD4) and parallel lower activity of the serotonin (5-HT) system may be involved in individuals who showed higher measures of spirituality (Comings et al., 2000; Kjaer et al., 2002; Previc, 2006). The latter postulated that their results might be due to the higher concentration of dopamine D4 receptor in the frontal cortex. However, it has been shown that the dopaminergic system is in part under the regulation of 5-HT projections. For instance, stimulating 5-HT1A or 5-HT2A receptors may elicit dopaminergic release (Diaz-Mataix et al., 2005). Therefore, it is too early to postulate a role for neurotransmitters in trance and religious experiences given the tiny number of studies conducted so far.

From a psychophysiological perspective of trance and dissociation, dissociation involves the disengaging of the cognitive processes from their executive, higher-order, volitional faculties (Winkelman, 2000). Generalized psychophysiological correlates of what might be described as trance with dissociative aspects involve hemispheric lateralization that favors (in right-handed people) the right hemisphere of the brain (more closely associated with intuitive, emotive, nonlogical, spatial, imaginative thought and perception) over the ordinarily dominant left hemisphere (associated with linguistic and rational processing).

Winkelman (1986), in his studies of indigenous shamans, suggested that a wide range of culturally patterned induction techniques lead to generalized parasympathetic dominance in which the frontal cortex exhibits high-voltage, slow-wave,

Table 1   Neuroimaging studies involving trance and similar experiences

Study	Method	Subjects	Paradigm	Decreases (↓) and Increases (↑) in Brain Activity
Herzog et al. (1990)	PET	8 Yoga meditators	Meditative yoga	↑ Frontal and occipital cortex
Jevning et al. (1996)	REG	10 Meditators	Transcendental meditation	↑ Frontal and occipital cortex
Lazar et al. (2000)	fMRI	5 Kindling meditators	Meditation	↑ Dorsolateral PFC, parietal cortices, hippocampus, temporal lobe, pregenual ACC, and striatum
Newberg et al. (2001)	SPECT	8 Tibetan Monks	Buddhist meditation	↑ ACC, inferior and orbital frontal cortex, DLPFC, and thalamus
Azari et al. (2001)	PET	6 Fundamentalist Christians	Religious experience	↑ DLPFC, dorsomedial frontal and medial parietal cortex
Newberg et al. (2003)	SPECT	8 Franciscan nuns	Prayer	↑ PFC, inferior frontal lobes and inferior parietal lobes
Beauregard and Paquette (2006)	fMRI	14 Carmelite nuns	Sense of union with God	↑ RL medial orbitofrontal cortex, R middle temporal cortex, RE inferior and superior parietal lobules, RL caudate, L medial PFC, L ACC, L insula, L brainstem, striate visual cortex
Newberg et al. (2006)	SPECT	9 Charismatic prayers	Glossolalia	↑ L caudate ↓ DLPFC, L Superior Parietal
Lutz et al. (2008)	fMRI	16 Long-term Buddhist meditators	Emotional and neutral sounds during the meditation	↑ Insula and ACC

Note: PET = positron emission tomography; REG = rheoencephalography; SPECT = single photon emission computed tomography; fMRI = functional magnetic resonance imaging; ACC = anterior cingulate cortex; PFC = prefrontal cortex; DLPFC = dorsolateral prefrontal cortex; R = right; L = left.

synchronous EEG patterns (e.g., theta rhythms) that originate in the limbic system and proceed to frontal regions via limbic-frontal innervations. Some ASCs, such as some forms of meditation and hypnosis, exhibit small variances in EEG patterning, and similar differences also exist between voluntary and spontaneously induced states.

Winkelman (1986) also indicated that involvement of the limbic system is an important part of the neural architecture of dissociative trance. For instance, it has been implicated in the modulation of a variety of functions including basic survival drives and hypothalamic/pituitary release of neurotransmitter and endogenous opiates. The hypothalamic action, in turn, influences, among other things, dissociation trance-related hallucinations, analgesia, and amnesia. The hypothalamus also controls sympathetic (excitatory) and parasympathetic (inhibitory) nervous systems; the latter being associated with decreased cortical excitation and increased hemispheric synchronization. Evidence shows that parasympathetic dominance can be induced through excessive sympathetic activation; such as through drumming, dancing, and chanting, all of which are common features of ritual practice and in which the homeostatic reciprocal action of the autonomic nervous system (ANS) collapses.

Lex (1979) suggested that the "*raison d'être* for rituals, often involved in trance, is the readjustment of dysphasic biological and social rhythms by manipulation of neurophysiological action under controlled conditions" (p. 144). Rituals, such as those associated with shamanism and mediumship, therefore, not only provide psychological relief from social and environmental stressors, they are mechanisms that employ driving techniques that "tune" the nervous system through hemispheric lateralization, parasympathetic dominance, and cortical synchronization.

In a field study conducted by Don and Moura (2000), topographic brain mapping at midline scalp locations of healer-mediums revealed increased brain activity when the healer-mediums reported being incorporated by a "spirit," compared to resting baseline conditions. These results suggest the presence of a hyperaroused brain state associated with the possession trance behaviors of the mediums. In contrast, a small sample of psychiatric patients monitored during involuntary possession trance revealed no high-frequency brain activity.

Rhythmic brain electrical oscillations as measured by EEG may also have functional implications for the dynamics associated with cortical networks. EEGs reflect changes in attention, sensory processing, and cognitive processes highlighting the different cortical network interactions (Lopes da Silva, 1991). In particular, alpha, theta, and beta wave activities have all been reported to be associated with different processes of alertness, focused attention, and awareness (Fanji et al., 2003). Giesbrecht et al. (2006) reported a correlation with self-reported dissociative experiences and theta power. Additionally, their results indicated a positive relation between dissociation and delta activity, whereas cortical power within the alpha range was inversely related to dissociative symptoms.

Consequently, the combining of neurophysiological and phenomenological assessments in a qualitative investigation of mediumistic experiences is essential to develop a more precise understanding of the neurobiological substrate of its manifestation and disruption of the integrated functions of consciousness.

For example, the evidence for associating dissociative identity disorder (multiple personality) and demonic possession with epilepsy is weak (Caixeta, Caixeta, and Barbosa, 2009). There are many examples of prolonged fugue states with behavioral alterations and subsequent amnesia as a sign or even as the only clinical manifestation of psychomotor epilepsy. Furthermore, paroxysmal abnormalities in EEGs have been described in at least one case of multiple personality (Horton and Miller, 1972). Although the clinical descriptions suggest that many additional cases in the earlier literature were also epileptic, this is difficult to demonstrate since EEGs were not obtained and since hysteroepileptic convulsions were considered common in cases of dissociative states.

Convulsions are frequently described in cases of demonic possession, but the relationship between epilepsy and possession is more difficult to surmise. Most of these convulsions may well have been hysterical in origin but, once again, this is difficult to demonstrate since EEGs were not obtained in most cases (Saver and Rabin, 1997). In 1968, Prince pointed out that possession states had not been studied physiologically although the unusual behavior and the ASCs that are associated with possession phenomena suggest an alteration of cerebral physiology. The confounding of involuntary possession and seizure has been seen since biblical times. For instance, in the frequently quoted passage from the New Testament (Mark 9:17–27), the "dumb spirit" who throws a man on the floor and makes him foam at the mouth seems to represent ordinary epilepsy, even though this passage is often quoted as an example of demonic possession and its successful exorcism.

Mesulan (1981) reported 12 cases with a clinical condition reminiscent of dissociative identity disorder and involuntary possession (seven with multiple personality and the other five with delusions of "supernatural intervention"). These patients' EEGs showed different degrees of abnormality, suggestive of focal electrical disturbance predominantly in the temporal lobes. Thus, Mesulan suggested that some cases of involuntary possession may be ascribed to disturbed electrical activity in regions of the brain related to the limbic system. However, the description of these patients as epileptic may be questioned in accordance with Mesulan's reporting absence of motor manifestations in this group. Flor-Henry et al. (1990) described two multiple personality cases on EEG analysis that were in a state of relative left hemisphere activation across all cerebral regions.

Many parapsychological-like experiences (sensed presence of another sentient being, out-of-body experiences, distortions in subjective time, religious reveries) have been reported in association with complex partial seizures with foci within the temporal lobes, particularly the hippocampus and amygdala (Gloor et al., 1982). Direct surgical stimulation of mesiobasal structures within the temporal lobes, particularly in the right hemisphere, evoked comparable experiences (Horowitz and Adams, 1970). Furthermore, individuals who are more prone to parapsychological-like experiences tend to show more prominent alpha rhythms over the temporal lobes (Makarec and Persinger, 1990).

In some traditional cultures, it is widely observed that ordinary, healthy participants in a ritual ceremony enter voluntary possession trance, with or without psychoactive drugs. Based on a survey of 488 human societies worldwide, Bourguignon (1973) reported that 89 percent had institutionalized ASCs and 57 percent associated these states with possession trance (which she differentiated from involuntary possession). Therefore biological mechanisms common to all human beings may well underlie possession and trance phenomena. Since trance and mediumship have so rarely been investigated from a neurobiological perspective, these mechanisms are not clear (Oohashi et al., 2002). The HWK and PAC teams therefore conducted the following studies of Brazilian mediums during trance states.

Studies with Brazilian Mediums

In Brazil, mediumship is a central component within the ritual practice of spiritistic religions of which Candomblé, Kardecismo, and Umbanda are the three major groupings (Hess, 1994). They hold a commonality of belief in the power and efficacy of "spirit agents" and the ability of humans to interact with and embody these agents through ritualized methods of dissociative trance, such as possession.

Mediumship is typically induced during what Westerners consider an ASC. In the case of the African-derived Candomblé and Umbanda practices, their mythologies are permeated with stories about a "Sky God" and his intermediaries, the *orixás* (or *orishas*), who symbolize the primordial forces of nature. The *orixás* are believed to be powerful and terrifying but also "human" in that they can be talked to, pleaded with, and cajoled through special offerings. Group members also believe that the *orixás* have the ability to take hold of the mind and body of a human through acts of spirit "incorporation." Practitioners of these African-based rituals believe that they gain access to supernatural power in three ways: (1) by making offerings to the *orixás*; (2) by "divining" (i.e., foretelling the future with the help of an *orixá*); and (3) by being taken over by an *orixá*, ancestral spirit, or other entity who—if benevolent—may warn the community about possible calamities, diagnose illnesses, and prescribe cures. The medium through which these spirits speak typically performs the task voluntarily and usually claims no remembrance of the experience. The trance required for this is usually brought about by dancing, singing, and drumming, as well as by using mind-altering substances, such as strong tobacco (Villoldo and Krippner, 1987).

Of all the Brazilian spiritist movements, Candomblé most closely resembles the original religions of Africa, retaining the original names and worship of many West African *orixás* (Bastide, 1960). In contrast, Umbanda gives greater emphasis to Brazil's Christian heritage than to the African *orixás*. Kardecismo (a variant of nineteenth century spiritualism), also called Espiritismo, is not to be confused with the general reference to Afro-Brazilian spiritistic traditions and draws heavily from the teachings of Allen Kardec (1861, 1867), a French pedagogue and spiritualist.

Despite the widespread popularity of spiritistic traditions in Brazil, the practice of mediumship has been largely denigrated as psychopathological in Brazil, similar to how these phenomena are largely negatively viewed in Europe and North America (Johnson, 2007). For example, Rodrigues (1896/1935) conducted extensive research on the various types of Afro-Brazilian mediumistic practices, interpreting such practices as hysterical phenomena resulting from profoundly superstitious personalities of its African-descended practitioners. Later, Xavier de Oliveira (1931) claimed that nearly 10 percent of patients hospitalized during a 12-year period in the University of Rio de Janeiro suffered psychosis from spiritistic traditions, while Pacheco e Silva (1936) maintained that existing psychotic tendencies are aggravated by spiritistic traditions. Two historical elements played a key role in these pathologizing viewpoints: the attempt by Brazilian intellectuals to create a modern Eurocentric nation through suppressing spiritistic practices, and the view that spiritism was the enemy of psychiatrists coming from Roman Catholic or materialist perspectives (Moreira-Almeida, Silva de Almeida, and Neto, 2005).

However, later work, such as that of Roger Bastide (1978) concluded psychopathology may explain some cases, but speculated that spiritism can be viewed as more normative based on social dynamics. Psychiatric theory thereafter developed a cultural sensibility also influenced by the development of transcultural psychiatry and ethnopsychiatry (Lewis-Fernandez and Kleinman, 1995). Within this evolving context, mediumship began to be seen by some as a skill that can empower its practitioners (e.g., women subjugated by a patriarchal culture) and provide support for community members suffering from anxiety, depression, and other afflictions (Krippner, 1997b).

Defining some terms related to spiritist traditions, such as "possession" and "dissociation," poses difficulties. For example, Leacock and Leacock (1972) studied the Batuque, an Afro-Brazilian tradition that used the expression "trance-possession," but these juxtaposed terms were not synonymous in that possession was viewed as "the presence in the human body of a supernatural being" and trance was viewed as "an altered psychological state" (p. 217). Bourguignon and her associates (1964, 1976, 1977) investigated the practice of "spirit possession," and differentiated it from possession and trance. In possession, a spirit has produced the changes in an individual's behavior, health, or disposition without an accompanying shift in awareness, but in possession trance, an individual loses conscious awareness while the invading spirit's own behavior, speech patterns, and body movements take over and can be observed by outsiders. However, trance was an ASC that includes the loss of conscious awareness but not the presence of a spirit or other outside entity.

In addition, the term "incorporation" is also used by the spiritistic groups in Brazil to describe situations in which practitioners allow themselves to be taken over by a spirit entity, exemplified by mediums who voluntarily allow the incorporation of an *orixá*. The term "possession," in contrast, is often used to define the experience of an involuntary takeover, typically perceived as distressful, unwelcome, and possibly long lasting (Negro, Palladino-Negro, and Louza, 2002, p. 65). Possession can also occur with or without the ASC known as dissociation (a separation of awareness that may impede memory). Possession frequently requires the intervention of a religious specialist who can exorcise the offending agent, but, in possession trance, the intrusive spirit may be benevolent, bringing new insights to the possessed individual by means of automatic writing, channeling, or mediumship. Sometimes the spirit even plays the role of a trickster, teaching the individual life lessons through embarrassment or humor. The results differ from cases where an invading entity takes over a victim's body as the result of a sorcerer's curse or to gratify the spirit entity's earthbound impulses and desires. These types of trance are extremely dissociative when the individual manifests experiences and behaviors that appear to be disconnected from the mainstream flow of conscious awareness, behavioral repertoire, and/or self-identity (Krippner, 1997a, 1997b).

Study One

The HWK team reported a study with two purported mediums from the Brazilian spiritistic traditions of Candomblé, Umbanda, and Kardecismo. Findings were interpreted by employing the high-risk model (Wickramasekera, 1991) as a theoretical framework for understanding incongruities between mind and body systems in individuals with mediumistic-like experiences. This study was completed with mediums who were held by their communities as capable of incorporating discarnate entities, as well as with a local tour guide not associated with any of the local spiritistic movements who served as an age-matched "control participant" from a similar culture. This strategy was selected since, when working with individuals with special abilities, it is useful to make intracultural comparisons (Murphy, 1969). Data were collected in a quiet, comfortable hotel room during a parapsychological conference in Recife in 1999. The two research participants received no money for their mediumistic activity or for taking part in this study.

One medium tested was Pai Ely (born in 1932 as Manoel Rabelo Pereira), a *pai-de-santo* in Recife, Brazil. Krippner had visited his *terreiro* or temple, The Lar de Ira Center (in 1990, 1991, 1993, 1995, 1997, and 1998), making observations and conducting interviews with him and members of his congregation. Pai Ely conducts both Candomblé and Umbanda services in the Center and is well versed in both traditions (Krippner, 1998/1999). Formerly, Pai Ely was a bank executive. In his early forties, he began to see and hear spirits and *orixás*. He was uncomfortable and fought the presence of the entities, especially when they told him he was being "called" to become a healer. As a result of such incidents, Pai Ely transformed his social identity from bank executive to *pai-de-santo*.

Pai Ely reported that his teacher, Master Oascati, in his 70s at the time of our visit, lived in Benin, Africa. Master Oascati once told Pai Ely that he must constantly work on himself to obtain clearer, purer information from the *orixás*. He explained that it is easy for one's own biases, experiences, and fantasies to contaminate the spiritual message. In Pai Ely's words, "The *orixá* paints only one small part of the picture; the medium must paint the rest." As a result, the client receives no "pure" information. According to Pai Ely, it is unusual for more than 25 percent of the *orixá's* message to get through. Furthermore, many of the messages are from lesser entities that are not "illuminated beings" and may unknowingly distort information or deliberately play tricks on the mediums and their clients. To prepare to receive the spirit, Pai Ely usually engaged in prayerful meditation or group prayer (Krippner, 1998/1999).

The other medium tested was José Jacques Andrade, born in 1945, who is a medium active in the Kardecismo movement. During a 1998 visit to his center, the Leonardo da Vinci Salon of Mediumistic Art, Krippner observed a ceremony that culminated in Andrade's incorporating several famous artists (e.g., Monet, da Vinci) and a few unknown to anyone including Andrade. In preparation, Andrade and his group sang hymns and prayed. Andrade, virtually deaf, did little singing as he prepared himself, through prayer, for the incorporation of his colleagues "on the other side." Once the spirits had been "called," Andrade dipped both of his hands into jars of paint and, with two canvasses in front of him, swiftly began to execute remarkably attractive landscapes, still lifes, and portraits, two at a time, which he claimed were produced as "mediumistic art." For example, with one hand, he produced a landscape signed "Monet," and with the other, a still life signed "Cezanne." The other artists under whose influence he claimed to paint that evening included Van Gogh, Manet, Picasso, da Vinci, Degas, Portinari, and Toulouse-Lautrec. Andrade produced these works at an extraordinary speed, each work taking no more than 10 minutes. Each painting bore at least a passing resemblance to the style of the artist being incorporated, some more than others.

Lima (1998) collected 107 paintings by Andrade during an approximate one-year period between 1994 and 1995, looking for similarities in the process itself, in the product, and in the signatures of the purported artists. Nearly 300 different artists were represented in this collection, the most frequent being Miro (3.7 percent of the total), Van Gogh (3.2 percent), and Dali (2.3 percent). Lima reported that before beginning to paint, Andrade hesitated for about 20 or 30 seconds; the average time spent on a painting was 6 minutes, 28 seconds. Other patterns Lima mentioned included Andrade's preference for using his right hand, although he would frequently use both hands, producing two paintings at the same time.

The control participant was E. O. S. (born in 1945), a tour guide and school-teacher. He assisted Krippner as a translator in 1993 and 1995 and was familiar with the spiritistic religions of the area. He was included as a control participant to explore if cultural constraints or environmental demand characteristics existed that could account, at least in part, for the results obtained from the two mediums. All research participants denied being on any form of medication before or during the testing.

Two psychological measures were used in the study: the Dissociative Experiences Scale (DES; Bernstein and Putnam, 1986), and a Portuguese translation of the Tellegen Absorption Scale (TAS; McIntyre, Klein, and Gonçalves, 2001). These were administered by Brazilian colleagues and scored by Krippner. The DES is used as a screening tool for both clinical and nonclinical populations to assess the frequency and intensity of dissociation in one's daily life. The higher the DES score, the more likely that the respondent has dissociative identity disorder; however, only 17 percent of those who score above 30 on the DES are diagnosed with the disorder (Carlson and Putnam, 1993). The TAS is used to measure an individual's capacity for experiences that involve both narrowing and broadening of attentional focus, which are characterized by marked restructuring of one's phenomenal self and the world (Tellegen, 1977; Tellegen and Atkinson, 1974).

Because data can be distorted by bodily movement, and imagery has been found to be efficacious in both performance enhancement and rehabilitation (e.g., Appel, 1992), the two mediums were instructed to imagine incorporating a spirit (rather than to engage in direct incorporation). Previous research, primarily in the field of sport psychology, has suggested that imagery rehearsal activates the same brain centers involved in actual performance (e.g., Feltz and Landers, 1983) and guided this methodological choice. The duration of the psychophysiological testing sessions were four minutes each and all were measured under two baseline resting conditions (eyes open, eyes closed). The two mediums were measured while imagining an incorporation from the "spirit world," and last, during the return to baseline conditions (eyes open; eyes closed), referred to as recovery. The following briefly describes the results of the study.

Psychological Measures

On the TAS absorption measure, only Pai Ely tested high. The Brazilian participants all claimed to be moved by songs that they enjoyed, professed to get caught up in the action while watching a movie, and liked to watch clouds take various shapes in the sky. However, only the medium Pai Ely claimed to anticipate statements from other people when discussing allegedly supernatural experiences, to feel imaginary matters with such intensity that they seemed real, and to have music evoke colorful pictures in his imagination. He also claimed to think in visual images, to be able to imagine his body becoming so heavy it would not move, and to occasionally feel "suspended in air" while listening to a band or an orchestra. Pai Ely's imagination was very vivid, and he moved his hands and arms frequently when he was, from his perspective, actually incorporating discarnate entities. In this respect, Pai Ely's behavior is consistent with his high score on the TAS.

It is not unusual for Brazilians to use such idioms as "I got caught up in the music," or "I was flying during that performance." In addition, the role of a medium may influence responses to tests of this nature. For example, when Pai Ely gave a positive response to the item regarding being "suspended in air" he may have simply been making a declaration concerning his abilities and what was expected of him as a *pai-de-santo*.

From a broader lens, individuals who make high scores on the TAS tend to report becoming fully absorbed while they are watching a movie, television program, or theatrical performance. They also tend to be able to suspend disbelief and to become empathic (Wickramasekera and Szlyk, 2003), especially when their companion (or, at times, a complete stranger) is undergoing stress. Those scoring high on absorption have many traits in common with highly hypnotizable people, deriving meaning from body language and personal mannerisms (Fernandez, 2001). This description is especially applicable to Pai Ely who deals daily with people under stress. There are members of his congregation, as well as many outsiders, who come to him for relief of some real or imagined misfortune, interpersonal conflict, or health problem. A frequent method of treatment involves incorporating entities from the spirit world, sometimes requesting that they give advice and aid, while at other times intervening to stop their purported malevolent actions against Pai Ely's clients. Of course, his test scores may be influenced by his culture and role expectations.

Andrade did not score as high on the TAS as Pai Ely, but he also does not deal as extensively or intimately with clients. In other words, the high score on the TAS might be related to the frequency with which the two practitioners engage in spirit incorporation. When Andrade incorporates his artistic colleagues from the spirit world, he often becomes so absorbed with the task that he claims not to recall the details when the discarnate entities leave the scene.

On the DES dissociative measure, both Brazilian mediums and their control tested as "severely dissociative." The term "severely dissociative" could be reframed as "intensively imaginative" when culture-bound beliefs and practices are taken into account. For example, all three Brazilian participants reported that they often "have the experience of sometimes remembering a past event so vividly that [it feels] as they were reliving that event," and reported that they often "have the experience of feeling that their body does not seem to belong to them." Pai Ely and Andrade have practiced mediumship for several decades and scored as "severely dissociative"; however, the fact that E. O. S. also received a high DES score supports the likelihood that idioms of expression influenced the results obtained on his dissociation measure as well. This highlights some caution in using a strict interpretation of high absorption and high dissociation as risk factors for somatization (e.g., psychosomatic illnesses) for multicultural research.

Another study with Kardec mediums in São Paulo, Brazil, by Negro, Palladino-Negro, and Louza (2002) reported that their mediums also attained high scores on dissociation (as assessed by the DES), and that there was a positive association between mediumship training and the control of the dissociated experiences. Hence, the capacity for dissociative self-experiences may play an important role in the ability to practice as a medium through differentiating and dissociating their normal identity states during their hypnotic-like procedures (Krippner, 2005).

Sociocognitive theorists of dissociation and hypnosis would probably suggest that the phenomenological experiences during mediumship are created in accordance with the previous expectancies and beliefs about the role of being a medium, and other contextual variables (Lynn, Pintar, and Rhue, 1997). The sociocognitive view on dissociation thus seems to be illustrated by Pai Ely's belief that as much as 75 percent of his experience during mediumship may be the result of his own biases, experiences, and fantasies. Pai Ely's description of his process of discernment of "pure" from "contaminated" information does seem to capture the sociocognitive explanation of how a person might construct a role and personal narrative about dissociative trance experiences as a kind of "believed-in imaging" (Sarbin, 1998).

Neodissociation theorists of hypnosis and dissociation might look at the importance of the hypnotic-like procedure (Krippner, 2005) itself in allowing access to the self-experience of the channeled identity state (Hilgard, 1994). A neodissociative or ego state's explanation of mediumship would probably highlight the normal poly-psychic nature of human identity (Frederick, 2005) so that it probably should not be too surprising that individuals might be able to encounter another ego state within them during a hypnotic-like procedure. Our experience of this normally inactive ego state may thus be activated by the hypnotic-like procedures of mediumship whether or not that ego state actually represents the presence of a spirit or deity. These theorists might then speculate that a simpler explanation of mediumship could be derived through focusing on the origin of the channeled identity as stem-ming from ego states or cognitive subsystems that are not properly integrated within the mediums' normal experience of identity.

Probably everyone has some trickster-like phenomena hidden away within their self-experience that they may not normally elicit but that mediums seem to develop as part of their training (Krippner, 2005). This polypsychic aspect of human identity may significantly contribute along with sociocognitive factors to the difficulty Pai Ely described in the attempt to discern pure from contaminated information. However, our data merely illustrate the sociocognitive and neodissociative perspectives on mediumship while a host of many other factors (including actual spirit incorpora-tion) may play a role as well if science were to accept the possibility of actual spirit incorporation.

It is important to be cautious about interpreting psychological measures used in research across cultures, since culture-bound beliefs and practices (e.g., idioms of expression) may influence how individuals from differing cultures score on dissocia-tion and absorption measures. For example, a tendency toward hyperbole may be more common among Latin Americans than among Europeans, Canadians, and individuals from the United States, a proposition congruent with Krippner and Weinhold's (2001) finding that Brazilian dream reports contain high levels of emo-tional content and Krippner and Faith's (2001) finding that twice as many "exotic" dream reports characterize Brazilian dream reports as those obtained from partici-pants in the United States. Dissociation must also be understood through a cultural lens because certain life experiences may be adaptive to life events that are culturally related (Calof, 2002; Krippner, 1997a).

Psychophysiological Measures

A variety of interesting psychophysiological measures were obtained. For example, Andrade had approximately a 5 degree Fahrenheit discrepancy between his left hand and right hand temperature during the baseline "eyes open" condition. When Andrade was asked to close his eyes and relax, there was at least a 1 degree drop in temperature in both hands, while the discrepancy between each hand decreased to about 4 degrees. During the fantasy of incorporating an artist session, his left hand dropped an additional degree, but his right hand temperature barely changed. When he relaxed after imagining an incorporation, his bilateral hand temperatures contin-ued to drop an additional degree in both the recovery conditions. A 4 degree discrepancy existed between both hand temperatures compared to the imagining session. Thus, Andrade tested with right hand temperature higher than left hand under all conditions.

Similarly, Andrade's electromyographic (EMG) baseline readings were about 5 microvolts higher than the optimal (3.1 microvolts). When instructed to close his eyes and relax, his EMG increased almost a microvolt, contrary to expectations. When instructed to imagine incorporating an artist, his EMG increased an additional 4 microvolts. During the eyes open recovery session, his EMG dropped over 6 microvolts, but his EMG increased over 2 microvolts during the eyes closed recovery. Again, this result is paradoxical.

In addition, Andrade's heart rate increased modestly in the baseline eyes closed condition, and in particular during the imagining of incorporation. His heart rate dropped during both recovery sessions with little difference between the eyes open and eyes closed conditions. In general, his heart rate (59–63 BPM) under all conditions was low for a person of his age although he increased his heart rate modestly in the eyes closed conditions.

Similarly in a paradoxical fashion, Andrade's mean skin conductance level (SCL) dropped across the entire session independent of other conditions and instructions. Generally, there was a greater sympathetic activation in his left hand than in his right hand.

Pai Ely reported that he had imagined incorporating a "gentle" *preto velho*. During baseline conditions before the imagination session, Pai Ely's EMG, EEG, and SCL measures were quite normal, but his heart rate was high (90–92 BPM). His bilateral hand temperatures were discrepant during the baseline, eyes open condition with the right hand about 2 degrees higher than the left. When Pai Ely was asked to close his eyes and relax, the results were similar. Hence, even before initiating the imagination task, there were notable incongruities in Pai Ely: his bilateral hand temperatures and an unusual heart rate.

The first collection of data during the imagination session was confounded by motor artifacts and could not be used because he moved his hands and arms frequently. When Pai Ely was asked to restrain himself while imagining that he was incorporating a discarnate entity, his left and right hand temperature remained stable. His EMG, SCL, and heart rate increased during the imagination condition, and generally remained elevated relative to the baseline data.

For the Brazilian control, there were fewer discrepancies among the EEG, EMG, hand temperature, SCL, and heart rate. All of E. O. S.'s scores were in the normal range and were essentially congruent.

A variety of EEG measures also were obtained. Andrade's EEG showed an increase in the percentage of theta brain waves from the eyes open to the eyes closed baseline conditions, but a drop in alpha percentage. During the imagination exercise, there was an increase in the percentage of alpha comparable to the eyes open condition. Paradoxically, the increase in the percentage of alpha was also associated with a sustained increase in beta percentage, even during recovery conditions. Pai Ely's percentage of theta brain waves increased in both the left and right cortical hemispheres.

E. O. S. showed a large increase in EEG alpha wave percentage in both eyes closed conditions.

For the EMG measures, both mediums increased muscle tension from the baseline eyes open condition to the baseline eyes closed condition. During the imagining of incorporation, all increased muscle tension with the exception of Pai Ely who decreased in muscle tension. During the recovery eyes open session, all decreased muscle tension. Pai Ely's muscle tension remained about the same for both recovery sessions, but E. O. S. and Andrade increased muscle tension in the recovery eyes closed session and each one returned almost to baseline (eyes open) in the recovery eyes closed condition.

Although each of the three decreased their left-hand temperature during the imagination session, E. O. S.'s right-hand temperature also decreased during the imagination session, whereas both mediums increased temperature in their right hand. For recovery in the eyes open condition, only Pai Ely increased temperature in the left hand, but both mediums increased temperature in their right hands. For the recovery eyes closed condition, both mediums increased bilateral hand temperatures. For the heart rate session, Andrade increased heart rate from the baseline eyes open condition to the baseline eyes closed condition, whereas Pai Ely and E. O. S. decreased their heart rate. Each of the three increased their heart rate during the imagining of incorporation, with the exception of E. O. S., whose heart rate remained almost exactly the same from the baseline eyes closed condition to both recovery conditions. Pai Ely increased heart rate substantially for the imagining session. However, Pai Ely and Andrade decreased their heart rate from the imagination to the recovery eyes open condition. In addition, Pai Ely and Andrade increased their heart rate from the recovery eyes open condition to the recovery eyes closed condition.

In general, the psychophysiological data obtained from Andrade reveals several incongruent findings. First of all, there was a general reduction in SCL across conditions. Since SCL is a measure of sympathetic activation or withdrawal, it is paradoxical to find it associated with peripheral vasoconstriction and increased EMG during the imagination task. Both sets of data suggest increased sympathetic activation in these response systems. Second, the increase in muscle tension during the eyes closed imagination condition and the associated increase in the percentage of alpha activity during imagination are also paradoxical; EMG and EEG are typically negatively correlated, not positively correlated. Andrade's increase in frontal EMG while imagining incorporation is consistent with a hypothesis of increased muscle tension that is possibly driven by intrusive cognitions and/or affect. Andrade's heart rate data are also consistent with the hypothesis of intrusive events occurring in the eyes closed conditions.

Pai Ely also showed incongruities between major physiological response systems, particularly during the imagination condition. Although sympathetic activation was observed in the ANS, relaxation was noted in the central nervous system (CNS), which both typically function in a more integrated manner.

E. O. S.'s large increase in EEG alpha wave percentage in both the eyes closed conditions is consistent with his moderate score on the TAS, which was exactly the same as Andrade's. The EEG data are probably consistent with E. O. S.'s hypnotic ability, although this was not tested. However, studies of the association of absorption with measured response to hypnosis demonstrate only a moderate relationship (Spiegel, 1990, p. 125).

There were markedly specific incongruities in the peripheral and central physiological response systems. In other words, there were deviations during Andrade's imagination condition that were discrepant from what is typically seen during an eyes closed imagination condition. This supports a previous finding that physiological incongruities are frequent outcomes of testing sessions with people claiming mediumistic abilities (Wickramasekera, 1991). Not only are there incongruities between the mediums' verbal reports and behavioral observations but between their psychophysiological response systems as well.

People with incongruities between CNS and ANS responses have been described by Wickramasekera (1986a) as living episodically in two worlds, one in which they are critical, rational, and practical, and another into which their fantasy and emotional reactivity expands and deepens. As such they often are "at risk" for somatization. Both sets of descriptors apply to Pai Ely, the *pai-de-santo* in our investigation who attained a high absorption score on the TAS. Not only does Pai Ely incorporate discarnate entities, he manages a large and successful enterprise, the Lar de Ita Center.

Wickramasekera's (1991) descriptors apply to some extent to the other psychic claimant, Andrade, who also displayed CNS/ANS incongruence. Andrade's duties at the Kardec temple are not as demanding as those of Pai Ely, nor does he spend the amount of time incorporating entities, as does the *pai-de-santo*. When we visited the Kardec temple, we observed a few dozen people in attendance; in contrast, Pai Ely's Candomblé/Umbanda temple was filled with several hundred people during each of our visits. In addition, we observed that Pai Ely has a team of mediums and trained assistants at his disposal at the temple. However, Wickramasekera's (1991) descriptors do not particularly apply to E. O. S. who showed no noticeable CNS/ANS incongruence. According to Wickramasekera (1986b, 1991), incongruence between CNS and ANS response systems are not unusual among spiritual practitioners. It is taken for granted that some practitioners, especially self-styled mediums and channelers, will demonstrate incongruence between their behavioral observations and verbal reports.

In addition, the incidence of individual response specificity among the Brazilian mediums and their control was noticeable. An example of this is that each predominately exhibited stress in their right hand temperatures, but Andrade exhibited SCL stress predominately with his left hand. Mediums and channelers both purport to be able to receive information that supposedly does not originate from consensual reality. Though they might appear calm and composed, while speaking of calamitous events from their clients' "past lives," from the lives of their clients' deceased relatives, or from scenarios of their clients' purported futures, physiological tests often indicate that they are under tension. The individual response specificity (Andreassi, 2000) may help clarify such incongruence and Stern and Sison's findings (1990) offer some insight, as those individuals who report a high degree of autonomic response typically also show a greater autonomic reactivity than those with a lower awareness of their autonomic response. Moreover, there is the tendency for the more aware individuals to exaggerate their degree of reactivity, while the lesser aware individuals tend to underestimate their reactivity.

Wickramasekera's (e.g., 1989, 1993, 1995, 1998) findings support the proposition that spiritual practitioners often are at risk for stress-related symptoms, in particular, when there are incongruities between verbal reports of low negative affect while ANS data indicate otherwise, profound temperature differences between the right and the left sides of the body (e.g., individual response specificity), and "flip-flops" between a repressive cognitive style and easy access to cognitive processing (Wickramasekera, Krippner, and Wickramasekera, 2001). Negro, Palladino-Negro, and Louza's (2002) study of Kardec mediums found that research participants characterized by extensive training attained favorable scores on measures of socialization and adaptation. However, pathological signs were detected among the group of younger mediums with less training; in addition, they evidenced poorer social support. Although stress for mediums may be modified by social support systems, other programs involving voluntary control of internal states (e.g., biofeedback, meditation) and regimens for healthy living (e.g., Krippner, Wickramasekera, and Tartz, 2002, pp. 59–60) may be utilized. There is some evidence that, at least in the United States, self-styled mediums and channelers may be at greater risk than healers and intuitives.

Study Two

The PAC team studied nine mediums (three males, six females; all with normal social functionality and no adjunct mental disorder) linked to the Brazilian Spiritist Federation of the State of Goiás. None of them were taking psychotropic medication or using ritual substances, so the EEG abnormalities in these cases could not conceivably be attributed to the effect of mind-altering substances. They had no psychiatric or neurological antecedents or history of using ritual substances or medical psychotropics and did not receive any money for their participation.

Two showed mediumship behavior related to "psychography" (an alleged spirit's manifestation using the writing of a medium), and one to "psychography" and "psychophony" (from the Greek *psyche* or soul, and the words "graph" and "phone," i.e., sound or voice), the names given by Kardec Spiritism (Kardecismo) and some other spiritualist traditions to the phenomena where a spirit uses the voice of a medium. The remaining six manifested only psychophony. All were fitted with an eight-channel EEG recording device, and two periods of 90-second continuous baseline resting and probing EEG were recorded (see Table 2 for partial results).

This study was designed to rule out epilepsy as a cause of most mediumship experience, since none of the cases had an EEG suggestive of either epileptic discharge

Table 2   EEG findings, type of mediumship, and gender of mediums

Mediums	Sex	Type of Mediumship	EEG Findings (pretrance)	EEG Findings (during trance)
Case 1	F	Psychophony	Normal	Slowing of right temporal delta and theta
Case 2	M	Psychophony	Normal	General slowing of right frontal temporal occipital theta and left frontal temporal theta
Case 3	M	Psychophony	Normal	Slowing of right frontal theta
Case 4	F	Psychography	Normal	Slowing of left temporal theta
Case 5	F	Psychography	Normal	Slowing of left temporal theta
Case 6	F	Psychophony	Normal	Normal
Case 7	F	Psychophony	Normal	Slowing of right occipital theta and left frontal theta
Case 8	F	Psychophony	Normal	Normal
Case 9	M	Psychography and psychophony	Normal	Normal

during mediumship activity or a clinical history of seizure disorder or alterations of ongoing EEG background activity.

EEG findings did not show a consistent pattern among the mediums, but ranged from absolutely normal electrical activity to some degree of EEG slowing. Oohashi et al. (2002) also reported an individual case during an episode of involuntary possession in which the EEG of the possessed subject did not show any pathological findings or epileptic discharges, but indicated enhanced power (increase) in the theta and alpha frequency bands during the trance. Hughes and Melville (1990), in another EEG study with 10-trance channelers, suggested that the trance channeling state is characterized by large, statistically significant increases in amount and percentage of beta, alpha, and theta brain-wave activity. These authors concluded that there appear to be definite neurophysiological correlates to the trance channeling state, and furthermore that there is some evidence that these correlates may be patterned, in contrast with our results.

None of our cases presented with electrical disturbance that resembled those found in Mesulan's cases (Mesulan, 1981), and it must be emphasized that none had a history of seizure disorders. In the face of these findings, it would be overly hasty to conclude that abnormal electrical activity was the cause of this phenomenon, or even an epiphenomenon since it may be a consequence. Mesulan also argued that the high incidence of these otherwise rare conditions at his behavior neurology unit and their association with abnormal EEGs raises the possibility that dissociative identity disorder and involuntary possession may be a behavioral manifestation of abnormal electrical activity in the temporal lobes. We disagree with this statement in the sense that these phenomena are not uncommon in certain cultures (particularly in Brazil, as well as in India and many other Southeast Asian countries) and are not significantly associated with any psychosocial dysfunction (Moreira-Almeida et al., 2008) or with epileptic disorders.

Although the present sample was not large enough to produce interactions of sufficient statistical power, the current results support the notion of an electrophysiological repercussion during mediumship activity in most of the mediums we studied. The current results should be interpreted cautiously, pending replication and extension to other samples.

Conclusion

Both of the studies presented in this chapter open more questions than they resolve, but they also point to the possible importance of using neurobiological data to explore extraordinary experiences, such as of those who claim to be mediums. The complicated patterns found undoubtedly require much additional research to clarify their fuller meanings.

However, there is a growing consensus that a respect for spiritual belief systems is an ethical duty for physicians and other health care providers and most modern health systems in general take no account of the belief in life after death held by most of the world's population (Peres et al., 2007a). The interest and pertinence of scientific investigations relating to mediumship, trance states, and spiritual experience are justified, given the importance of their impact on people's quality of life. For example, health and disease are cardinal concepts in all areas that deal with human suffering, and conceptual inaccuracies about the myriad of elements that constitute human nature may lead to partial diagnosis and even erroneous therapeutic conduct.

Human nature awaits further elucidation, so scientific research must continue to examine this complex field involving spirit communication and life after death. What we have reported is simply a beginning. However, the preliminary results argue for its continuation and expansion.

References

Almeida, A. A. S. (2007). *"Uma fábrica de loucos": Psiquiatria x espiritismo no Brasil (1900–1950)* ["An insanity factory": Psychiatry and spiritism in Brazil]. Unpublished Doctoral dissertation, University of Campinas, Sao Paulo, Brazil. Retrieved from http://www.hoje.org.br/bves.

Almeida, A. M., and Lotufo Neto, F. (2004). A mediunidade vista por alguns pioneiros da área da saúde mental [Mediumship as seen by some pioneers in the area of mental health]. *Revista de Psiquiatria Clínica, 31,* 132–141.

Andreassi, J. L. (2000). *Psychophysiology: Human behavior & physiological response.* Mahwah, NJ: Lawrence Erlbaum.

Appel, P. R. (1992). Performance enhancement in physical medicine and rehabilitation. *American Journal of Clinical Hypnosis, 35,* 11–19.

Azari, N. P., Nickel, J., Wunderlich, G., Niedeggen, M., Hefter, H., and Tellmann, L. (2001). Neural correlates of religious experience. *European Journal of Neuroscience, 13,* 1649–1652.

Bastide, R. (1960). *Les religions Africaines au Brésil* [The African religions of Brazil]. Paris: Press Universitaires de France.

Bastide, R. (1978). *The African religions of Brazil: Toward a sociology of the interpenetration of civilizations.* Baltimore, MD: Johns Hopkins University Press.

Beauregard, M. (2007). Mind does really matter: Evidence from neuroimaging studies of emotional self-regulation, psychotherapy, and placebo effect. *Progress in Neurobiology, 81,* 218–236.

Beauregard, M., and Paquette, V. (2006). Neural correlates of a mystical experience in Carmelite nuns. *Neuroscience Letters, 405,* 186–190.

Bernstein, E. M., and Putnam, F. W. (1986). Development, reliability, and validity of a dissociation scale. *Journal of Nervous and Mental Disease, 174,* 727–735.

Bourguignon, E. (1964). The self, the behavioral environment, and the theory of spirit possession. In M. Spiro (Ed.), *Context and meaning in cultural anthropology* (pp. 39–60). New York: Free Press.

Bourguignon, E. (1973). A framework for the comparative study of altered states of consciousness. In E. Bourguignon (Ed.), *Religion, altered states of consciousness, and social change* (pp. 3–38). Columbus: Ohio State University Press.

Bourguignon, E. (1976). *Possession.* San Francisco: Chandler & Sharp.

Bourguignon, E., and Evascu, T. (1977). Altered states of consciousness within a general evolutionary perspective: A holocultural analysis. *Behavior Science Research, 12,* 199–216.

Caixeta, L., Caixeta, M., and Barbosa, E. (2009). Phenomenological and neurophysiological studies of Brazilian spiritist mediums. Manuscript submitted for publication.

Calof, D. L. (2002). *Dissociation: Nature's tincture of numbing and forgetting.* Retrieved December 7, 2002, from http://www.carleton.ca/~whovdest/calof.html.

Cardeña, E., Lewis-Fernandez, R., Beahr, D., Pakianathan, I., and Siegel, D. (1996). Dissociative disorders. In T. A. Widiger, A. J. Frances, H. J. Pincus, R. Ross, M. B. First, and W. W. Davis (Eds.), *Sourcebook for the DSM-IV* (Vol. II, pp. 973–1005). Washington, DC: American Psychiatric Press.

Carlson, E. G., and Putnam, F. W. (1993). An update on the Dissociative Experiences Scale. *Dissociation, 6,* 16–27.

Chibeni, S. S., and Moreira-Almeida, A. (2007). Remarks on the scientific exploration of "anomalous" psychiatric phenomena. *Revista de Psiquiatria Clínica, 34* (suppl. 1), 8–16.

Comings, D. E., Gonzales, N., Saucier, G., Johnson, J. P., and MacMurray, J. P. (2000). The DRD4 gene and the spiritual transcendence scale of the character temperament index. *Psychiatric Genetics, 10,* 185–189.

Diaz-Mataix, L., Scorza, M. C., Bortolozzi, A., Toth, M., Celada, P., and Artigas, F. (2005). Involvement of 5-HT1A receptors in prefrontal cortex modulation of dopaminergic activity. *Journal of Neuroscience, 25,* 10831–10843.

Don, N. S., and Moura, G. (2000). Trance surgery in Brazil. *Alternative Therapies, 6*(4), 39–48.

Duncan, G. (2000). Mind-body dualism and the biopsychosocial model of pain: What did Descartes really say? *Journal of Medicine and Philosophy, 25,* 485–513.

Fanji, G., Xin, M., Shen, E., and Zhijie, C. (2003). Can we measure consciousness with EEG complexities? *International Journal of Bifurcation and Chaos, 13,* 733–742.

Feltz, D. L., and Landers, D. M. (1983). The effects of mental practice on motor skills learning and performance: A meta analysis. *Journal of Sport Psychology, 5,* 25–57.

Fernandez, L. (2001). The worldview of the Grade V hypnotizable person. *Hypnos, 28,* 207–208.

Flor-Henry, P., Tomer, R., Kumpula, I., Koles, Z. J., and Yeudall, L. T. (1990). Neurophysiological and neuropsychological study of two cases of multiple personality syndrome and comparison with chronic hysteria. *International Journal of Psychophysiology, 10,* 151–161.

Frederick, C. (2005). Selected topics in ego state therapy. *International Journal of Clinical and Experimental Hypnosis, 53,* 339–429.

Giesbrect, T., Jongen, E. M. M., Smulders, F. T. Y., and Merckelbach, H. (2006). Dissociation, resting EEG and subjective sleep experiences in undergraduates. *Journal of Nervous and Mental Disease, 194,* 362–368.

Gloor, P., Olivier, A., Quesney, L. F., Andermann, F., and Horowitz, S. (1982). The role of the limbic system in experiential phenomena of temporal lobe epilepsy. *Annals of Neurology, 12,* 129–144.

Greyson, B. (2007). Near-death experiences: Clinical implications. *Revista de Psiquiatria Clinica, 34* (suppl. 1), 49–57.

Hageman, J. H., Krippner, S., and Wickramasekera, I., II. (2009, in press). Sympathetic reactivity during meditation. *International Journal of Subtle Energies, 19*(2).

Hastings, A. (1991). *With the tongues of men and angels: A study of channeling.* Fort Worth, TX: Holt, Rinehart and Winston.

Herzog, H., Lele, V. R., Kuwert, T., Langen, K. J., Rota Kops, E., and Feinendegen, L. E. (1990). Changed pattern of regional glucose metabolism during yoga meditative relaxation. *Neuropsychobiology, 23,* 182–187.

Hess, D. J. (1994). *Samba in the night: Spiritism in Brazil.* New York: Columbia University Press.

Hilgard, E. R. (1994). Neodissociation theory. In S. J. Lynn and J. W. Rhue (Eds.), *Dissociation, clinical and theoretical perspectives* (pp. 32–79). New York: Guilford.

Horowitz, M. J., and Adams, J. E. (1970). Hallucinations on brain stimulation: Evidence for revision of the Penfield hypothesis. In W. Keup (Ed.), *Origin and mechanisms of hallucinations* (pp. 13–22). New York: Plenum.

Horton, P., and Miller, D. (1972). The etiology of multiple personality. *Comprehensive Psychiatry, 13,* 151–159.

Hughes, D. J., and Melville, N. T. (1990). Changes in brainwave activity during trance channeling: A pilot study. *Journal of Interpersonal Psychology, 22,* 175–189.

Jevning, R., Anand, R., Biedebach, M., and Fernando, G. (1996). Effects on regional cerebral blood flow of transcendental meditation. *Physiology & Behavior, 59,* 399–402.

Johnson, B. L. (2007). Spirits on the stage: Public mediums, spiritualist theater, and American Culture, 1848–1893. *Dissertation Abstracts, 68*(7). (UMI No. AAT 3273027)

Kardec, A. (1861). *Le livre des esprits: Contenant les principes de la doctrine spirite* [The book of the spirits: Containing the principles of spiritistic doctrine] (10th ed.). Paris: Didier et Cie.

Kardec, A. (1867). *Le livre des mediums ou guide des mediums et des Évocateurs* [The book of mediums or guide of mediums and the evocative ones]. Pars: Didier et Cie.

Kelly, E. F., Kelly, E. W., Crabtree, A., Gauld, A., Grosso, M., and Greyson, B. (2007). *Irreducible mind: Toward a psychology for the 21st century.* Lanham, MD: Rowman & Littlefield.

Kirkebøen, G. (2001). Descartes' embodied psychology: Descartes' or Damasio's error? *Journal of the History of the Neurosciences, 10,* 173–191.

Kjaer, T. W., Bertelsen, C., Piccini, P., Brooks, D., Alving, J., and Lou, H. C. (2002). Increased dopamine tone during meditation-induced change of consciousness. *Cognitive Brain Research, 13,* 255–259.

Klimo, J. (1998).*Channeling: Investigations on receiving information from paranormal sources.* Berkeley, CA: North Atlantic Books.

Krippner, S. (1997a). Dissociation in many times and places. In S. Krippner and S. M. Powers (Eds.), *Broken images, broken selves: Dissociative narratives in clinical practice* (pp. 3–40). Washington, DC: Brunner/ Mazel.

Krippner, S. (1997b). The varieties of dissociative experience. In S. Krippner and S. M. Powers (Eds.), *Broken images, broken selves: Dissociative narratives in clinical practice* (pp. 336–362). Washington, DC: Brunner/ Mazel.

Krippner, S. (1998/1999). Transcultural and psychotherapeutic aspects of a Candomblé practice in Recife, Brazil. In S. Krippner and H. Kalweit (Eds.), *Yearbook of cross-cultural medicine and psychotherapy: Mythology, medicine, and healing: Transcultural perspectives* (pp. 67–86). Berlin: Verlag fur Wissenschaft und Bildung.

Krippner, S. (2005). Trance and the trickster: Hypnosis as a liminal phenomenon. *International Journal of Clinical and Experimental Hypnosis, 53,* 97–118.

Krippner, S., and Faith, L. (2001). Exotic dreams: A cross-cultural study. *Dreaming, 11,* 73–82.

Krippner, S., and Weinhold, J. (2001). Gender differences in the content analysis of 240 dream reports from Brazilian participants in dream seminars. *Dreaming, 11,* 35–42.

Krippner, S., Wickramasekera, I., and Tartz, R. (2002). Scoring thick and scoring thin: The boundaries of psychic claimants. *Journal of Subtle Energy, 11*(1), 43–61.

Lazar, S. W., Bush, G., Gollub, R. L., Fricchione, G. L., Khalsa, G., and Benson, H. (2000). Functional brain mapping of the relaxation response and meditation. *Neuroreport, 11,* 1581–1585.

Leacock, S., and Leacock, R. (1972). *Spirits of the deep: A study of an Afro-Brazilian cult.* Garden City, NY: Doubleday Natural History Press.

Lewis-Fernandez, R., and Kleinman, A. (1995). Cultural psychiatry: Theoretical, clinical and research issues. *Psychiatric Clinics of North America, 18,* 433–448.

Lex, B. (1979). The neurobiology of ritual trance. In E. G. d'Aquili, C. D. Laughlin Jr., and J. McManus (Eds.), *The spectrum of ritual: A biogenetic structural analysis* (pp. 117–151). New York: Columbia University Press.

Lima, I. W. R. (1998). Pesquisa de atividade psicopictorafica de Jacques Andrade [Research into the psychic paintings of Jacques Andrade]. *Papels del Tercer Encuentro Psi 1998* (pp. 121–124). Curitiba, Brazil: Instituto de Psicología Paranormal.

Lopes da Silva, F. (1991). Neural mechanisms underlying brain waves: From neural membranes to networks. *EEG Clinical Neurophysiology, 79,* 81–93.

Lutz, A., Brefczynski-Lewis, J., Johnstone, T., and Davidson, R. J. (2008). Regulation of the neural circuitry of emotion by compassion meditation: Effects of meditative expertise. *Public Library of Science One, 26*(3e), 18–97.

Lynn, S. J., Pintar, J., and Rhue, J. W. (1997). Fantasy proneness, dissociation, and narrative construction. In S. Krippner and S. M. Powers (Eds.), *Broken images, broken selves: Dissociative narratives in clinical practice* (pp. 274–302). Washington, DC: Brunner/ Mazel.

Macmillan, M. (2000). Restoring Phineas Gage: A 150th retrospective. *Journal of the History of the Neurosciences, 9*, 46–66.

Makarec, K., and Persinger, M. A. (1990). Electroencephalographic validation of a temporal lobe signs inventory in a normal population. *Journal of Research in Personality, 24*, 323–327.

Martinez-Taboas, A. (1995). The use of the Dissociative Experiences Scale in Puerto Rico. *Dissociation, 8*, 14–23.

McIntyre, T. M., Klein, J. M., and Gonçalves, F. (2001). *Escala de Tellegen* (Portuguese translation of the Tellegen Absorption Scale). Braga, Portugal: University of Minho.

Mesulan, M. M. (1981). Dissociative states with abnormal temporal lobe EEG: Multiple personality and the illusion of possession. *Archives of Neurology, 38*, 176–181.

Moreira-Almeida, A., Almeida, A. A. S., and Lotufo Neto, F. (2005). History of "spiritist madness" in Brazil. *History of Psychiatry, 16*, 5–25.

Moreira-Almeida, A., and Koenig, H. G. (2008). [Review of the book *Irreducible Mind*: Toward a psychology for the 21st century]. *Journal of Nervous and Mental Disease, 196*, 345–346.

Moreira-Almeida, A., Lotufo Neto, F., and Cardeña, E. (2008). Comparison of Brazilian spiritist mediumship and dissociative identity disorder. *Journal of Nervous and Mental Disease, 196*, 420–424.

Moreira-Almeida, A., Lotufo Neto, F., and Greyson, B. (2007). Dissociative and psychotic experiences in Brazilian spiritist mediums. *Psychotherapy and Psychosomatics, 76*, 57–58. Erratum in *Psychotherapy and Psychosomatics, 76*, 185.

Moreira-Almeida, A., Silva de Almeida, A. A., and Neto, F. L. (2005). History of "spiritist madness" in Brazil. *History of Psychiatry, 16*, 5–25.

Murphy, G. (1969). The discovery of gifted sensitives. *Journal of the American Society of Psychical Research, 63*, 3–20.

Negro, P. J., Jr., Palladino-Negro, P., and Louza, M. R. (2002). Do religious mediumship dissociative experiences conform to the sociocognitive theory of dissociation? *Journal of Trauma and Dissociation, 3*, 51–73.

Newberg, A., Alavi, A., Baime, M., Pourdehnad, M., Santanna, J., and d'Aquili, E. (2001). The measurement of regional cerebral blood flow during the complex cognitive task of meditation: A preliminary SPECT study. *Psychiatry Research, 10*, 113–122.

Newberg, A., Pourdehnad, M., Alavi, A., and d'Aquili, E. G. (2003). Cerebral blood flow during meditative prayer: Preliminary findings and methodological issues. *Perceptual and Motor Skills, 97*, 625–630.

Newberg, A. B., Wintering, N. A., Morgan, D., and Waldman, M. R. (2006). The measurement of regional cerebral blood flow during glossolalia: A preliminary SPECT study. *Psychiatry Research, 22*, 148, 67–71.

Oliveira, X. de (1931). *Espiritismo e loucura* [Spiritism and madness]. Rio de Janeiro: A. Coelho Franco Filho.

Oohashi, T., Kawai, N., Honda, M., Nakamura, S., Morimoto, M., Nishina, E., and Maekawa, T. (2002). Electroencephalographic measurement of possession trance in the field. *Clinical Neurophysiology, 113*, 435–445.

Pacheco e Silva, A. C. (1936). *Problemas de higiene mental* [Problems of mental hygiene]. São Paulo: Oficinas Graficas do Juqueri.

Parnia, S. (2007). Do reports of consciousness during cardiac arrest hold the key to discovering the nature of consciousness? *Medical Hypotheses, 69*, 933–937.

Penfield, W. (1978). *The mystery of mind: A critical study of consciousness and the human brain.* Princeton, NJ: Princeton University Press.

Peres, J. F. P., Moreira-Almeida, A., and Nasello, A. G. (2007a). Spirituality, religiousness and psychotherapy. *Revista de Psiquiatria Clínica, 34*, 136–145.

Peres, J. F. P., Moreira-Almeida, A., Nasello, A. G., and Koenig, H. G. (2007b). Spirituality and resilience in trauma victims. *Journal of Religion and Health, 46*, 343–350.

Popper, K. R., and Eccles, J. (1977). *The self and its brain.* Berlin: Springer Verlag.

Previc, F. H. (2006). The role of extrapersonal brain systems in religious activity. *Conciousness and Cognition, 15*, 500–539.

Prince, R. (1968). Can the EEG be used in the study of possession states? In R. Prince (Ed.), *Trance and possession states* (pp. 121–137). Montreal: R. M. Bucke Memorial Society.

Rodrigues, N. (1935). *O animismo fetichista dos negros Bahíanas* [The animistic fetish of Bahían negros]. Rio de Janeiro: Civilizacao Brasileira. (Original work published 1896.)

Sarbin, T. R. (1998). Believed in imaginings: A narrative approach. In J. R. Rivera and T. R. Sarbin (Eds.), *Believed-in imaginings: The narrative construction of reality* (pp. 15–30). Washington, DC: American Psychological Association.

Saver, J. L., and Rabin, J. (1997). The neural substrates of religious experience. *Journal of Neuropsychiatry and Clinical Neuroscience, 9*, 498–510.

Spiegel, D. (1990). Hypnosis, dissociation, and trauma: Hidden and overt observers. In J. Singer (Ed.), *Repression and dissociation: Implications for personality theory, psychopathology, and health* (pp. 232–243). Chicago: University of Chicago Press.

Stern, R., and Sison, E. E. E. (1990). Response patterning. In J. T. Cacioppo and I. G. Tassinary (Eds.), *Principles of psychophysiology: Physical, social, and inferential elements* (pp. 193–215). New York: Cambridge University Press.

Tellegen, A. (1977). *The Multidimensional Personality Questionnaire.* Minneapolis: National Computing Systems.

Tellegen, A., and Atkinson, G. (1974). Openness to absorbing and self-altering experience ("absorption"), a trait related to hypnotic susceptibility. *Journal of Abnormal Psychology, 83*, 268–277.

Villoldo, A., and Krippner, S. (1987). *Healing states.* New York: Fireside/Simon & Schuster.

Wickramasekera, I. (1986a). Risk factors for parapsychological verbal reports, hypnotizability and somatic complaints. In B. Shapin and L. Coly (Eds.), *Parapsychology and human nature* (pp. 19–35). New York: Parapsychology Foundation.

Wickramasekera, I. (1986b). A model of people at high risk to develop chronic stress related somatic symptoms: Some predictions. *Professional Psychology: Research and Practice, 17*, 437–447.

Wickramasekera, I. (1989). Is hypnotic ability a risk factor for subjective (verbal report) psi, somatization, and health care costs? In L. Coly and J. D. S. McMahon (Eds.), *Psi and clinical practice* (pp. 184–191). New York: Parapsychological Foundation.

Wickramasekera, I. (1991). Model of the relationship between hypnotic ability, psi, and sexuality. *Journal of Parapsychology, 55*, 159–174.

Wickramasekera, I. (1993). Assessment and treatment of somatization disorders: The high risk model of threat perception. In J. W. Rhue, S. J. Lynn, and I. Kirsch (Eds.), *Handbook of clinical hypnosis* (pp. 587–621). Washington, DC: American Psychological Association.

Wickramasekera, I. (1995). Somatization: Concepts, data and predictions from the high risk model of threat perception. *Journal of Nervous and Mental Disorders, 183*, 15–30.

Wickramasekera, I. (1998, Spring). Out of mind is not out of body: Somatization, the high risk model, and psychophysiological psychotherapy. *Biofeedback*, pp. 8–11, 32.

Wickramasekera, I., Krippner, S., and Wickramasekera, J. (2001). *Case studies of "psychic sensitives": Testing predictions from a model of threat perception.* Unpublished case studies. San Francisco, CA: Saybrook Graduate School and Research Center.

Wickramasekera, I. E., II, and Szlyk, J. (2003). Could empathy be a predictor of hypnotic ability? *International Journal of Clinical and Experimental Hypnosis, 51*(4), 390–399.

Winkelman, M. (1986). Trance states: A theoretical model and cross-cultural analysis. *Ethos, 14*, 174–203.

Winkelman, M. (2000). *Shamanism: The neural ecology of consciousness and healing.* Westport, CT: Bergin & Garvey.

Wulf, D. M. (2000). Mystical experience. In E. Cardeña, S. J. Lynn, and S. Krippner (Eds.), *Varieties of anomalous experience: Examining the scientific evidence* (pp. 397–440). Washington, DC: American Psychological Association.

Field Day

CHAPTER 6

Electrical Activity in the Brain and the Extraordinary Mind

Norman S. Don

For a quarter of a century, my colleagues and I have conducted studies of brain electrical activity and cognition. In some studies we recorded event-related brain potentials (ERPs), which are minute fluctuations in brain activity produced as a response to stimuli or cognitive activity. In other studies we recorded natural brain rhythms, such as alpha or beta waves. Many of these studies involved ordinary cognition and participants who were not selected for psychic ability. Other studies focused on parapsychological questions and involved well-known psychic claimants, among them Malcolm Bessent and Olof Jonsson. In addition, we conducted field work in Brazil, observing and recording brain waves from "trance surgeons" and people in altered conscious states—some induced by *ayahuasca*, a legal hallucinogen used by some shamans and religious groups. We also carried out a brain-wave study of 13 people in trance who claimed that they had learned to enter a hyperaroused state (in which brain waves speed up) while allegedly being abducted by alien beings. This range of research has led us to certain basic conclusions about psi and the neurobiology of the extraordinary people who claim to manifest it.

A word on the limitations of our studies: When we began our work in the early 1980s, there had been only three previous studies of psi and ERPs (Lloyd, 1973; Millar, 1979; Silverman and Buchsbaum, 1970). At that time, many EEG machines used in ERP research had only five electrodes. By the time we initiated our work in Brazil in the 1990s, the EEG typically came with 19 electrodes or more. Similar limitations were common in the conventions of analyzing frequencies. Although EEG machines in the 1980s were capable of registering up to 40 Hz (40 Hertz, shorthand for the gamma band, which can extend from 30 to 70 Hz), few researchers measured frequencies in this range. Daniel Sheer (1984) in the mid-1980s was the first to investigate the higher frequencies. It was some 10 years after Sheer's research that 40 Hz became a salient concern.

Conscious Failures and Unconscious Achievements: The ERP Experiments

In the course of roughly a decade, my colleagues and I conducted a series of four experiments with research participants engaged in guessing tasks in which psychic ability (as measured by a statistically significant number of correct guesses) might be involved. In addition to collecting basic information concerning correct and incorrect guesses, our experiments were designed to measure EEG data in the form of ERPs. At various sites on the scalp, electrodes used in an ERP study measure the voltage (in microvolts) and the timing (in milliseconds) of the brain's response to a stimulus. Multiple responses are averaged to produce the final ERP. (See Figure 6-1, an ERP plotted from data recorded in our laboratory.)

We were aware of two relatively well-known psychic claimants who, in other laboratories, had scored at above chance levels on the psi task of guessing target images from nontargets. We chose one of them, Malcolm Bessent, to be the research participant in our first experiment. Previously, he was a major participant in the

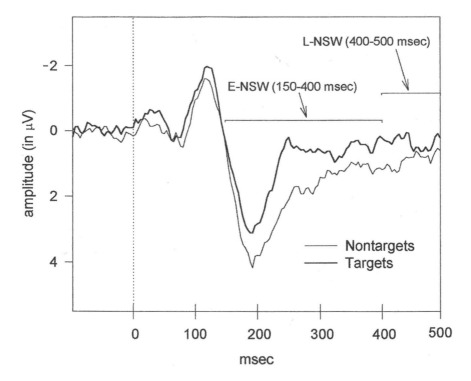

Figure 6-1   Early and late negative slow wave data

We wish to thank John Palmer, Ph.D., editor of *The Journal of Parapsychology*, for permission to reprint Figure 1 from *The Journal of Parapsychology*, 62 (June 1998): 133.

well-known dream ESP experiments at Maimonides Medical Center (e.g., Ullman and Krippner, 1989). Also, he had repeatedly achieved statistically significant scores in well-controlled laboratory experiments (Honorton, 1987). He was fully aware that we intended to test his alleged psychic abilities at target guessing and that we would be recording his brain's response to the various images used in the study.

An ESPerciser, an automated, computer-controlled system, was used for the experiment (Psychophysical Research Laboratories, 1985). Four images were flashed on a screen sequentially, and the EEG recorded his brain's electrical response to each image. Then the four images appeared together, and Bessent used a mouse-like pointer to select one of them as the target image. In about half the trials, the target was selected by a random number generator (RNG) before the experimental run, thus providing a test of the psychic's clairvoyance. In the other half, the target was selected by a RNG after the run, providing a test of the participant's precognitive abilities. Bessent was not informed whether a run was presented in the clairvoyant or precognitive modes until the run was completed. We conducted 20 runs of 10 trials each (Warren, McDonough, and Don, 1990).

Initially, we felt that the results we obtained for this experiment were disappointing. Our participant's conscious guessing of targets as compared with nontargets fell just at chance levels, and no psi appeared to be involved. However, upon inspecting the ERPs, we found that the subject's brain responded differently to targets than to nontargets, and that this was true of both clairvoyant and precognitive trials. On the graph of results, for example, we noted what researchers refer to as a "negative slow wave" arising about 150 milliseconds (msec) and persisting to 500 msec. No such reaction appeared for the average of the nontarget responses.

In the research literature concerning ERPs, a negative slow wave is often found in studies involving selective attention. The ERPs Bessent produced looked indistinguishable from these. But in our study, selective attention did not appear to be involved; Bessent's conscious choices were without significance because he failed to score above chance. It takes about 500 msec for a thought to become conscious. The negative slow waves we were seeing appeared earlier than this—at 150 msec. The rapidity of the response, then, served as an additional indicator that the reaction our participant was registering was either unconscious or preconscious. What was happening? Were Bessent's supposed abilities retreating to an unconscious level? Or were we encountering evidence for the unconscious nature of psi itself?

A second experiment (Warren, McDonough, and Don, 1992) with the same participant (in both clairvoyant and precognitive modes) replicated findings from the first. Again, our participant's conscious guessing was not different from chance. However, one of the two major findings of the first experiment dealing with the participant's unconscious reaction to the targets (the negative slow wave) was replicated. Our participant's brain was unconsciously registering different reactions to targets than to nontargets. Did he have a unique, though unconscious, ability? Was he neurobiologically different from other people, or did other people have this unconscious ability as well?

We decided to perform a third experiment using 25 participants unselected for psychic ability (Don, McDonough, and Warren, 1995a, 1998). In our third experiment, we ensured that our participants were blind to any test of psi; they were told our study was about gambling. They were given 50 cents to wager on each trial. We ran the trials only in the precognitive mode to increase the stringency of our testing. For a third time, the conscious guessing task was a failure; the number of correct choices was no greater than chance. However, for a third time, we found that averaged brain reactions to targets were different from those to nontargets. Once again, we observed negative slow waves, this time appearing 150–400 msec after the target images were selected. The results of our third experiment led us to conclude that Bessent was not alone in his precognitive abilities. The population at large, even those with no conscious ability, might still have an unconscious ability to manifest psi. The ERP plotted in Figure 6-1 was generated by data from this experiment.

Our fourth study (McDonough, Don, and Warren, 2002) involved 20 new participants and, like the third, was presented as a gambling experiment. The protocol was identical to that of the third experiment, and it ran only in the precognitive mode. By the time of the fourth experiment, however, we had noticed that the slow wave actually began at 150 msec and extended beyond 500 msec. We thus redefined the slow wave to include these parameters. Our results were again replicated. There was a statistically significant difference between targets and nontargets, measured by what is called the Stimulus Category by Hemisphere interaction. The effect was found over the right hemisphere sites (McDonough et al., 2002, pp. 194–195).

Our ERP studies lead us to suggest that psi is an unconscious and ubiquitous psychological function. The average person differs little from the accomplished psychic claimant or medium in his or her initial or unconscious reception of psi information. And, once psi-generated information enters the brain, it appears to be processed in much the same way the brain processes ordinary perceptual and cognitive data, although psi does appear to favor right hemisphere processing. How then, or in what way, do the minds of psychic claimants and mediums differ from the minds of ordinary people? Do extraordinary people have a greater ability to bring precognitive or unconscious information into consciousness? And if so, how do they do it? We do not know for sure, but, as we shall see, it might have something to do with the frequency of their brain waves.

Neurobiological Effects in the Frequency Domain

In the early 1980s we had the opportunity to work extensively with another well-known psychic claimant, Olof Jonsson. He had participated in an ESP test performed by astronaut Edgar Mitchell aboard the Apollo 14 space capsule while Jonsson remained on earth (Mitchell, 1971). He also performed significantly above-chance on a computer-controlled experiment in our laboratory (Don, McDonough, and Warren, 1992). Jonsson reported that from a very early age, perhaps five or six, he could perceive a "subtle energy" that circulated around his body.

He also claimed that a similar circulation of "subtle energy" existed for all material objects and living things. According to Jonsson, it was by controlling these circulations with his imagination that he learned to affect material objects and his own state of consciousness. (Somewhat similar practices of circulating "subtle energy" are found in Chinese Taoist yoga, but Jonsson claimed no knowledge of them.)

In explaining his work as a psychic claimant, Jonsson asserted that there were three major states of consciousness associated with psi. He termed these states Condition One (CD1), Condition Two (CD2), and Condition Three (CD3). CD2 and CD3 were the prime states for successful psychic work. Jonsson claimed that he sometimes could control his state of consciousness by controlling the "subtle circulation" and so could voluntarily enter into any of these three conditions. We therefore had him repeatedly cycle through the three conditions while his brain activity was monitored by the EEG. The EEG did, in fact, discriminate three states based on the frequency of Jonsson's brain waves (Don, Warren, McDonough, and Collura, 1988).

Intrigued with this information, we devised an additional study. Data were collected while Jonsson cycled repeatedly through the three conditions and later engaged in a forced-choice guessing task in addition to a "serial-sevens" mental arithmetic control condition. A total of 405 state of consciousness (State) trials and 140 forced-choice guessing (Prediction) trials were collected. These were extensively edited for EEG artifacts and potential scalp-muscle activity (EMG). After editing, 282 State and 96 Prediction trials remained. These were analyzed into frequency components using a Fast Fourier Transform (FFT) (Bracewell, 1986). Next, Stepwise Discriminant Analysis (SDA) (Dixon, 1985) was performed to classify the data into different categories, such as the different conditions and correct and incorrect guessing on the prediction task. Our statistical tests strongly suggested that CD1, CD2, and CD3 are a continuum of states of consciousness. However, to simplify our final analysis, we did statistical testing only on CD1, CD3, correct and incorrect guesses, and the mental-arithmetic control condition.

We found that CD3 is an altered state much further removed from the ordinary waking state (as represented by the mental-arithmetic control condition) than is CD1, which, however, is also an altered state. Additionally, we determined that both CD3 and correct clairvoyance involved a reduction or reversal of left hemisphere dominance as indicated by broad changes in EEG power. We also found that a pattern of heightened activity at the occipital (visual) region of the brain had appeared, as indicated by increased power, particularly in the 40 Hz region. This was thought to reflect concentration or visualization techniques employed by Jonsson and was observed for CD3 relative to CD1 and for correct relative to incorrect trials. It is worth noting that the finding of greater power in the theta and 40 Hz bands at the right hemisphere for correct compared to incorrect trials during the prediction task has been replicated in our laboratory with another participant performing a similar clairvoyant task (McDonough, Don, and Warren, 1988). Finally, an SDA model was developed for the different EEG electrodes, one that would discriminate the CD1 from CD3 State trials. This model was then applied to data from the prediction task and was able to correctly classify correct as opposed to incorrect guesses

with 90 percent or greater accuracy at all five electrodes. Therefore, with this participant, psi task performance was closely linked to his state of consciousness; when
Jonsson was in CD3—a state characterized by 40 Hz frequencies—he was almost
always correct in his predictions. Thus, though several studies have been published
that relate psi to the lower frequency brain rhythms, such as alpha and theta (e.g.,
Healy, 1986; Honorton, Davidson, and Bindler, 1971), we found that the high-
frequency rhythms—40 Hz or the gamma band—may be a much more powerful
indicator of the presence of psi than the lower frequencies.

40 Hz Gamma Brain Activity in Our ERP Data

The idea that 40 Hz might be significantly associated with psi led us to review
some of our other studies. We decided to subject data from our third ERP experiment to frequency analysis (Warren, Don, and McDonough, 1997). As we had done
in previous work, we restricted our analysis to data from the 36 to 44 Hz frequency
band, partly to replicate Sheer's (1984) pioneering work investigating the gamma
band. ERP data from the 150 to 500 msec poststimulus period were selected in
advance, since our previous study indicated that the negative ERP successfully dis-
criminated target from nontarget events (Don et al., 1995a). These data were tested
for potential scalp muscle artifacts; data failing the test were excluded from further
analysis.

We performed what statisticians term a "4-factor ANOVA" on the remaining
gamma-frequency data. There was significantly more 40 Hz EEG activity for target
card imagery than for nontarget imagery. Again, the target was later selected randomly by the computer, indicating that these differential brain responses were precognitive. Also, the gamma activity was statistically independent from the 150 to
500 msec ERP brain activity discussed earlier, and unlike that activity, gamma was
a significant discriminator only over right frontal and right posterior regions of the
brain. (One recalls that Jonsson showed a reversal or reduction of left hemisphere
dominance in CD3, suggesting, again, that the right hemisphere has greater importance in psychic perception.)

In the above study of Jonsson's three conditions and in the analysis of the third
ERP study with 25 gamblers, it is worth noting that 40 Hz activity accompanied
unconscious psi in participants unselected for psychic ability, but conscious psi in a
gifted participant selected for psychic ability. We should also note that the participants unselected for psi showed 40 Hz at two electrode sites, while Jonsson showed
40 Hz activity at all five electrode sites, a more global effect.

Many neuroscientists hold that conscious experience depends upon a linking of
widely separated brain loci by coherent or in-phase gamma waves, which produce a
"global workspace" for the brain (Baars, 1996). Thus, gamma band activity has taken
on a central role in explaining the synthesis of perceptual and cognitive unities we
know as "consciousness." Llinás and Ribary (1993) proposed that 40 Hz may underlie hyperattentiveness to internal stimuli. It could be that a globalization of 40 Hz

across the cortex is a precondition for, or in some other way reflects, the movement of unconscious psi toward conscious levels.

Additional suggestions may lie in the details. Our experiment was run in two modes—wager and nonwager. There was more extensive 40 Hz in the wager condition than in the nonwager, and conscious guessing accuracy tended to be above chance in wager trials, though not robust enough to attain statistical significance. Thus, there was a trend suggesting that the accuracy of conscious psi could be related to the presence of 40 Hz frequencies, or that these frequencies help to translate psi information into conscious awareness.

Was Jonsson's brain neurologically different in his ability to manifest 40 Hz frequencies across all electrodes? Was it this ability that allowed him to become conscious of what is ordinarily considered to be unconscious extrasensory perceptions? Do other extraordinary people manifest such frequencies? And, if so, how do they manifest?

40 Hz Found in Field Studies in Brazil

We made several trips to Brazil in the 1990s to observe and record brain waves from groups engaging in differing altered states of consciousness (ASCs). We did not perform controlled tests for psi, but we found increased gamma brain activity in each group, suggesting hyperaroused ASCs.

Santo Daime

The Santo Daime Church is a well-known spiritual group in Brazil, one that uses the hallucinogenic mixture *ayahuasca* in its rituals. (The Santo Daime Church prefers the term *daime*.) The use of ayahuasca for sacramental purposes, in order to access spiritual knowledge, is legal in Brazil. The mixture's main ingredients are dimethyltryptamine (DMT) and β-carbolines such as harmine. We were invited to record brain waves from members of a Santo Daime center in Rio de Janeiro both shortly before and 45 minutes after ingestion. We found significantly increased 36–44 Hz brain activity over the visual cortex (posterior cortex) of the brain, an area that processes visual information. This is consistent with reports of enhanced internal visual imagery after ayahuasca ingestion. The mixture is widely used by shamans in the Amazon region who often claim that it facilitates psychic ability; however, there have been no controlled tests of this claim, although the substance has also been termed *telepathine*. As far as we can determine, our study of the effects of a hallucinogen on the human EEG was the first to be published since the 1960s (Don et al., 1998).

Trance Surgery

There are many Brazilian mediums engaging in what many anthropologists term "possession trance," a practice that is found widely throughout the world in which it is believed that spirits take possession of a person's body (e.g., Bourguignon,

1979). However, since 1950, there have been a small number of Brazilian mediums also performing crude forms of surgery, usually employing sharp instruments such as scalpels, but without anesthesia or sterile procedures. We term this practice trance surgery. In widely separated places in Brazil, during the 1990s, we recorded EEGs from nine trance surgeons and several patients undergoing surgery. We also videotaped many surgeries. While many incisions were superficial, many others were not. The first trance surgeon we observed employed a handheld circular saw (meant for cutting wood) to open up his patients, in some cases into the peritoneal cavity. We found that for all the surgical mediums in trance whose brain-wave activity we recorded, there was an abundance of 40 Hz or gamma activity; therefore, these were hyperaroused trances. EEG data from a few patients undergoing surgery were also recorded, revealing slow brain rhythms such as alpha, suggesting a relaxed, pain-free condition, which is exactly what we observed.

Treatment efficacy under fieldwork conditions is very difficult to assess. However, it is clear that the completely unsanitary conditions and the crude techniques should have produced considerable blood loss and left many patients in shock. We found no evidence of this. How the hyperaroused trances of the surgical mediums, with abundant 40 Hz brain activity, allows them to inflict what would normally be considered significant insult to their patients' bodies is not understood. It may be relevant that for one of the surgical mediums we covertly ran an electronic random event generator (REG). During his trance, the REG became significantly nonrandom, perhaps suggesting a field effect of the trance state. (For a more complete treatment of trance surgery, see Don and Moura, 2000.)

UFO Experiencers

In addition to the trance surgeons, we were able to study another Brazilian group exhibiting hyperaroused trance (Don and Moura, 1997). Our purpose was only to examine their EEGs during trance, which pilot data suggested were unusual. It was beyond our capability to validate or disprove their claims of abductions by—or contact with—extraterrestrial "aliens" and unidentified flying objects (UFOs). A group of 13 participants was selected for our study. Their ages ranged from 19 to 72; the mean age was 47.2 years. All reported having conscious memories of being abducted or having contact with extraterrestrial, nonhuman beings. From our pilot work with people claiming contact or abduction, we found some who could enter an ASC, which reportedly commenced with the UFO experience. In order to be included in the study, participants had to be able to voluntarily enter a hyperaroused state as measured by the EEG. In this state, they maintained muscular relaxation and immobility. Their EEGs, at all 19 electrodes, showed high-frequency activity, but maximally over the prefrontal and adjacent areas. Examination of prefrontal/frontal data revealed intermittent trains of *rhythmic*, approximately 40 Hz activity, at times exceeding 40 microvolts. This activity was distinct from faster brain waves (over 70 Hz) with different morphologies, which we attributed to scalp muscle EMG. Midline EEG analysis (where EMG contamination would be minimized, and statistically controlling for EMG activity) revealed significantly more 40 Hz in trance than baseline ($p < .006$). That is, there were less than six chances in 1,000 that this occurred just by chance. Also, the frequency of the dominant alpha frequency significantly increased in trance ($p < .01$), which is another indication of hyperarousal. There was no evidence of epilepsy or schizophrenia, either of which might have confounded these results.

As in the trance surgery studies, we covertly ran an electronic REG. During the hyperaroused conditions, the REG outputs were significantly nonrandom, again suggesting a field effect associated with high-frequency gamma activity. The participants in the study were diverse (including a 70-year-old grandmother and her 19-year-old grandson, who claimed to have been abducted together). None were meditators, and all claimed that their ASC began with their abduction or encounters with nonhumans.

It may be significant that in the research literature, voltages of 40 microvolts (and above) gamma waves have been reported only three times previously. First, this was reported in a study of an Indian guru in Calcutta engaged in a meditative practice known in yoga as "raising the kundalini" in order to achieve a "unitive state of consciousness" (Das and Gastaut, 1957). A second report of high voltages involved inhalation of nitrous oxide, which induced up to 100-microvolt gamma activity at 34 Hz (Yamamura, Fukuda, Takeya, Goto, and Furukawa, 1981). The third report of approximately 40-microvolt gamma was a study of eight Tibetan Buddhist meditators with 15–40 years of practice (Lutz, Greischar, Rawlings, Ricard, and Davidson, 2004). It is interesting that our Brazilian subjects, without meditative training or nitrous oxide, could produce 40–50-microvolt gamma waves. This, of course, does not validate their claim that their brains were altered during their reported abductions or encounters.

40 Hz and Mysterious Minds

Conclusions remain difficult. When we examine frequency, we see that, for participants unselected for psi, correct guessing of targets or "conscious psi" appears to be related to the presence of 40 Hz at the right frontal and right posterior regions of the brain. In the case of Jonsson, we have seen that correct guessing of targets or "conscious psi" would appear to be strongly related to the presence of 40 Hz at disparate regions of the brain.

While it is tempting to think that 40 Hz can explain consciousness or the amplification of unconscious psi to conscious levels, it would be reductive to equate consciousness with gamma wave activity. The number of near-death experients who report events in the physical world while remaining technically "unconscious" confounds the equation; apparently, some forms of awareness are not biodegradable. This type of evidence does not support the prevailing "neural monist" view among neuroscientists, that mind can be totally explained as an output of a well-functioning brain. Perhaps 40 Hz—at high enough voltages and phase coherence

—may be one pathway through which human minds become capable of mysterious activities.

Correlation Waves

The usual evidence for psi involves some kind of target to be correctly identified or affected in some nonordinary manner. However, if psi transcends space and time, perhaps the "focused" model of psi has misled parapsychologists for a long time. Perhaps psi is not a signal or a form of energy, but a wave of correlation that creates meaningful wholes.

Experiment 1

Some time after completing our laboratory experiments with Jonsson, we decided to try a long-distance ESP card guessing experiment with him. I conducted the experiment from our laboratory, 1,500 miles from Jonsson's home. We used the standard precautions and double-blind controls, and the procedure was straightforward: Count the hits and misses and compute the statistical probability of the result. (For experimental details, see Don, McDonough, and Warren, 1995b.) Jonsson scored eight correct identifications or "hits" out of the 25 guesses. It would have taken nine hits to be statistically significant. No further tests were planned, and I set the results aside.

Several weeks later, I had a sudden idea that perhaps it would be worthwhile to make a table of targets versus guesses to see if any kind of two-dimensional pattern would emerge. I plotted the targets and guesses on x–y coordinates, using one-letter characters for each of the ESP cards. For example, if the fifth guess were "star," then across the fifth row of the table, in each of the five columns labeled "star," I would place a checkmark. When the table was completed, I looked at the diagonal stretching from the lower right corner to the upper left of the page; a two-dimensional wave seemed to spread across the graph, similar to water waves in a pond. (This table is accurately reproduced in Don, McDonough, and Warren, 1996.)

To confirm the presence of a wave, we needed to analyze our existing data mathematically, with methods capable of determining the presence of periodicities. We turned to a complex set of statistical procedures known as signal analysis. It is beyond the scope of this chapter to explain these statistical transformations in any detail, but mention of them may be helpful to readers.

First, we ruled out the possibility that the target list itself contained periodicities by conducting an autocorrelation test. No periodicities were found. Then we cross-correlated the guesses with the targets. Initially, this cross-correlation proceeded in a linear fashion. We placed our vertical list of guesses parallel to our vertical list of targets and moved or "lagged" one list up a row for each of the 25 trials, counting the matches at each lag and dividing by the number of possible matches to arrive at the "hit densities." We then computed the power spectral density (PSD) of the hit densities with a FFT (Bracewell, 1986) to quantify any periodicities in the data. These methods analyze the entire range of all data from an experiment.

We found three power peaks. The power in the maximum power peak was ranked in comparison to 1,000 computer simulations of our experiment with random data, yielding 1,000 power values. These were ranked from smallest to largest. Our experimental max power was only exceeded by 47 simulated experiments, yielding $p < .048$, which is usually considered to be statistically significant. Therefore, the mathematical analysis tended to validate our conjecture that there was a wave pattern in the data.

Experiment 2

We decided to conduct additional research to test for this hypothesized pattern. A month later, we repeated the first long-distance experiment with Jonsson. It was immediately clear that on-target hits and wave power are independent measures. There were seven hits out of a possible 25, a score less statistically significant than that of the first experiment. However, though Experiment 2 yielded weaker evidence of conscious psi than Experiment 1, paradoxically it revealed more power in the wave that correlated guesses with targets ($p < .009$).

Experiments 3 and 4

We conducted two additional experiments in our laboratory and with our staff. These were variants of the experiments mentioned above and involved the intent to match the symbol order in two decks of ESP cards (Don et al., 1995b). Experiment 3 had seven hits but insignificant power in the correlation wave. (In contrast, Experiment 2 above, also with seven hits, had high power in its correlation wave.) Experiment 4 replicated Experiment 3; but there were nine focal hits and significant correlation wave power ($p < .046$).

Experiment 5: Pearce-Pratt Data

Experiments 1–4 all involved our laboratory staff. We decided that a data sample from outside our lab was indicated. We knew that data from some of J. B. Rhine's experiments with the high-scoring subject Hubert Pearce were archived in the Duke University library (Rhine and Pratt, 1954). We drew a random sample from this archived collection and analyzed the data, as above. There were 10 focal hits on the 25 ESP card targets ($p < .017$). Using new simulated data, the correlation wave power was quite significant ($p < .011$).

Experiment 6: Mean Maximum Power for Experiments 2–5 as a Group: Linear Correlation

So as not to contaminate our attempts at replicating our initial experiment, we excluded the "pilot data" of Experiment 1, and averaged the maximum wave power of our data from Experiments 2 through 5. We drew random samples of size four (one power maximum from each experiment) from the 1,000-value Monte Carlo simulations we had used in evaluating Experiments 2–5 and computed their means. Only one of the 1,000 simulated means ($p < .002$) exceeded the average power maximum for Experiments 2–5. Thus, we had now replicated and confirmed our original hypothesis about the correlation wave in an entirely new and independent data set.

Circular Correlation: Mean Maximum Power for Experiments 1–5 as a Group

In linear cross-correlation, the number of possible matches decreases after each lag, thus incrementally raising the "standard error." We decided to perform yet another analysis upon all the previous data in an attempt to decrease the standard error. For this analysis, we switched to a form of circular correlation with guesses and targets arranged in concentric circles. This format preserved an n of 25 for each step of the analysis (Oppenheim and Schafer, 1989). Circular correlation directly addresses whether or not there are periodicities throughout the whole two-dimensional table of guesses and targets. By arranging the data in continuous circles, any periodicity found would be continuous across data boundaries. Thus, distinctions of precognition (ESP of future occurrences) and retrocognition (ESP of past occurrences) vanish because there is no longer any directionality to causality. We computed the circular correlation and PSD for each of the five data sets. Then we compared the mean of the maximum-power spectral lines from the five data sets to another 1,000-value Monte Carlo simulation. The mean of the maximum powers exceeded all of the data from circular correlation simulations ($p < .001$). Our results strongly supported the correlation wave hypothesis.

Circular Correlation of Data from 52 Students

We also analyzed some additional forced-choice data, lent to us by Professor James Crandall (1987), for the existence of a correlation wave. The participants were 52 undergraduate students who were classified as having either a visual or a verbal cognitive style on the basis of scores on Paivio's (1971) Individual Differences Questionnaire; a list of low- and high-imagery words served as psi targets. We used the same type of analysis described above, except that we substituted circular convolution (a variant of circular correlation that reverses its order) for circular correlation itself (Bracewell, 1986). The mean maximum spectral power was significant for the 14 participants classified as visualizers when guessing high-imagery targets at any above-chance level of accuracy ($p < .037$). For the 12 visualizers scoring at below-chance levels of accuracy on the same targets, the mean maximum spectral power was $p < .063$. Both sets of visualizers had nonsignificant effects when guessing "low-imagery" targets. All participants with verbal cognitive styles had nonsignificant effects with all data. Thus, it was only the participants whose cognitive style was visual rather than verbal whose guesses produced correlation waves.

Although we did not attempt to focus on psi's association with brain laterality—and what data we have on this issue are ambiguous—the correlation wave revealed its holistic nature and link to visual processes. Both of these are associated with the right cerebral hemisphere. But the phenomenon clearly goes beyond a simple interpretation that these effects are outputs of the right hemisphere. Instead, the underlying mathematical unity, of a coherent two-dimensional pattern—of the thoughts of 52 unselected subjects and the word lists they were guessing—suggests that psi is woven into the very fabric of nature.

Denouement

We do not agree with mainstream neurobiologists that coherent 40 Hz *is* consciousness, or is a *sine qua non* for conscious experience. Many reports of consciousness during "near-death" and "out-of-body" experiences make this unlikely (Kelly et al., 2007, pp. 367–421). However, ample data support the claim that coherent 40 Hz is a major factor in ordinary conscious experience. The extraordinary people we dealt with, or referred to, had high to very high 40 Hz voltage. For some of these people, wave coherence was also measured and was at high levels. So, perhaps, coherent, high-voltage 40 Hz is present for people who have conscious access to the underlying unity we found expressed by correlation waves. For the extraordinary people we investigated, this unity appeared.

References

Baars, B. J. (1996). *In the theater of consciousness: The workplace of the mind.* New York: Oxford University Press.

Bourguignon, E. (1979). *Psychological anthropology.* New York: Holt, Rinehart and Winston.

Bracewell, R. (1986). *The Fourier transform and its applications.* New York: McGraw-Hill.

Crandall, J. E. (1987). Effects of cognitive style and type of target on displacements. *Journal of Parapsychology, 51,* 191–215.

Das, N. N., and Gastaut, H. (1957). Variations de lactivité électrique du cerveau, du coeur et des muscles squelettiques au cours de la méditation et de la lextase yogique. *Electroencephalography and Clinical Neurophysiology,* Supplement No. 6, 211.

Dixon, W. J. (Ed.). (1985). *BMD statistical software* (pp. 519–537). Berkeley: University of California Press.

Don, N. S., McDonough, B. E., Moura, G., Warren, C. A., Kawanishi, K., Tomita, H., Tachibana, Y., Bohlke, M., and Farnsworth, N. R. (1998). Effects of "ayahuasca" on the human EEG. *Journal of Phytomedicine, 5*(2), 87–96.

Don, N. S., McDonough, B. E., and Warren, C. A. (1992). Psi testing of a controversial psychic under controlled conditions. *Journal of Parapsychology, 56,* 87–96.

Don, N. S., McDonough, B. E., and Warren, C. A. (1995a). Differential brain responses to targets and nontargets in a precognitive, forced-choice task. *Proceedings of the 38th Annual Convention of the Parapsychological Association,* 113–121.

Don, N. S., McDonough, B. E., and Warren, C. A. (1995b). Signal processing analysis of forced-choice ESP data: Evidence for psi as a wave of correlation. *Journal of Parapsychology, 59,* 357–380.

Don, N. S., McDonough, B. E., and Warren, C. A. (1996). Erratum. *Journal of Parapsychology, 60,* 80.

Don, N. S., McDonough, B. E., and Warren, C. A. (1998). Event-related brain potential (ERP) indicators of unconscious psi: A replication using subjects unselected for psi. *Journal of Parapsychology, 62,* 127–145.

Don, N. S., and Moura, G. (1997). Topographic brain mapping of UFO experiencers. *Journal of Scientific Exploration, 11,* 435–453.

Don, N. S., and Moura, G. (2000). Trance surgery in Brazil. *Alternative Therapies in Health and Medicine, 6*(4), 39–48.

Don, N. S., Warren, C. A., McDonough, B. E., and Collura, T. F. (1988). Event-related brain potentials and a phenomenological model of psi-conducive states. In D. H. Weiner and R. L. Morris (Eds.), *Research in parapsychology 1987* (pp. 72–76). Metuchen, NJ: Scarecrow Press.

Healy, J. (1986). Hippocampal kindling, theta resonance, and psi. *Journal of the Society for Psychical Research, 53,* 352–368.

Honorton, C. (1987). Precognition and real-time ESP performance in a computer task with an exceptional subject. *Journal of Parapsychology, 51,* 291–321.

Honorton, C., Davidson, R., and Bindler, P. (1971). Feedback-augmented EEG alpha, shifts in subjective state, and ESP card guessing performance. *Journal of the American Society for Psychical Research, 65,* 308–323.

Kelly, E. F., Kelly, E. W., Crabtree, A., Gauld, A., Grosso, M., and Greyson, B. (2007). *Irreducible mind: Toward a psychology for the 21st century.* Lanham, MD: Rowman & Littlefield.

Llinás, R., and Ribary, U. (1993). Coherent 40-Hz oscillation characterizes dream state in humans. *Proceedings of the National Academy of Science, 90,* 2078–2081.

Lloyd, D. H. (Pseudonym) (1973). Objective events in the brain correlating with psychic phenomena. *New Horizons, 1*(2), 69–75.

Lutz, A., Greischar, L. L., Rawlings, N. B., Ricard, M., and Davidson, R. J. (2004). Long-term meditators self-induce high-amplitude gamma synchrony during mental practice. *Proceedings of the National Academy of Sciences, USA, 101,* 16369–16373.

McDonough, B. E., Don, N. S., and Warren, C. A. (1988). EEG frequency domain analysis during a clairvoyant task in a single-subject design: An exploratory study. *Proceedings of the 31st Annual Convention of the Parapsychological Association,* 124–132.

McDonough, B. E., Don, N. S., and Warren, C. A. (2002). Differential event-related potentials to targets and decoys in a guessing task. *Journal of Scientific Exploration, 16,* 187–206.

Millar, B. (1979). The Lloyd effect. *European Journal of Parapsychology, 2,* 381–395.

Mitchell, E. D. (1971). An ESP test from Apollo 14. *Journal of Parapsychology, 35,* 89–107.

Oppenheim, A. V., and Shafer, R. W. (1989). *Discrete-time signal processing.* Englewood Cliffs, NJ: Prentice-Hall.

Paivio, A. (1971). *Imagery and verbal processes.* New York: Holt, Rinehart & Winston.

Psychophysical Research Laboratories. (1985). *Psilab II user's manual.* Princeton, NJ: Psychophysical Research Laboratories.

Rhine, J. B., and Pratt, J. G. (1954). A review of the Pearce-Pratt distance series of ESP tests. *Journal of Parapsychology, 18,* 165–177.

Sheer, D. E. (1984). Focused arousal, 40 Hz EEG, and dysfunction. In T. Elbert, B. Rockstroh, and W. Lutzenberger (Eds.), *Functional brain imaging* (pp. 64–84). New York: Springer.

Silverman, J., and Buchsbaum, M. (1970). Perceptual correlates of consciousness: A conceptual model and its technical implications for psi research. In R. Cavanna (Ed.), *Psi favorable states of consciousness: Proceedings of an international conference on methodology in psi research* (pp. 143–169). New York: Parapsychological Foundation.

Ullman, M., and Krippner, S. (1989). *Dream telepathy* (2nd ed.). Jefferson, NC: McFarland.

Warren, C. A., McDonough, B. E., and Don, N. S. (1990). Single subject event-related brain potential changes in a psi task. *Proceedings of the 33rd Annual Convention of the Parapsychological Association*, 344–360.

Warren, C. A., McDonough, B. E., and Don, N. S. (1992). Partial replication of single subject event-related potential effects in a psi task. *Proceedings of the 35th Annual Convention of the Parapsychological Association*, 169–181.

Warren, C. A., Don, N. S., and McDonough, B. E. (1997). "40 Hz" and attention to psi information. *Proceedings of the 40th Annual Convention of the Parapsychological Association*, 454–463.

Yamamura, T., Fukuda, M., Takeya, H., Goto, Y., and Furukawa, K. (1981). Fast oscillatory EEG activity induced by analgesic concentrations of nitrous oxide in man. *Anesthesia and Analgesia, 60*, 283–288.

Classic Decadence

CHAPTER 7

Neurobiology, Brain Reductionism, and Subjective Experience

Vernon M. Neppe

It would certainly be gratifying to neuroscientists if we could explain ourselves away as simply being a mass of microtubules and controlled, but amorphous, protoplasm. We would then be able to tame the ineffable concepts of "life," "consciousness," "reality," "identity," "self," and even "creativity," "genius," and "intuition." We would once and for all pack that ghost into the machine and heave a sigh of relief that we need not "unthink" anything we have thought before (Neppe, 2008c).

Or maybe we will, once again, doubt that our world is so simple. Maybe we will even look at the cogent evidence that has accumulated over the past quarter century or so, and truly wonder about our origins. Maybe the purely monistic and physicalistic presuppositions will tumble and we will realize we need to replace our carefully built neurobiologically based edifice or at least augment it. This chapter explores various relationships between neurobiology and subjective experiences related to what has often been seen as mysterious.

The best way to examine such ideas is to examine the fabric of the subjective experiences that are among the most threatening to our current worldview, namely *subjective paranormal experiences* (SPEs) (Neppe, 1980a). In the 1980s I developed the nonprejudicial term "SPE" to examine such phenomena. This way, I could evaluate ostensibly anomalous or psychic or intuitive experiences with a similar face validity approach that I have used in my examination of auditory hallucinations (Neppe, 1982a). The approach, then, neither confirms nor denies the veridicality of the SPE itself, nor does it label SPEs as "pathological" or "normal." Instead, the SPE term allows for analyzing links with areas of the brain in order to understand the deeper aspects of the experience.

Brain Stimulation and the Out-of-Body Experience

Tart (1967) was the first modern investigator of electroencephalographic (EEG) correlates of out-of-body experiences (OBEs), a term he articulated in the 1960s. Tart (1998) pointed out that naturally occurring OBEs are psychologically important since they are a primary cause of the belief in postmortem survival. Whether the specific findings here eventually will be shown to be part of the causal mechanism of OBEs is unknown, but future research should study the full-scale OBE complex, not only each possible component (Tart, personal correspondence, November 4, 2007).

This area has become particularly controversial since 2002, when the stimulation of a particular area of the brain (the angular gyrus) in a patient with a right temporal seizure disorder produced the subjective report of the patient saying she was out of her body (Blanke, Ortigue, Landis, and Seeck, 2002). This report was replicated on further stimulation. Subsequently, the same researchers (Blanke and Arzy, 2005; Blanke, Landis, Spinelli, and Seeck, 2004; Blanke and Mohr, 2005; Blanke et al., 2005; Bunning and Blanke, 2005) and others (Tong, 2003) have reported stimulation of similar, but slightly different, areas of the brain's right hemisphere (Booth, Koren, and Persinger, 2005), producing reported OBEs. Persistent tinnitus (ear ringing) often was linked with such experiences.

In fact, such reports are not new. Penfield (1958) described how he induced such an experience in the brain, as did Munro and Persinger (1992). And a more recent stimulation case producing OBEs has been replicated in a patient with intractable tinnitus who described a "sense of disembodiment" (De Ridder, Van Laere, Dupont, Menovsky, and Van de Heyning, 2007).

How do we approach these subjective OBE reports? The cited investigations postulated possible brain sites for the OBE, suggesting that the mystery had been solved. However, when one analyzes OBEs induced by brain stimulation, they are sufficiently atypical to question whether, phenomenologically, they are the same as spontaneously occurring OBEs. In comparison with spontaneous, noninduced OBEs described by experients, they are incomplete in that the whole body is not experienced as being "outside." Further, experients of induced OBEs often continue to perceive the environment from the visual perspective of the physical body.

The latter experients variably produced trivial illusion phenomena (Greyson, Parnia, and Fenwick, 2008): distorted body image, depersonalization and derealization, visual perceptions of specific fixed location, and other associated parietotemporal state or trait features. These descriptions differ markedly from thousands of spontaneous OBE reports. These OBEs frequently involve extracorporeal awareness with locality-dependent perceptual experiences, clear imagery, polymodal perceptions, and profound cognitive reports. The environment (including the body itself) is accurately perceived from an extracorporeal perspective, and this disembodied center of consciousness may move about independently of the physical body (Gabbard and

Twemlow, 1984; Gabbard, Twemlow, and Jones, 1982). These descriptions are often reported by individuals with such brain dysfunctions as seizure foci or tinnitus (Neppe, 2006).

Additionally, when analyzing OBEs and for that matter comparable phenomena such as déjà vu, no single localization can be found (Neppe, 1983c, 2006; Neppe and Funkhouser, 2006). We can learn from these other experiences that at least four distinct nosological subtypes of déjà vu exist (Neppe and Bradu, 2006). Similar research on OBEs needs to be performed to determine its subtypes (Neppe, 2003).

The following guidelines seek to ensure the phenomenological description of the data and associate them with identified diagnostic or special research groups (Neppe, 2002). (1) Analyze these SPEs in as much detail as possible and compare them with the typical features of SPEs of those who have no history of brain dysfunction. (2) Realize that with any brain pathology, the experiential report has a specific pathophysiological context. (3) Do not generalize single cases to other humans. (4) Compare the literature and initiate detailed research, learning from past knowledge. (5) Search for sources of single localization for specific phenomena, but recognize the existence of nosological subtypes (e.g., as found in déjà vu). (6) Realize that, even when findings are referable to specific brain functioning, they neither confirm nor deny actual origins within the brain: one explanation for events may be endogenous origins within the brain (e.g., pathological hallucinations), but another brain function or pattern may allow consideration for the experience of an outside, usually covert, reality. (7) Methodologically, consider that associative links do not imply causality; to consolidate the causality hypothesis one should analyze both normal populations for specific brain changes and also the converse (e.g., find patients with those brain changes and determine if they report the same SPEs).

Thus, these dichotomous epiphenomena of subjectively interpreted OBEs require careful phenomenological differentiation. The induced OBE apparently differs from the spontaneous OBE; using one term for both endpoint expressions could produce incorrect clustering of different phenomena (e.g., spontaneous OBEs versus complex partial symptoms). Without determining the possible subtypes of OBEs, different origins and etiologies could be inappropriately interpreted as one syndrome (Alvarado, 2000; Neppe, 2002).

The Near-Death Experience

Plato's famous cave allegory may be an important warning that brain waves and other neurobiological measurements reflect very little of what we assume. The OBE research on brain stimulation is closely linked with similar investigations of so-called near-death experiences (NDEs) in which individuals report unusual perceptions and cognitions while near death (e.g., coma, cardiac resuscitation). These reports vary, but have some consistency: the presence of nonphysical beings, tunnel and light experiences, or being out of body (Morse, Castillo, Venecia, Milstein, and Tyler, 1986; Sabom, 1980). Since the initial volley of reports was published by physicians and psychologists, the origins of these experiences have been debated.

The neurophysiological basis of the NDE is unknown. Do they originate with a lack of oxygen in the brain, from a rush of endorphins (Jansen, 1990), from imbalances of neurotransmitters (Bonta, 2004), or from temporal lobe activity (Neppe, 1989)? How is it possible that these experiences can occur when memories during comas are typically lost (Morse and Neppe, 1991; Sabom, 1980, 1998)?

One controversy links NDEs to a stage of sleep called rapid eye movement (REM) intrusion, a sleep stage characterized by vivid dreams and accompanied by sleep paralysis, which may occur during wakefulness or such clinical conditions as narcolepsy (Nelson, Mattingly, Lee, and Schmitt, 2006). Again, many neuroscientists have ostensibly explained the NDE as purely brain-linked.

The original article (Nelson, Mattingly, Lee, and Schmitt, 2006) linking NDEs and REM intrusion has become so significant that it is critical to understand its limitations, while also using it as a jumping ground for further research. Nelson et al. argued that NDE phenomena can be explained by REM intrusion, evoked by cardio-respiratory afferents in an arousal system predisposed to intrusion of REM activity. They showed that the lifetime prevalence of REM intrusion in 55 NDE subjects compared with an age/gender-matched control group (who also reported sleep paralysis, as well as sleep-related visual and auditory hallucinations) was substantially more common in subjects reporting NDEs. These findings suggest that under circumstances of peril, an NDE would be more likely in those with a history of REM intrusion, hence promoting subjective aspects of NDE and associated syncope. Suppression of an activated locus caeruleus (involved with norepinephrine) could be central to an arousal system predisposed to both REM intrusion and NDEs.

There are methodological problems with this study, however. It had a retrospective design; only 64 patients out of 446 patients, from the large Internet site that recruited subjects, responded to the author's query. The NDE experients chosen were people who also had contributed their experiences to a Web site. Therefore, they may have been more likely to overendorse questions about unusual experiences, thinking that the investigators were looking for them. Moreover, the REMs of NDE experients were compared to a sample of hospital workers who may have been particularly reluctant to admit any accompanying bizarre symptoms for fear of job discrimination. A more suitable control group would have been composed of people who had been near death but did not have an NDE.

But let us assume the sample was adequate for illustrative purposes. Even then, we would still have to face several questions: Is the NDE simply an endogenous physiological phenomenon or, alternatively, does it have implications for the survival of consciousness after death?

The important challenge to such NDE research is Occam's razor, and we should approach other anomalous phenomenon in a parsimonious way. However, we must be aware of what has aptly been called *premature parsimony*—a premature conceptual reduction by investigators that can distort our understanding. The object of such inquiry is to find appropriate explanations, not just the simplest. The explanation must be fruitful, explaining all, not just a few aspects, of a phenomenon.

In Nelson's (Nelson, Mattingly, Lee, and Schmitt, 2006) research, the data are post hoc, as they did not compare the NDE experients' REM intrusions before and after the NDE. Could the NDE experients, as a consequence of their NDEs, have experienced neurological insults that increased the rates for a variety of symptoms? Was the REM state intrusion the *result* of experiencing a NDE rather than the *cause* of an NDE?

Personally, I believe that this scenario is unlikely. The narcoleptic syndrome has sleep paralysis as a major feature. But REM intrusion could also arise during the pre-sleep hypnagogic and postsleep hypnopompic states, as well as during the cataplexic and diplopic states we commonly see in narcolepsy and certainly during the over-whelming short daytime sleepiness in narcolepsy. The reason for all these links is that the proportions of REM intrusion, as in narcoleptic syndromes (Mignot et al., 2006), seem to have a solid linkage to sleep onset. So there is precedent (Planelles et al., 1997), and I suspect this predisposition is constitutionally based since in my clinical practice I have never encountered brain injury producing such changes. But we also see here a variety of other bizarre symptoms such as hallucinatory experiences (Douglass, Hays, Pazderka, and Russell, 1991). In fact, my working hypothesis is that the narcoleptic-like condition may be associated with SPEs, just as there is a link between SPEs and anomalous temporal lobe activity.

However, there is a terminological aspect in that the label "REM intrusion" is not commonly used. I suspect it should be limited to demonstrable REM occurring on polysomnography, not based on historical interviews or questionnaire data about symptoms. This, in itself, creates a further level of error. If the authors had used the less provocative term "sleep paralysis" as a correlate of NDE, then we might have raised no objection. Sleep paralysis is a major epiphenomenal expression of REM intrusion, but this would not have been the correct dressing for newsworthy salience. The parallel is an important one; if we were to find that a cohort of patients with NDEs had a more rapid pulse than a control group, it would make a scientific con-tribution but would not make the evening news.

But let us now look at the other side of the topic. First, we need to reexamine fun-damentals. NDE experients frequently change their spiritual attitudes, yet this phe-nomenon often is disregarded by most medical journals. Second, we must be careful to make few assumptions when reading about REM intrusion experiences unless there has been an EEG or brain wave study of the research participant's wake-fulness/sleep cycle. If not, the reported experiences are simply subjective and less credible, not having been objectively validated on such measures as sleep polysom-nography. Next, the presence of so-called REM intrusion in a state of coma is physio-logically dubious; comatose people are unlikely to manifest REMs or to report dreams. Finally, the fact that REM intrusion or sleep paralysis correlates with NDEs does not make them causal, and they are unlikely to be so in the vast majority of NDEs.

There is no immediate reason why we need to spend thousands of dollars on complex equipment when the medical approach has been based on taking a case history and making a medical examination. History includes the eliciting of symptoms—those that are occurring at the same time as the feature being examined—as well as trait signs, in which any symptoms or features that occur over an extended period or even a lifetime are examined, but which do not occur typically, for example, with either sleep paralysis or NDEs. In the Nelson (Nelson, Mattingly, Lee, and Schmitt, 2006) study, only trait features were examined, limiting interpretations of the links with medical conditions or changes in specific foci of the brain. Additionally, as with almost all models, the unidirectional approach was used (i.e., near death experients were evaluated for their REM intrusion symptoms by medical history). The bidirectional approach would examine, in contrast, those patents presenting with REM intrusion features, as well as looking at NDE correlates.

Functional Magnetic Resonance Imaging and ESP

There is a new phase of research opportunities presented through the advent of functional magnetic resonance imaging (fMRI) scanners for attempting imaging and visualization of SPEs, addressing whether our very being might amount to a mere mass of microtubules. Research has become very sophisticated, illustrated by a Harvard fMRI study that attempted to demonstrate the veridicality of ESP (Moulton and Kosslyn, 2008). Because there were no neurobiological markers for matches between participants' guesses and a concealed target, the experimenters concluded that ESP was most likely illusory.

However, in fMRI studies, we attempt to demonstrate the functional (as opposed to anatomical) correlates of certain physiological changes (e.g., thinking, hallucinations, delusions, changes in emotion). We can experimentally study, for instance, the brain's expression of what happens when people laugh or cry. The technology is truly remarkable, but still in its early stages. Moulton and Kosslyn (2008) argued that their special methodology was the first to actually demonstrate that ESP does *not* occur, assuming ESP would have to be processed by the brain if it were more than a subjective experience. Moulton and Kosslyn could find no differences between the brain activity of research participants attempting to elicit telepathy, clairvoyance, or precognition compared with brain activity of a control group making no such attempt.

These research results have evoked enormous media reactions; in fact, Harvard University issued a press release about the study (Lavoie, 2008). Superficially, the research looks persuasive until one examines this "new method" and the conclusions drawn, as well as reexamines the earlier but unmentioned literature in which positive results were obtained with the use of psychophysiological equipment.

Moulton and Kosslyn (2008) used fMRI in an effort to document the existence or nonexistence of ESP. The researchers believed that fMRI would be more sensitive than using indirect behavioral methods and designed an experiment that they felt would increase the sensitivity of studying any significant results from tests for telepathy, clairvoyance, and precognition. Statistical results on the ESP measures they obtained, however, hovered around the expected chance score of 50 percent (i.e., they did not find evidence for ESP in their research). The researchers also reported that there was no fMRI difference when the participants attempted to evoke ESP compared with participants who were making no such attempt. Does this conclusively demonstrate that ESP is illusory? As quoted in the Harvard University press release, Moulton, the principal author, remarked,

> You cannot affirm the null hypothesis. But at the same time, some null results are stronger than others. This is the best evidence to date against the existence of ESP. Perhaps most important, this study offers scientists a new way to study ESP that avoids the pitfalls of past approaches. (Lavoie, 2008, no page specified)

Ironically, if they had found a neurobiological change, would that change have reflected all types of ESP or just one specific kind? Moulton and Kosslyn's complex design reflected different tests for so-called "contemporaneous telepathy," "contemporaneous clairvoyance," as well as precognition. Despite major problems that characterize the Moulton and Kosslyn (2008) study, their methodology was innovative, even though the study did not integrate lessons from previous research in the area, nor important theoretical applications such as "psi conduciveness" (Braud and Braud, 1973). For example, the researchers did not find above-chance ESP scores in 15 of the 16 pairs they tested. But an absence of ESP and a lack of physiological changes related to attempts to produce ESP suggest that the few correct ESP scores found could have been due to chance. If so, no fMRI changes would have been expected. However, even if above-chance ESP scores had been reported and there were still no physiological changes, this might simply have meant that the researchers had not located the appropriate anatomical correlates.

Ironically, Moulton and Kosslyn (2008) just may have hit a home run despite these flaws, namely one related to unexpected changes on the fMRI. The sixteenth pair of participants, the only pair demonstrating above-chance ESP scores, yielded provocative neurobiological results (i.e., less activity in several brain areas with most reduction, notably, being in the temporal lobe) during correct ESP trials as compared with incorrect ESP trials. The researchers explained this away as a "scanning artifact" and concluded that the results were not relevant. While this explanation could be correct, this "artifact" could have been associated with ESP. Paradoxically, Moulton and Kosslyn may have explained away their one positive result! If one positive result can be explained away, why is it not possible to explain away 15 negative results (see Radin, 2008)?

The researchers used biologically or emotionally related participants and emotional stimuli in an effort to maximize experimental conditions that are purportedly conducive to psi. Important, too, are effects of the participants' expectations, degree of psi conduciveness of the psychological conditions (Braud and Braud, 1973), and experimenter effects. These factors may dampen or accentuate results (Green and Thorpe, 1993; Neppe, 1982b). Also, the signal-to-noise ratio in fMRI studies (Logethetis, 2003) may be a legitimate explanation of negative results. If research participants are asked to think about an apple and an orange, the fMRI scans may demonstrate no differences between the two types of events. They are still different thoughts, but are not demonstrable because fMRI design is potentially insensitive to subtle psychological effects.

Finally, Moulton and Kosslyn (2008) did not cite the extant literature on ESP and fMRI. Eventually, Moulton asked the parapsychologist Dean Radin to delineate the literature they had missed and Radin (2008) cited several positive fMRI studies relating to ESP (e.g., Bierman, 2000; Radin, 2006; Bierman and Scholte, 2002; Richards, Kozak, Johnson, and Standish, 2005; Standish, Johnson, Kozak, and Richards, 2003). The Richards experiment (Richards, Kozak, Johnson, and Standish, 2005) represents a utilization of both the use of fMRI technology and the EEG. Extreme care was taken to isolate the subjects from each other and to automate the experiment to avoid any added experimenter error. There were still limitations (e.g., limited sample size), but because a correlated signal could be detected and replicated in the non-stimulated partner by using two independent neurophysiologic measures of brain function (EEG and fMRI), the evidence is strong that an anomalous phenomenon (not just a recording artifact) may have been at play in this study. Interestingly, brain changes occurred with the flashing 6 Hz stimulus, despite it not being detected by the subject visually.

In another study, Achterberg, Cooke, Richards, Standish, Kozak, and Lake (2005) found significant differences between experimental ("sending") and control ("no sending") procedures using self-designated healers. Areas activated during these experimental procedures included the anterior and middle cingulate area, precuneus, and frontal area. In an extension of this experiment, Achterberg examined purported "distant healing intention" using 11 self-identified healers and a "sensitive partner" selected by each healer. The healer's "intention" conditions were significantly correlated with "bold" signals in most of their partners' fMRIs while the healers sent "distant healing intention" at "on and off" random periods.

Results from a pilot study (Standish, Johnson, Kozak, and Richards, 2003) to test the feasibility of using an EEG experimental design for an fMRI study were also positive. An increase in blood oxygenation level was observed in the visual cortex of the nonstimulated subject. This was correlated to the stimulus-on condition of the stimulated partner. No such signal was observed when the stimulated partner was presented with the stimulus-off condition or when the participants reversed their roles.

In addition, Bierman's (2000) study of eight experienced meditators (and members of a control group) used randomly shown images. The time course of response measured by qualitative analyses (peak counting) demonstrated dynamic changes on fMRI (described as a "presentiment") about 4 seconds prior to actually being exposed to some of the emotionally stimulating (either violent or erotic) pictures. During meditation, presentiment was significantly linked with erotic stimuli, while the nonmeditators' presentiments correlated more highly with violent pictures (Bierman, 2000; Radin, 2006). A problem with such presentiment research is one of interpretive difficulty, the most radical being the possibility of "retrocausality," a backward shift in cause and effect. Alternatively, some writers consider "immediate precognition" and other explanations at quantum levels. A related problem is that neuroscientists can as easily claim that presentiment is, in fact, an expression of the same physiological event measured a fraction of a second prior to its registered actualization (Wegner, 2003).

These latter experiments were described as "preliminary" or as "pilot studies" and none of their authors issued press releases claiming they had demonstrated the reality of ESP. In fact, these authors simply stated that more research was warranted. Moulton and Kosslyn (2008) published their results (accompanied by a Harvard press release) while they were apparently unaware of the previous studies, even though they had all been published by peer-reviewed journals and indexed in Medline.

The Temporal Lobe and Subjective Paranormal Experiences

Reducing a system to its parts and discarding the critical synergism and Gestalt relationships may cause a loss of perspective. Reductionism in science is an appropriate methodology, but it must include complex and possibly, at this stage, ineffable concepts such as "reality," "self and identity," "consciousness," and even "life" itself. We must continue to study these topics empirically and in controlled laboratory settings, being careful to recognize our interpretations as limited and without prematurely applying theoretical paradigms to the results available. Sometimes that laboratory setting is simply the clinical medical evaluation, but this too can yield valuable data.

The clinical symptomatology approach has been a fruitful direction of interest for the neuroscience researcher. One benefit is that it is much less expensive than fMRI apparatus, which can be extremely costly. Hence, sample size can be much larger, and more clinical parameters can be measured. This approach emphasizes the phenomenological aspect of neuroscience, examining symptoms and clinical features so they can be correlated with the particular subgroup being analyzed. For example, detailed information on olfactory hallucinations can be correlated with temporal lobe epilepsy (Neppe, 1983a, 2008a, 2008b). This approach also illustrates the bidirectional model of causality. It applies what has been an unrecognized but standard medical model for centuries by allowing statements about correlations to reflect a cause, an effect, or both.

Are such SPEs merely a manifestation of the brain playing tricks on us? If so, is there an area of the brain where these tricks occur? Our understanding of SPEs from a physiological point of view would be greatly enhanced if we could pinpoint a section of the brain in which psi mediation (i.e., ESP, PK) occurs, or at least an area that plays a primary role. Such knowledge would provide at least three concrete benefits. First, by considering the functions performed by this part of the brain, we could develop more incisive insights about how psi manifests. For instance, if the area plays a crucial role in the activation of memories, credence would be lent to the hypothesis that psi occurs by activating stored memories. Second, if momentary brain states could be found to correlate with the accuracy of discrete psi responses, progress could be made in predicting which particular psi responses (e.g., guesses on a card test) will appear to be correct. Third, attempts could be made through biofeedback, drugs, or other means to alter the functioning of this part of the brain to enhance psi performance (Palmer and Neppe, 2003, 2004).

We can apply these same analogies directly to psi and the brain. Can we use a methodology based on the clinical medical model to assist our studies here? Let me whet your appetite by briefly discussing my own research on the temporal lobe, which, with respect, pioneered this approach in the context of SPEs (Neppe, 1980b, 2003). This research required the development of a measuring instrument, the Neppe Temporal Lobe Questionnaire (TLQ), to elicit symptoms that could be attributed to the temporal lobe of the brain; I designated them as Possible Temporal Lobe Symptoms (PTLSs). Our later work used an upgrade of this instrument, the Inventory of Neppe of Symptoms of Epilepsy and the Temporal Lobe (INSET) (Palmer and Neppe, 2003, 2004).

Similarly the research required development of measures to screen for so-called psychic experiences and thereafter to go into great detail to elicit whether participants had spontaneous SPEs and to use criteria for levels of subjective validation of the experiences. Again, in no way does this imply the experiences objectively occurred as interpreted. The essence of such phenomenological research is to be nonprejudicial and to approach experience in the same way as one would approach subjective reports of pain, dizziness, or hallucinations. There are ways of quantifying experience, and this approach offers the ability to develop comparative experimental and control groups. In our later work, the INSET incorporated such data.

The original work was my retrospective pilot study in South Africa. This examined whether more PTLSs are associated with ostensibly normal subjects claiming a large number of SPEs than with subjects claiming none, and if so, whether any specific PTLSs stood out. Both state and trait symptoms were examined. If PTLSs occurred during or just before or after the SPEs, then this would be a Temporal Lobe/SPE state; conversely, if they occurred at other times (as with the Nelson et al. [2006] research on REM intrusion), these would be trait phenomena that may imply a constellation of several symptoms.

In the initial Neppe study, despite a small endpoint sample size, SPE experients exhibited significantly more PTLSs than SPE nonexperients, with olfactory hallucinations being particularly common. These findings suggest an anomalous kind of temporal lobe functioning among the SPE experients, but would neither confirm nor deny the veridicality of their SPEs. This work is theoretically very important as, for the first time since Descartes misrepresented the pineal gland, an anatomical area could reliably be regarded as a kind of interaction zone for mind and brain—whether or not that "mind" may still be brain or would allow an appreciation of such experience.

Subsequently, this work was replicated in a different population by Persinger in Canada, again in normal populations (Persinger and Valliant, 1985). I did further work on SPE experients demonstrating a detailed qualitative kind of olfactory hallucination that overlapped with PTLSs, but were also different (Neppe, 1983a); the particular type of olfactory hallucination associated with SPEs has a pleasant and perfumy odor but commonly coexists with unpleasant burnt-smelling or foul-smelling temporal lobe type hallucinations. Similarly, I extended this work to the déjà vu phenomenon demonstrating that there were at least four qualitatively distinct, homogeneous categories of déjà vu (Neppe, 1983c): Subjective paranormal déjà vu experience was characterized by its time distortions and specific predictions component and occurred in SPE experients; associative déjà vu occurred in "normals" and essentially was vague with a lack of memorable and outstanding features; in the neuropsychiatric group, déjà vu experienced by temporal lobe epileptics was characterized by postictal (postseizure) features and associated PTLSs; and this type of experience did not occur in schizophrenics, whose déjà vu experiences were characterized by psychotic intrusions.

A study in this direction was our analysis of two families with ostensible psi abilities and temporal lobe dysfunction (Hurst and Neppe, 1981, 1982). This study may suggest familial links to PTLSs combined with SPEs. However, case reports may reflect exceptions and the data are only suggestive. These kinds of findings also reflect correlations only. To establish a higher probability of causality, one needs bidirectionality. This means using a novel methodology by applying the two converse rules: first, examine SPE experients (and a suitable comparative nonexperient group) for temporal lobe state and trait phenomena; and second, apply the converse by looking at patients with temporal lobe dysfunction and their SPEs. My colleague, John Palmer, and I did this by demonstrating that those with temporal lobe dysfunction have more SPEs than did a comparative population (Palmer and Neppe, 2003, 2004).

This produced what I call the *bidirectional medical model of causality*. Effectively, physicians have been applying the "bidirectional medical model of causality" through the ages. For example, in the model of malaria, the condition can be diagnosed clinically, and then confirmed by isolating plasmodium. Conversely, a malaria diagnosis may be made based on plasmodium in the blood and then finding correlates with clinical malaria. This moves correlation closer to causality. Even though this is still subjective, the subjective experience model in no way diminishes attempts to correlate it with objective events. Even when such causal links like the temporal lobe research (above) are found, this is just *one necessary but insufficient requirement* for SPEs to be expressed in the brain. We may have a functioning brain, but we still cannot walk without legs.

The Frontal Lobes and Other Anatomical Organs: Theoretical Bases

One can certainly argue that the lack of adequate frontal lobe functioning allows reduced self-awareness that may facilitate effects of intentionality on physical phenomena (Dobyns, 2003; Freedman, Jeffers, Saeger, Binns, and Black, 2003). This general state as hypothesized by Ehrenwald (1975) allows reception of psi-related information from outside (Bergson, 1914) because psi cortical filters are impaired (Neppe, 1990). However, if one looks at the model of temporal lobe functioning, it does not necessarily require dysfunction for individuals to experience significant SPEs. I have suggested that it requires a different kind of anomalous temporal lobe functioning that may be facilitated or correlated with dysfunction of seizures, but may also occur in ostensibly normal SPE experients.

If one uses the same parallel with the frontal lobe, a correlation with psi may not necessarily imply a feature reflecting a more generalized dysfunction, in this regard impaired self-awareness. It does not necessarily involve dysfunction of the frontal lobes even if we find a correlation of frontal lobe symptomatology with SPEs. We would need to use the same bidirectional, causal, medical, hypothetical model to link the two and, if so, we should examine SPE experients to establish if there are frontal lobe symptomatology links.

This kind of research is critical because I have previously hypothesized that the frontal lobes could correlate with efferent psi (i.e., PK) function (Neppe, 1990). The logic behind the hypothesis is that PK abilities are motor/efferent functions. The frontal lobe is the classical *executive* cerebral cortical organ. It is involved with every level of higher brain motor function. It is the logical candidate either alone or with the anterior temporal lobe for efferent psi phenomena.

Also relevant is the fact that unconscious psi phenomena sometimes occur. How does one measure presentiment on an EEG if indeed this is some kind of precognitive phenomenon or, even more radically, retrocausality? How does one measure autonomic changes in percipients correlating these changes with stimuli known only to the transmitters or agents? How does one correlate brain function with so-called spontaneous telesomatic phenomena (e.g., an itchy left foot known to the experient as an indication of danger to the family)? Essentially, these same principles apply as described: this does not necessarily reflect focal or generalized dysfunction of the brain (Neppe, 1983b). Instead this may reflect a pattern of functioning, global, or specific foci (localized in the brain) that correlates with a pattern allowing for anomalous events to be experienced or influenced (Neppe, 2002, 2003, 2008c). Such correlations of SPEs neither confirm nor deny the veridicality of psi and such correlations may derive from a specific bodily organ, or may be impacted through that organ (Neppe, 1983b, 2003). Only a bidirectional approach can establish some potential causal correlation, adequate controls have to be set up to appropriately make sense of the results, and these controls are sometimes very difficult to implement (Neppe, 2003). In addition, interpretations should not go beyond what is tested, such that subjective sleep paralysis should not be interpreted using more scientific sounding terms such as REM intrusion (see Nelson, Mattingly, Lee, and Schmitt, 2006), or, if ESP is not demonstrated, then we cannot argue that REM does not exist (e.g., Moulton and Kosslyn, 2008) or OBEs should be appropriately considered with all the OBE features, so that misinterpretations may not result (e.g., Blanke and Arzy, 2005).

All said, if unconscious psi has occurred, I will make some further predictions: the logical brain organ for such a correlation is the thalamus for afferent unconscious psi (as in so-called ESP) and for the hypothalamus to refer to endocrine linked psi, and for an unconscious efferent motor series of cerebral neurons to be involved. One example may possibly be the basal ganglia for unconscious efferent psi (i.e., PK). I will not at this point argue that these are all nondominant hemisphere-related functions. The brain works holistically in multiple ways.

I will make the following comparison using a baseball analogy. I am deliberately being farcical here because it illustrates so well the problems of methodology, the need for detail, the complexities of interpretations, and the ostensible double standards. I am a great admirer of Ken Griffey Jr., whose career began in Seattle, so choosing him in this farce reflects my admiration for this baseball icon. Let us suppose that we want to examine the brain correlates of Griffey's home-run swing. Griffey is appropriately tested with the most sophisticated apparatus around. But he does not hit a home run. Do we conclude that there is no change in his brain during his home-run swing? Of course not. *But many counteradvocates often do this with psi.* Now we test him again. This time he hits a home run. Our apparatus shows some change, but we find that this same change occurs during other states that others have exhibited. Do we conclude that he has not really hit a home run because others who do not hit home runs also show that change? Of course not. Or do we say we will study a large sample of home runs and compare it with a large sample of non-home-run swings in which he made an out? Fair enough. We may find Griffey shows no demonstrable change. Do we conclude that his home-run swing does not really exist? After all, we cannot demonstrate it in the brain. Of course not. We know it exists. We may say that our specific apparatus is not sensitive enough to differentiate his home-run swing from his non-home-run swing. *But many counteradvocates do this with psi.* Now, Griffey hits a home run again. This time he exhibits some unique change. The researchers notice it is one specific kind of home run he hits, only the longer ones to the left side. They are proud that they are realizing there is a need to subtype this "kind" of home run and conclude that they need to study this specific feature more extensively, otherwise how do they know these specific home-run findings really are linked with the brain changes? This seems legitimate but time consuming and difficult. But they have the financial resources to fund it, so they go ahead. They allocate complex mathematical analyses (e.g., multidimensional scaling, correspondence analyses) to ensure that they understand the differences between the subtypes they have analyzed. Hopefully some of the critics' protests can be seen more clearly through this baseball comparison. And counteradvocates might think: "Wow, if we study psi we might have to subclassify some events as well." But they quickly put that out of their minds because they "know" psi phenomena do not exist. However, I used multidimensional scaling in 22 dimensions to examine the déjà vu phenomenon in great detail and to demonstrate correlations of particular kinds of déjà vu with specific subtypes (Neppe, 2006; Neppe and Bradu, 2006; Neppe and Funkhouser, 2006).

Another concern is that researchers want to replicate their study. Replication is critically important in behavioral research. The difficulties often relate to exact conditions being replicated. They know there is a complex system of neurobiology at work and maybe even a dogged anomaly that they cannot measure. They may even realize that this anomaly is correlative, not causal. But if these were SPEs would they conclude that the brain changes are the causal links for the specific SPE features indicated? They look at the cited research on stimulating the brain and producing OBEs, on REM intrusion causing NDEs, on fMRI showing or not showing any kind of ESP, and wonder why causality rather than correlations were emphasized. They also examined the temporal lobe and its links to SPEs and noted the care taken to emphasize correlations, not causality.

The researchers in the farcical example would, of course, not conclude that Griffey's home runs actually do not really exist and are instead fantasies and imaginings. They know there are independent spectators who saw these home runs and that they are not just mass hallucinations. Yet, bizarrely, many critics do all of this regarding psi, even when statistical data for methodologies achieve highly believable levels. Rejecting all that evidence for their conclusions would be as ridiculous as saying Griffey's home runs were not hit, instead of saying "We don't quite know in what way they were hit." What can we conclude? Can we say that a certain pattern of brain function allows individuals to hit home runs? No, after all this, we cannot even say that. All we can say is that there appears to be a *correlate* of a distinct pattern of brain functioning when individuals strike the ball hard enough to hit a "special" kind of home run. This neither *demonstrates* nor denies the causal link of the underlying subjective experience of the hitter, or the objective brain experience that the individuals concerned may have when they hit a home run. Indeed, when a home run is hit, far more than cerebral cortical mechanisms are involved. A whole, possibly perfectly synchronous sensorimotor loop is involved in the properly trained individual. That one tiny finding in the brain in this extensive study may be simply an epiphenomenon of something far more complex. And so the researchers learn about the utter complexity of the real world, and the difficulties of doing such research—and the focus they need to only measure home runs. By substituting "home runs" with "psi," it becomes an apparent paradox that only in the discipline commonly called "parapsychology" (a discipline I believe should more correctly be called "dimensional biopsychophysics") would counteradvocates dare to write without assiduous examination of the appropriate literature and succeed with approbation, such as in the Harvard study (Moulton and Kosslyn, 2008) that has received so much attention, despite its flaws.

Concluding Comments on a Multiaxial, Classificatory, and Phenomenological Model

There is an urgent need to subdivide all apparently anomalous experiences into greater detail from the outset using a phenomenological approach. This may allow analyses that ultimately will provide the parapsychological researcher, phenomenological psychiatrist, anomalistic psychologist, and dimensional biopsychophysicist greater insight into the presence of homogeneous entities. This has been empirically demonstrated in my previous research on the déjà vu phenomenon, temporal lobe symptomatology and psi, and olfactory hallucinations. Whereas some researchers may not believe their work is relevant to such analyses now, a future researcher doing meta-analyses decades from now may thank them.

Psychiatrists have for many years attempted to detail their diagnosis with other factors that may be relevant. Diagnosis is commonly linked, for example, with predisposing, precipitating, and perpetuating factors in relation to the illness. The American Psychiatric Association (1994) has, in fact, formalized diagnosis into five axes, namely I (psychopathology), II (personality), III (organicity), IV (social precipitants), and V (recent functionality) with specific diagnostic (or operational) criteria adopted within each axis, producing the internationally recognized *Diagnostic and Statistical Manual* (DSM) in its various forms, including DSM-V (in development). I believe that a similar multiaxial schema can be applied in the phenomenological description of anomalous events (i.e., happenings that apparently do not fit within our conventional psychophysical framework). The schema that I propose includes an axis with neurobiological components, assessed by probing for possible temporal lobe symptomatology using measures such as the INSET (Neppe, 2008c). It could also include other information leading to neurological and psychiatric diagnoses and labels, including pharmacological responsiveness, a key being toleration and response to antipsychotic doses of medication (Neppe, 1988a, 1988b; Neppe and Smith, 1982; Neppe and Wessels, 1979), genetic components (e.g., family pedigree), neurobiological correlates (e.g., interictal EEG), results from various kinds of neurological testing (e.g., evoked potential measures), and anatomical measures (e.g., magnetic resonance imaging level or computerized tomography of the head). Also relevant may be medical diagnoses and the patient's syndromes, symptoms, and signs (e.g., does the subject have a known temporal lobe seizure disorder; is there a delirious state; was there a NDE or was someone in a prolonged coma or under anesthesia; etc.?)

Outside factors may also be relevant, including asking the following: "What was the sidereal time of the experience?" "What time and space elements, such as pertaining to electromagnetism and geomagnetism, existed at the time?" "How was the broader research done (e.g., Ganzfeld setups; was the setting public or private)?" "How were interpersonal aspects relevant?" Before explaining or describing something as ostensibly psi, the anomalistic psychologist must consider what I call globally "quasifamiliar" explanations (Neppe, 1980c), including the "subliminal" (latent familiarity), "organic," and "dynamic" explanations. These incorporate three alternatives to psi as an explanation for a happening that appears anomalous, namely: (1) subliminal stimuli or "latent familiarity," organic explanations such as a hallucination or memory disturbance (paramnesia; Devereux, 1974); (2) Neppe's "pseudofamiliarity" (Neppe, 1985, 1980c); and (3) psychological nonorganic explanations based at the level of the unconscious (i.e., psychodynamic, or simply "dynamic" or antecedent events (i.e., "antefamiliarity"; Neppe, 1980c). These three allow a hierarchy of parsimonious explanations prior to interpreting any quasifamiliar externally objectively validated event as a psi experience: If that psi can be regarded as such a kind that a modification of our present Newtonian laws of physics is necessary, this would be "parafamiliarity"—implying an extension of our natural laws; if it requires rejection of current laws, this implies a "metafamiliar" explanation ("meta-" refers to nonphysical explanations; Devereux, 1974). Finally, the experience may be anomalous because of its apparent acausal synchronicity, which I have called "prefamiliarity" (Neppe, 1980c) and possibly psi embraces it. If uncertain whether meta- or parafamiliar, or prefamiliar, this is "queryfamiliarity" (Neppe, 1980c). Because these anomalous levels—latent, dynamic, organic, psi—may be difficult to differentiate, I have suggested including such questions and concerns in research to more comprehensively classify and describe SPEs as either single spontaneous ones or clusters. This system is based on what was previously called Neppe's Anomalous Multiaxial

Event System (NAMES; Neppe, 1980c) and could benefit research and clinical applications, especially by increasing awareness of their possible neurobiological aspects. In conclusion, the interplay between neurobiology and SPEs, such as OBEs, NDEs, and various types of psi, are an exciting area in which many breakthroughs in understanding are likely on the horizon.

References

Achterberg, J., Cooke, K., Richards, T., Standish, L. J., Kozak, L., and Lake, J. (2005). Evidence for correlations between distant intentionality and brain function in recipients: A functional magnetic resonance imaging analysis. *Journal of Alternative and Complementary Medicine, 11*, 965–971.

Alvarado, C. S. (2000). Out-of-body experiences. In E. Cardeña, S. J. Lynn, and S. Krippner (Eds.), *Varieties of anomalous experience: Examining the scientific evidence* (pp. 183–218). Washington, DC: American Psychological Association.

American Psychiatric Association. (1994). *Diagnostic and statistical manual of mental disorders* (4th ed.). Washington, DC: American Psychiatric Association.

Bergson, H. (1914). Presidential address 1913. *Proceedings of the Society for Psychical Research, 27*, 157–175.

Bierman, D. (2000). *Anomalous baseline effects in mainstream emotion research using psychophysiological variables.* Paper presented at the 43rd Annual Convention of the Parapsychological Association, Freiberg Breslau, Germany, August 17–20.

Bierman, D. J., and Scholte, H. S. (2002). Anomalous anticipatory brain activation preceding exposure of emotional and neutral pictures. *Proceedings of Presented Papers: The Parapsychological Association 45th Annual Convention* (pp. 25–36). Cary, NC: Parapsychological Association.

Blanke, O., and Arzy, S. (2005). The out-of-body experience: Disturbed self-processing at the temporo-parietal junction. *Neuroscientist, 11*(1), 16–24.

Blanke, O., Landis, T., Spinelli, L., and Seeck, M. (2004). Out-of-body experience and autoscopy of neurological origin. *Brain, 127*, 243–258.

Blanke, O., and Mohr, C. (2005). Out-of-body experience, heautoscopy, and autoscopic hallucination of neurological origin: Implications for neurocognitive mechanisms of corporeal awareness and self-consciousness. *Brain Research Review, 50*(1), 184–199.

Blanke, O., Mohr, C., Michel, C. M., Pascual-Leone, A., Brugger, P., Seeck, M., et al. (2005). Linking out-of-body experience and self processing to mental own-body imagery at the temporoparietal junction. *Journal of Neuroscience, 25*, 550–557.

Blanke, O., Ortigue, S., Landis, T., and Seeck, M. (2002). Stimulating illusory own-body perceptions. *Nature, 419*, 269–270.

Bonta, I. L. (2004). Schizophrenia, dissociative anaesthesia and near-death experience: Three events meeting at the NMDA receptor. *Medical Hypotheses, 62*(1), 23–28.

Booth, J. N., Koren, S. A., and Persinger, M. A. (2005). Increased feelings of the sensed presence and increased geomagnetic activity at the time of the experience during exposures to transcerebral weak complex magnetic fields. *International Journal of Neuroscience, 115*(7), 1053–1079.

Braud, W. G., and Braud, L. W. (1973). Preliminary explorations of psi-conducive states: Progressive muscular relaxation. *Journal of the American Society for Psychical Research, 67*, 6–46.

Bunning, S., and Blanke, O. (2005). The out-of-body experience: Precipitating factors and neural correlates. *Progressive Brain Research, 150*, 331–350.

De Ridder, D., Van Laere, K., Dupont, P., Menovsky, T., and Van de Heyning, P. (2007). Visualizing out-of-body experience in the brain. *New England Journal of Medicine, 357*, 1829–1833.

Devereux, G. (1974). Extrasensory perception and psychoanalytic epistemology. In G. Devereux (Ed.), *Psychoanalysis and the occult* (pp. 16–46). London: Souvenir Press.

Dobyns, Y. H. (2003). Commentary: Comments on Freedman, Jeffers, Saeger, Binns, and Black: "Effects of frontal lobe lesions on intentionality and random physical phenomena." *Journal of Scientific Exploration, 17*, 669–685.

Douglass, A. B., Hays, P., Pazderka, F., and Russell, J. M. (1991). Florid refractory schizophrenias that turn out to be treatable variants of HLA-associated narcolepsy. *Journal of Nervous and Mental Disease, 179*, 12–17.

Ehrenwald, J. (1975). Cerebral localization and the psi syndrome. *Journal of Nervous and Mental Disease, 161*, 393–398.

Freedman, M., Jeffers, S., Saeger, K., Binns, M., and Black, S. (2003). Effects of frontal lobe lesions on intentionality and random physical phenomena. *Journal of Scientific Exploration, 17*, 651–668.

Gabbard, G. O., and Twemlow, S. W. (1984). *With the eyes of the mind: An empirical analysis of out-of-body states*. New York: Praeger.

Gabbard, G. O., Twemlow, S. W., and Jones, F. C. (1982). Differential diagnosis of altered mind/body perception. *Psychiatry, 45*, 361–369.

Green, P. R., and Thorpe, P. H. (1993). Tests for PK effects in imprinted chicks. *Journal of the Society for Psychical Research, 59*, 48–60.

Greyson, B., Parnia, S., and Fenwick, P. (2008). Visualizing out-of-body experience in the brain. *New England Journal of Medicine, 358*, 855–856.

Hurst, L. A., and Neppe, V. M. (1981). A familial study of subjective paranormal experience in temporal lobe dysfunction subjects. *Parapsychological Journal of South Africa, 2*(2), 56–64.

Hurst, L. A., and Neppe, V. M. (1982). Psi-genetics: An organic perspective. *Parapsychological Journal of South Africa, 3*, 54–57.

Jansen, K. L. (1990). Neuroscience and the near-death experience: Roles for the NMSA-PCP receptor, the sigma receptor and the endopsychosins. *Medical Hypotheses, 31*(1), 25–29.

Lavoie, A. (2008). *Researchers use neuroimaging to study ESP* (Press Release). Cambridge, MA: Harvard University. Retrieved January 5, 2009, from http://www.eurekalert.org/pub _releases/2008-01/hu-run010308.php.

Logethetis, N. K. (2003). The neural basis of the blood-oxygen-level-dependent functional magnetic resonance imaging signal. In A. Parker, A. Derrington, and C. Blakemore (Eds.), *The physiology of cognitive processes* (pp. 62–116). New York: Oxford University Press.

Mignot, E., Lin, L., Finn, L., Lopes, C., Pluff, K., Sundstrom, M. L., et al. (2006). Correlates of sleep-onset REM periods during the Multiple Sleep Latency Test in community adults. *Brain, 129*, 1609–1623.

Morse, M., Castillo, P., Venecia, D., Milstein, J., and Tyler, D. C. (1986). Childhood near-death experiences. *American Journal of Diseases of Children, 140*, 1110–1114.

Morse, M. L., and Neppe, V. (1991). Near-death experiences. *The Lancet, 337*, 386.

Moulton, S. T., and Kosslyn, S. M. (2008). Using neuroimaging to resolve the psi debate. *Journal of Cognitive Neuroscience, 20*, 182–192.

Munro, C., and Persinger, M. A. (1992). Relative right temporal-lobe theta activity correlates with Vingiano's hemispheric quotient and the "sensed presence." *Perceptual & Motor Skills, 75*, 899–903.

Nelson, K. R., Mattingly, M., Lee, S. A., and Schmitt, F. A. (2006). Does the arousal system contribute to near death experience? *Neurology, 66*, 1003–1009.

Neppe, V. M. (1980a). Subjective paranormal experience. *Psi, 2*(3), 2–3.

Neppe, V. M. (1980b). Subjective paranormal experience and temporal lobe symptomatology. *Parapsychological Journal of South Africa, 1*(2), 78–98.

Neppe, V. M. (1980c). Parapsychology: A conceptual overview. *Parapsychological Journal of South Africa, 1*(1), 1–16.

Neppe, V. M. (1982a). Psychiatric interpretations of subjective paranormal perception. *Parapsychological Journal of South Africa, 3*(1), 6–17.

Neppe, V. M. (1982b). The experimenter effect in medical research. *South African Medical Journal, 62*(3), 81.

Neppe, V. M. (1983a). Anomalies of smell in the subjective paranormal experient. *Psychoenergetics: Journal of Psychophysical Systems, 5*, 11–27.

Neppe, V. M. (1983b). Temporal lobe symptomatology in subjective paranormal experients. *Journal of the American Society for Psychical Research, 77*, 1–30.

Neppe, V. M. (1983c). *The psychology of déjà vu: Have I been here before?* Johannesburg: Witwatersrand University Press.

Neppe, V. M. (1985). A multiaxial classificatory system for anomalous experience. *Parapsychological Journal of South Africa, 6*(1), 57–72.

Neppe, V. M. (1988a). Psychopathology of psi: II. A new classification system for psi experience. *Parapsychology Review, 19*(6), 8–11.

Neppe, V. M. (1988b). Psychopathology of psi: I. A perspective. *Parapsychology Review, 19*(5), 1–3.

Neppe, V. M. (1989). Near-death experiences: A new challenge in temporal lobe phenomenology? Comments on "A neurobiological model for near-death experiences." *Journal of Near Death Studies, 7*, 243–248.

Neppe, V. M. (1990). Anomalistic experience and the cerebral cortex. In S. Krippner (Ed.), *Advances in parapsychological research 6* (pp. 168–183). Jefferson, NC: McFarland.

Neppe, V. M. (2002). Out-of-body experiences (OBEs) and brain localisation: A perspective. *Australian Journal of Parapsychology, 2*(2), 85–96.

Neppe, V. M. (2003, August). Parapsychological approaches to interpreting anomalous brain function and subjective paranormal experience: The out-of-body experience as an example. Paper presented at the Proceedings of the 46th Annual Parapsychological Association Convention, Vancouver, BC, Canada.

Neppe, V. M. (2006). *Déjà vu revisited*. Seattle: Brainvoyage Online Store.

Neppe, V. M. (2008a). Brain, reductionism, neuroscience, controversy and data. *Telicom, 21* (1), 31–48.

Neppe, V. M. (2008b). Re-examining current neuroscience research controversies. *Australian Journal of Parapsychology, 8*(2), 128–156.

Neppe, V. M. (2008c). Paroxysmal disorders: The INSET as a subjective screen: (Part 4). *Telicom, 21*(2), 24–28.

Neppe, V. M., and Bradu, D. (2006). Déjà vu subtypes: Four challenges for researchers. In V. Neppe and A. T. Funkhouser (Eds.), *Déjà vu: A second look* (pp. 52–67). Seattle: Brainvoyage Online Store.

Neppe, V. M., and Funkhouser, A. T. (Eds.). (2006). *Déjà vu: A second look*. Seattle: Brainvoyage Online Store.

Neppe, V. M., and Smith, M. E. (1982). Culture, psychopathology and psi: A clinical relationship. *Parapsychological Journal of South Africa, 3*(1), 1–5.

Neppe, V. M., and Wessels, W. H. (1979). Psychotic toleration of neuroleptic medication. *South African Medical Journal, 56*, 1147.

Palmer, J., and Neppe, V. M. (2003). Subjective paranormal experiences and temporal lobe dysfunction in a neuropsychiatric population: Analyses of refined predictors. *Journal of Parapsychology, 67*, 75–98.

Palmer, J., and Neppe, V. M. (2004). Exploratory analyses of refined predictors of subjective ESP experiences and temporal lobe dysfunction in a neuropsychiatric population. *European Journal of Parapsychology, 19*, 44–65.

Penfield, W. (1958). Functional localization in temporal and deep Sylvian areas. *Research in Nervous and Mental Disease, 36*, 210–226.

Persinger, M. A., and Valliant, P. M. (1985). Temporal lobe signs and reports of subjective paranormal experiences in a normal population: A replication. *Perceptual & Motor Skills, 60*, 903–909.

Planelles, D., Puig, N., Beneto, A., Gomez, E., Rubio, P., Mirabet, V., et al. (1997). HLA-DQA, -DQB and -DRB allele contribution to narcolepsy susceptibility. *European Journal of Immunogenetics, 24*, 409–421.

Plato. (n.d.). *Book VII: Plato's cave*. Boston: Internet Classics Archive MIT Media.

Radin, D. (2006). Bierman's brain. *Entangled minds* (pp. 176–179). New York: Paraview.

Radin, D. (2008). *January entries*. Retrieved on February 5, 2009, from http://deanradin.blogspot.com/2008_01_01_archive.html

Richards, T. L., Kozak, L., Johnson, L. C., and Standish, L. J. (2005). Replicable functional magnetic resonance imaging evidence of correlated brain signals between physically and sensory isolated subjects. *Journal of Alternative and Complementary Medicine, 11*, 955–963.

Sabom, M. B. (1980). The near-death experience. *Journal of the American Medical Association, 244*, 29–30.

Sabom, M. B. (1998). *Light and death*. Grand Rapids, MI: Zondervan.

Standish, L. J., Johnson, L. C., Kozak, L., and Richards, T. (2003). Evidence of correlated functional magnetic resonance imaging signals between distant human brains. *Alternative Therapies in Health and Medicine, 9*, 122–125.

Tart, C. (1967). A psychophysiological study of out-of-the-body experiences in a selected subject. *International Journal of Parapsychology, 9*, 251–258.

Tart, C. (1998). Six studies of out-of-body experiences. *Journal of Near-Death Studies, 17,* 73–99.

Tong, F. (2003). Out-of-body experiences: From Penfield to present. *Trends in Cognitive Science, 7,* 104–106.

Wegner, D. M. (2003). *The illusion of conscious will.* Cambridge, MA: Bradford.

The Gift

CHAPTER 8

Psi and the Brain

Morris Freedman

Despite an extensive literature on psi, there has been little emphasis on the role of selective brain systems as a key factor in the mechanisms underlying this poorly understood and controversial phenomenon. In keeping with successful approaches in other areas of behavioral neurobiology, defining the brain-behavior relations mediating psi may serve to significantly advance knowledge in this field. However, this endeavor will require the development of neurobiological models that are solidly based in neuroanatomy. Although the term "psi" covers a broad range of phenomena, including putative telepathy, clairvoyance, precognition, and psychokinesis, it is important to distinguish subjective paranormal experiences (SPEs) that have been studied without judgment about the validity of the experiences (Neppe, 1980, 1983, 1990) from psi effects that are presumed to be objective occurrences. This chapter will focus on the latter and will review current knowledge related to the neuroanatomy of psi. The emphasis will be on recent research related to the concept of frontal lobe function as an inhibitory factor that may suppress manifestations of psi in humans, using mind-matter interactions as a model (Freedman, Jeffers, Saeger, Binns, and Black, 2003).

Although the data are limited, several brain regions have been postulated to have a possible role in mediating psi effects. These include the reticular formation (Ehrenwald, 1975), right parietal and occipital areas, and occipital regions, primarily the right (Persinger, 2001; Persinger, Roll, Tiller, Koren, and Cook, 2002). There are also data on brain laterality favoring a role for the right hemisphere (Ehrenwald, 1975, 1978, p. 223; Schmeidler, 1994), although there is a suggestion that the left hemisphere may also be involved in psi-related processes (Schmeidler, 1994). In contrast to the small literature on the neuroanatomy of presumed objective psi effects, there are more extensive data on brain-behavior relations underlying SPEs. Neuroanatomical correlates of these events include primarily the temporal lobes (Neppe, 1983, 1990; Palmer and Neppe, 2003; Persinger, 1989; Persinger and Valliant, 1985) with little evidence for a role of other cerebral cortical areas (Neppe, 1990; Krippner, 2004, 2005).

Freedman et al. (2003) studied the effects of frontal lobe lesions on intentionality and random physical phenomena (i.e., mind-matter interactions or psychokinesis) and suggested that frontal lobe function might have an inhibitory role. The concept of an inhibitory factor restricting mind-matter interactions, if in fact these are genuine, arises from the need to explain why reported effects of such biologically important phenomena are so small (Bosch, Steinkamp, and Boller, 2006) and hard to replicate in experimental studies (Jahn et al., 2000; Walach and Jonas, 2007). One might postulate that the ability to influence physical events through conscious intention would be of such great significance that this would have evolved as a prominent human trait. Thus there would have to be an overriding biological advantage for the evolution of neural mechanisms designed to suppress these abilities, as well as other psi phenomena. In this regard, the evolutionary benefits for the development of psi-inhibitory brain systems might be to prevent exposure to constant bombardment with stimuli, many of which would be irrelevant and serve to divert attention away from critical stimuli that are important for day-to-day function and ultimately for survival. The evolution of neural inhibitory systems to screen out psi effects would thus offer protection from these distractions.

This speculation is in keeping with the concept proposed in the early 1900s by the philosopher, Henri Bergson, during his presidential address to the Society for Psychical Research (Bergson, 1914; Ehrenwald, 1978, pp. 215–217). In his "attention to life" theory, Bergson postulated that the nervous system serves to screen from consciousness all that is of no interest or benefit to the experient, including psychic abilities. He suggested that a deficit in these inhibitory mechanisms might lead to the emergence of psychic phenomena.

Using mind-matter interactions as a model, it might be useful to address the concept of psi inhibition as a protective neural mechanism by examining the conditions under which these interactions might most readily be demonstrated. Based on their extensive research using a random event generator (REG), Jahn and his colleagues at the Princeton Engineering Anomalies Research (PEAR) laboratory accumulated a wealth of data in support of mind-matter interactions as genuine phenomena (Jahn, Dunne, Nelson, Dobyns, and Bradish, 1997). Jahn and Dunne (1987, p. 142) suggested that success in influencing a REG through conscious intention may be associated with a state of immersion in the process that leads to a loss of awareness of oneself and the immediate surroundings. Extrapolating from this suggestion, it may be postulated that reduced self-awareness may facilitate mind-matter interactions. Since a state of reduced self-awareness is difficult for most individuals to attain, this may explain why mind-matter interactions are not readily observed under ordinary circumstances and why the effects are small and difficult to reproduce under controlled experimental conditions. This may also help to explain the reported occurrence of psi phenomena in association with altered mental states, such as meditation (Honorton, 1977) and hypnosis (Honorton, 1977; Stanford and Stein, 1994), in which there may be decreased self-awareness (Vaitl et al., 2005).

The suggestion that reduced self-awareness may facilitate mind-matter interactions has important implications for neuroanatomical models of the effects of conscious intention on physical phenomena, and more generally for models of other forms of psi. There is a well-established literature relating frontal lobe function to self-awareness, and lesions in the frontal lobes to a reduction in this function (Stuss, 1991; Stuss and Benson, 1986; Stuss and Levine, 2002). A neuroanatomical model may thus be postulated in which the frontal lobes of the brain, through the mediation of self-awareness, serve to inhibit the emergence of psi abilities.

The concept that frontal lobe function inhibits psi suggests that phenomena such as mind-matter interactions, telepathy, clairvoyance, and precognition would be difficult to detect in individuals with normal brain function and that any observable effects would tend to be small. This fits with the literature and suggests that scientists studying psi in normal subjects may be targeting a population in which the chances of demonstrating effects are greatly reduced. Instead of studying normal individuals, a neuroanatomical model incorporating frontal lobe inhibition of psi suggests that examining subjects with neurological damage to brain structures mediating self-awareness may maximize the chance of detecting psi effects. This novel approach may facilitate the significant and as yet unattained advancements that will be required to bring psi-related research into the realm of mainstream science.

Based on the concept that frontal lobe lesions may enhance psi effects, Freedman et al. (2003) carried out a study on mind-matter interactions in six patients with damage to their frontal lobes. Four subjects had bilateral brain lesions due to subarachnoid hemorrhage ($n = 2$) and frontal leucotomy ($n = 2$). The remaining two subjects had unilateral frontal lobe damage. One had a left frontal (LF) lesion due to a tension pneumocephalus and the other had a right frontal (RF) lesion due to a stroke. In addition to patients with frontal lesions, there were six normal control subjects. The focus on mind-matter interactions was based on the extensive work carried out by Jahn and his colleagues at the PEAR lab suggesting that individuals can affect the output of a REG through conscious intention (Jahn et al., 1997).

As described in more detail elsewhere (Jahn and Dunne, 1987, pp. 91–103; Freedman et al., 2003), the methodology involved the use of a REG that produced a random series of 0s and 1s based upon a sampling of an electronic noise pattern at preset regular intervals. The rate of sampling was 200 per second. The data were summed as 200-sample bits with expected numerical value of 100 due to a 50 percent chance of the REG producing a 0 or 1 at each sampling. A trial was composed of a sample of 200 bits of data. The REG used for the study was supplied by the PEAR laboratory and was a portable model of the larger device that has been used in that laboratory.

In the experimental design used in the PEAR lab, subjects sit in front of the REG and try to influence its output to achieve a higher value than the theoretical mean of 100; to achieve a lower value than the theoretical mean; or not to influence the output (Jahn et al., 1997). Since this type of task might have been too difficult for patients with damage to the frontal lobes of their brain, the methodology was modified. As described elsewhere (Freedman et al., 2003), the REG output was represented by an image (i.e., an arrow or bar) that moved on a computer screen to the right or left according to the cumulative mean of the output. Research participants sat in front of a computer screen and were asked to concentrate on moving the image to the right or left, or not to influence its movement, depending on the experimental intention. When the intention was to the right, there was an arrow on the screen that pointed to the right. For the leftward intention, the arrow pointed to the left. The midline represented a cumulative mean of 100. If the cumulative mean was greater than 100, the arrow tip was to the right of midline. If the cumulative mean was below 100, the tip was to the left of midline. For the baseline intention, in which subjects were instructed not to influence the movement of the image on the screen, there was a bar instead of an arrow (Figure 8-1a–c). The purpose of representing the REG output by an arrow or bar was to help subjects maintain attention on the task. The right, left, and baseline intentions each consisted of 10 blocks of 100 trials and lasted approximately 15 minutes. The position of the arrow tip and bar was reset to the midline after each block of 100 trials. Since there were differences in the time that subjects were able to devote to testing, the total number of trials varied across subjects. The order of the intentions (i.e., right, left, or baseline) followed a predetermined sequence.

A major difference between the methodology used by the PEAR group and the design used by Freedman et al. (2003) involved the control condition (Dobyns, 2003). The PEAR group compared experimental data during each intention to a theoretical mean and examined the difference between the high-intention and low-intention outputs. In contrast, Freedman et al. (2003) compared the data produced by the REG during the period when a participant was trying to influence the device's output to a control condition composed of REG output generated without the subject in the room. The participant was thus in the study room for each intention session (i.e., right, left, baseline). After completing a session, the participant left the room while a control run was carried out.

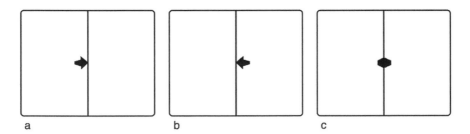

a   b   c

Figure 8-1   Computer screen showing initial position of arrow or bar for each intention: (a) Intention Right; (b) Intention Left; and (c) Intention Baseline.

This figure first appeared in the *Journal of Scientific Exploration*, vol. 17, no. 4, pp. 651–668, 2003, under the title "Effects of frontal lobe lesions on intentionality and random physical phenomena."

For the data analyses, a conservative correction for multiple comparisons was used (i.e., a Bonferroni correction). The purpose was to reduce the chance of considering that an observed difference was significant when in fact it was due to chance. For the bilateral frontal (BF) subjects, RF subject, and normal subjects, the analyses showed no significant differences between the intention and control conditions for the right, left, or baseline intentions. There were also no significant differences between the intention and control conditions for the pooled group of frontal patients or the entire sample of frontal and normal participants combined. In contrast, for the participant with LF damage, there was a significant difference between the intention and control conditions for the right intention that was in the direction of intention. This was significant even after a Bonferroni correction for multiple comparisons. However, in the LF participant, there were no significant differences between the intention and control conditions for the left or baseline intention (Figure 8-2a–c).

Although there was a significant effect in the LF participant that was in the direction of intention, and contralateral to his brain lesion, this finding was interpreted with great caution and a second study was carried out to determine whether the findings could be replicated. The results showed that the participant again demonstrated a significant effect for the right intention with the arrow moving in the direction of intention. As before, there were no significant effects for the left or baseline intentions (Figure 8-3). The data from the replication study were examined in consecutive 1,000 trial sessions for each intention (Figure 8-4a–c). For the right intention, the REG output showed a fairly consistent pattern in which the means were either higher or about the same on most pairs of 1,000 trial blocks compared to control output, whereas for the left and baseline intentions there was a pattern with less separation between conditions.

The patient with the LF lesion had a tension pneumocephalus. His case has been reported elsewhere (Marras, Kalaparambath, Black, and Rowed, 1998). Neuroimaging is shown in Figure 8-5. MRI at two-and-half years after initial presentation revealed an extensive lesion in the LF lobe, whereas the RF lobe appeared normal. Single photon emission computed tomography (SPECT) showed the addition of subtle RF dysfunction. Psychometric testing also suggested the addition of RF dysfunction. The patient was first tested in the study on mind-matter interactions approximately five years after developing the tension pneumocephalus.

The mechanisms underlying the unidirectional effect in the patient with the LF lesion warrant discussion in the context of a neuroanatomical model incorporating frontal lobe inhibition of psi. As discussed elsewhere (Freedman et al., 2003), processes underlying self-awareness are mediated by brain regions that include the frontal lobes, particularly on the right (Stuss and Alexander, 2000a, 2000b; Stuss, Gallup, and Alexander, 2001; Stuss, Picton, and Alexander, 2001). Although the patient had right-sided brain dysfunction, this may have been insufficient to produce impaired self-awareness. However, his extensive lesion on the left may have resulted in reduced self-awareness when attention was directed toward the right (i.e.,

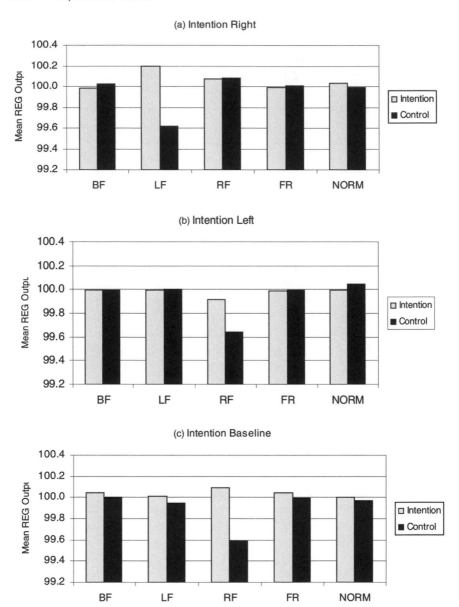

Figure 8-2   Mean REG output for patients with brain lesions in bilateral frontal (BF), left frontal (LF), and right frontal (RF) regions, frontal patients pooled (FR), and normal subjects (NORM): (a) Intention Right; (b) Intention Left; and (c) Intention Baseline.

This figure first appeared in the *Journal of Scientific Exploration*, vol. 17, no. 4, pp. 651–668, 2003, under the title "Effects of frontal lobe lesions on intentionality and random physical phenomena."

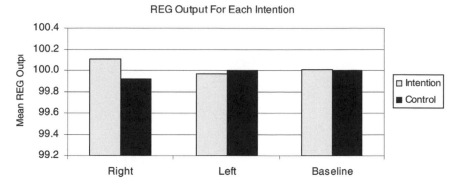

Figure 8-3   Mean REG output for the left frontal patient in replication study.

This figure first appeared in the *Journal of Scientific Exploration*, vol. 17, no. 4, pp. 651–668, 2003, under the title "Effects of frontal lobe lesions on intentionality and random physical phenomena."

contralateral to his lesion). The question arises why there were negative findings in the patients with bilateral lesions and in the patient with the RF lesion. One suggestion is that the mechanisms required for facilitating psi effects include reduced self-awareness in the setting of attentional mechanisms that are relatively intact. Attention, however, is not a unitary function (Stuss and Levine, 2002). Instead, there are separate attentional processes, each associated with a different anatomical localization within the frontal lobes (Stuss and Alexander, 2007). Attentional processes involved in trying to influence movement of an arrow on a computer screen, as in the study by Freedman et al. (2003), include initiating and sustaining a response, as well as monitoring. Bilateral frontal lesions, with some evidence for a more important role for the right hemisphere, are associated with deficits in initiation and sustained attention (energization), whereas RF lesions are related to deficits in monitoring (Stuss and Alexander, 2007). Thus participants with right hemisphere lesions may not demonstrate enhanced psi effects due to impaired function in these aspects of attention. This concept is in keeping with the suggested role of the right hemisphere in psi (Ehrenwald, 1975, 1978, pp. 223; Schmeidler, 1994) and may explain the negative findings in the patients with right sided brain lesions.

In conclusion, the concept that normal frontal lobe brain function may inhibit psi has been presented and may form the basis of a neuroanatomical model that will serve to significantly advance research in the field of psi. The findings reported and replicated by Freedman et al. (2003) support the further development of such a model and suggest that studying patients with frontal lobe lesions, particularly on the left, may facilitate the detection of psi in well-controlled experimental settings. However, there remains a strong cautionary note highlighting the need for further replication of psi effects in subjects with frontal lobe brain damage.

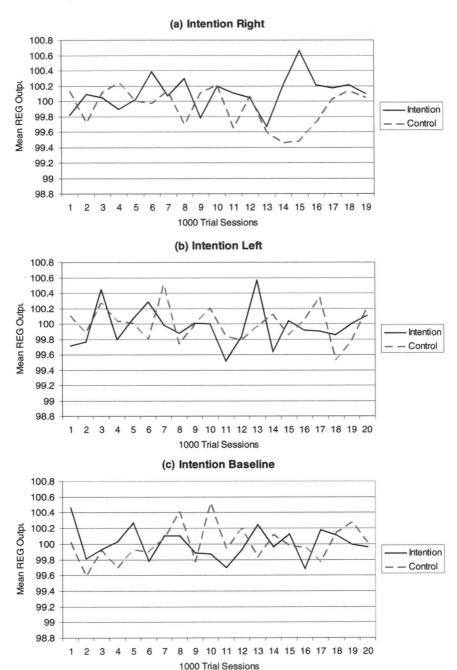

Figure 8-4   Mean REG output for each 1,000 trial session in replication study: (a) Intention Right; (b) Intention Left; and (c) Intention Baseline.

This figure first appeared in the *Journal of Scientific Exploration*, vol. 17, no. 4, pp. 651–668, 2003, under the title "Effects of frontal lobe lesions on intentionality and random physical phenomena."

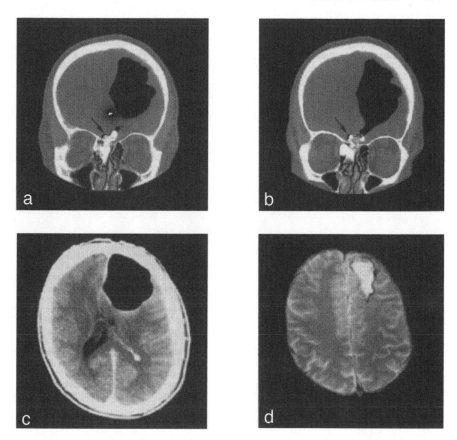

Figure 8-5   (a+b) Coronal images demonstrate the osteoma in RF-ethmoid sinus (arrows) with intracranial extension to the left of midline contiguous with the intracranial air; (c) Axial noncontrast CT head at presentation showing tension pneumocephalus with displacement of LF lobe; (d) T2-weighted MR axial image demonstrating LF encephalomalacia at 2.5 years follow up.

Reprinted with permission from Marras et al., *Canadian Journal of Neurological Sciences*, vol. 25, pp. 79–81, 1998.

References

Bergson, H. (1914). Presidential Address 1913. *Proceedings of the Society for Psychical Research, 27*, 157–175.

Bosch, H., Steinkamp, F., and Boller, E. (2006). Examining psychokinesis: The interaction of human intention with random number generators—a meta-analysis. *Psychological Bulletin, 132*, 497–523.

Dobyns, Y. H. (2003). Comments on Freedman, Jeffers, Saeger, Binns, and Black: "Effects of frontal lobe lesions on intentionality and random physical phenomena." *Journal of Scientific Exploration, 17*, 669–685.

Ehrenwald, J. (1975). Cerebral localization and the psi syndrome. *Journal of Nervous & Mental Disease, 161*, 393–398.

Ehrenwald, J. (1978). *The ESP experience: A psychiatric validation.* New York: Basic Books.

Freedman, M., Jeffers, S., Saeger, K., Binns, M., and Black, S. (2003). Effects of frontal lobe lesions on intentionality and random physical phenomena. *Journal of Scientific Exploration, 17*, 651–668.

Honorton, C. (1977). Psi and internal attention states. In B. B. Wolman (Ed.), *Handbook of parapsychology* (pp. 435–472). New York: Van Nostrand Reinhold.

Jahn, R., Dunne, B., Bradish, G., Dobyns, Y., Lettieri, A., Nelson, R., et al. (2000). Mind/machine interaction consortium: PortREG replication experiments. *Journal of Scientific Exploration, 14*, 499–555.

Jahn, R. G., and Dunne, B. J. (1987). *Margins of reality: The role of consciousness in the physical world.* Orlando, FL: Harcourt Brace Jovanovich.

Jahn, R. G., Dunne, B. J., Nelson, R. D., Dobyns, Y. H., and Bradish, G. J. (1997). Correlations of random binary sequences with pre-stated operator intention: A review of a 12-year program. *Journal of Scientific Exploration, 11*, 345–367.

Krippner, S. (2004). Psi research and the human brain's "reserve capacities." In A. Combs, M. Germine, and B. Goertzel (Eds.), *Mind in time: The dynamics of thought, reality, and consciousness* (pp. 313–329). Cresskill, NJ: Hampton Press.

Krippner, S. (2005). Psychoneurological dimensions of anomalous experience in relation to religious belief and spiritual practice. In K. Bulkeley (Ed.), *Soul, psyche, brain: New directions in the study of religion and brain-mind science* (pp. 61–92). New York: Palgrave MacMillan.

Marras, L. C., Kalaparambath, T. P., Black, S. E., and Rowed, D. W. (1998). Severe tension pneumocephalus complicating frontal sinus osteoma. *Canadian Journal of Neurological Sciences, 25*, 79–81.

Neppe, V. M. (1980). Subjective paranormal experience. *Psi, 2*, 2–3.

Neppe, V. M. (1983). Temporal lobe symptomatology in subjective paranormal experients. *Journal of the American Society for Psychical Research, 77*, 1–29.

Neppe, V. M. (1990). Anomalistic experience and the cerebral cortex. In S. Krippner (Ed.), *Advances in parapsychological research* (Vol. 6, pp. 168–183). Jefferson, NC: McFarland.

Palmer, J., and Neppe, V. M. (2003). A controlled analysis of subjective paranormal experiences in temporal lobe dysfunction in a neuropsychiatric population. *Journal of Parapsychology, 67*, 75–97.

Persinger, M. A. (1989). Psi phenomena and temporal lobe activity: The geomagnetic factor. In L. A. Henkel and R. E. Berger (Eds.), *Research in parapsychology 1988* (pp. 121–156). Metuchen, NJ: Scarecrow Press.

Persinger, M. A. (2001). The neuropsychiatry of paranormal experiences. *Journal of Neuropsychiatry & Clinical Neurosciences, 13*, 515–524.

Persinger, M. A., Roll, W. G., Tiller, S. G., Koren, S. A., and Cook, C. M. (2002). Remote viewing with the artist Ingo Swann: Neuropsychological profile, electroencephalographic correlates, magnetic resonance imaging (MRI), and possible mechanisms. *Perceptual & Motor Skills, 94*, 927–949.

Persinger, M. A., and Valliant, P. M. (1985). Temporal lobe signs and reports of subjective paranormal experiences in a normal population: A replication. *Perceptual & Motor Skills, 60*, 903–909.

Schmeidler, G. R. (1994). ESP experiments 1978–1992: The glass is half full. In S. Krippner (Ed.), *Advances in parapsychological research* (Vol. 7, pp. 104–197). Jefferson, NC: McFarland.

Stanford, R. G., and Stein, A. G. (1994). A meta-analysis of ESP studies contrasting hypnosis and a comparison condition. *Journal of Parapsychology, 58,* 235–269.

Stuss, D. T. (1991). Self, awareness, and the frontal lobes: A neuropsychological perspective. In J. Strauss and G. R. Goethals (Eds.), *The self: Interdisciplinary approaches* (pp. 255–278). New York: Springer-Verlag.

Stuss, D. T., and Alexander, M. P. (2000a). Affectively burnt in: A proposed role of the right frontal lobe. In E. Tulving (Ed.), *Memory, consciousness, and the brain: The Tallinn Conference* (pp. 215–227). Philadelphia: Psychology Press.

Stuss, D. T., and Alexander, M. P. (2000b). The anatomical basis of affective behavior, emotion and self-awareness: A specific role of the right frontal lobe. In G. Hatano, N. Okada, and H. Tanabe (Eds.), *Affective minds: The 13th Toyota Conference* (pp. 13–25). Amsterdam: Elsevier.

Stuss, D. T., and Alexander, M. P. (2007). Is there a dysexecutive syndrome? *Philosophical Transactions of the Royal Society of London—Series B: Biological Sciences, 362,* 901–915.

Stuss, D. T., and Benson, D. F. (1986). *The frontal lobes* (pp. 246–248). New York: Raven Press.

Stuss, D. T., Gallup, G. G. J., and Alexander, M. P. (2001). The frontal lobes are necessary for "theory of mind." *Brain, 124,* 279–286.

Stuss, D. T., and Levine, B. (2002). Adult clinical neuropsychology: lessons from studies of the frontal lobes. *Annual Review of Psychology, 53,* 401–433.

Stuss, D. T., Picton, T. W., and Alexander, M. P. (2001). Consciousness, self-awareness, and the frontal lobes. In S. P. Salloway, P. F. Malloy, and J. D. Duffy (Eds.), *The frontal lobes and neuropsychiatric illness* (pp. 101–109). Washington, DC: American Psychiatric Association.

Vaitl, D., Birbaumer, N., Gruzelier, J., Jamieson, G. A., Kotchoubey, B., Kubler, A., et al. (2005). Psychobiology of altered states of consciousness. *Psychological Bulletin, 131,* 98–127.

Walach, H., and Jonas, W. B. (2007). From parapsychology to spirituality: The legacy of the PEAR database. *Explore: The Journal of Science & Healing, 3*(3), 197–199.

Countervail

CHAPTER 9

The Neurochemistry of Psi Reports and Associated Experiences

David Luke and Harris L. Friedman

This chapter speculates on the possible neurochemistry underlying a number of extraordinary experiences falling within the domain of parapsychology, namely telepathy, precognition, and clairvoyance (known collectively as extrasensory perception [ESP]), as well as psychokinesis (PK), which together are subsumed under the umbrella terms "psychic" and "psi." Related anomalous phenomena, such as out-of-body experiences (OBEs), near-death experiences (NDEs), and "encounter" experiences with alleged discarnate entities are also considered in this chapter. Following the lead of Krippner and Achterberg (2000), we use the term "experience" to describe reports of anomalous phenomena and reserve the term "events" to refer to putative psi obtained under controlled conditions, usually in experimental settings.

Practically everything that is known about the neurochemistry of psi and these associated processes has arisen out of research into the effects of a class of psychoactive substances capable of inducing visionary and trance-like experiences, including a number of drugs and sacramental substances (e.g., LSD, mescaline, psilocybin, ayahuasca, marijuana, ketamine) but excluding others (e.g., alcohol, opiates, cocaine). The former have most commonly been called "psychedelics," meaning mind manifesting (Osmond, 1961), and are defined as follows:

> [Substances] which, without causing physical addiction, craving, major physiological disturbances, delirium, disorientation, or amnesia, more or less reliably produce thought, mood, and perceptual changes otherwise rarely experienced except in dreams, contemplative and religious exaltation, flashes of vivid involuntary memory, and acute psychoses. (Grinspoon and Bakalar, 1998, p. 9)

There is a wealth of nonexperimental data (e.g., anecdotal, anthropological, clinical, historical, survey) that testify to the apparent increased occurrence of these extraordinary experiences following the ingestion of psychedelics.

For instance, the anthropological literature is replete with examples of extraordinary phenomena apparently occurring with the traditional use of numerous psychedelic plants. An example would be the reports of telepathy and clairvoyance with the psychoactive Amazonian decoction, ayahuasca (e.g., Bianchi, 1994; Gorman, 1992; Kensinger, 1973; Luna and White, 2000; McGovern, 1927; Metzner, 2006; Shannon, 2002; Weil, Metzner, and Leary, 1965; Wilson, 1949). Such plants have long been taken by indigenous peoples in a ritual context for the express purpose of accessing altered states conducive to clairvoyance, precognition, telepathy, out-of-body travel, psychic diagnosis, psychic healing, and spirit communication (Dobkin de Rios, 1972; Schultes and Hofmann, 1992). Archaeological evidence suggests that such practices have existed the world over for millennia (Devereux, 1997), incorporating numerous plants and virtually every culture ever studied anthropologically (Dobkin de Rios, 1990).

Such visionary substances also have had clinical applications in the modern world. Psychedelic-assisted psychotherapy in the United States was practiced from the 1950s until its prohibition in the late 1960s and is now once again receiving attention as a treatment for a variety for ailments, such as alcohol and drug addiction (Kolp, Friedman, Young, and Krupitsky, 2006; Winkelman and Roberts, 2007) and death anxiety (Kolp, Young, Friedman, Krupitsky, Jansen, and O'Connor, 2007). In line with the traditional magico-religious use of psychedelics, ostensible ESP phenomena have been reported to have occurred spontaneously during psychedelic-assisted therapy by numerous observers (e.g., Eisner, 1995; Laidlaw, 1961; Stolaroff, 2004), especially with the use of LSD (e.g., Grof, 1975, 1980, 1990, 2001; Harman, 1963; Holzinger, 1964; Levine, 1968; Masters and Houston, 1966; Pahnke, 1968). A survey from one of the 1960s most productive psychedelic psychotherapy clinics, the International Foundation for Advanced Study, reported that spontaneous ESP experiences occurred in 2 percent of therapy sessions (Levine, 1968), which is a considerably higher incidence than that reported to have occurred in nonpsychedelic psychotherapy (Tornatore, 1977a, 1977b). As one specific example of this line of research, the percentage of clients reporting telepathic communication during LSD-assisted therapy changed from 49 percent in the first psychotherapy session to 80 percent in the second session (Blewett and Chwelos, 1959).

Further support for the notion that psychedelics can induce ostensible psychic phenomena comes from numerous survey reports. For instance, findings from surveys utilizing the Anomalous Experiences Inventory (AEI) consistently indicate a small positive relationship between "belief in the paranormal" and drug use, with a similar relationship between drug use and reported psychic experiences (Gallagher, Kumar, and Pekala, 1994; Houran and Williams, 1998; Simmonds and Roe, 2000; Thalbourne, 2001). This latter trend is corroborated by other surveys and is more pronounced with psychedelics than with other psychoactive drugs, such as cocaine, heroin, and alcohol (Luke and Kittenis, 2005). Furthermore, those respondents reporting ESP, apparitions, and other anomalous experiences were found to be significantly more likely to have used psychedelics (Palmer, 1979; Usha and Pasricha, 1989a, 1989b). Additionally, 18–83 percent of those reporting the use of psychedelics also reported psychic experiences—most commonly telepathy but also precognition—occurring under the influence of psychedelics (Palmer, 1979; Tart, 1970, 1993; Usha and Pasricha, 1989a, 1989b), with heavier users reporting more experiences (Kjellgren and Norlander, 2000–2001). The most commonly surveyed and perhaps the most commonly reported anomalous experience is the OBE (e.g., Blackmore, 1982, 1984; Blackmore and Harris, 1983; Myers, Austrin, Grisso, and Nickeson, 1983), which is reported to occur with a very wide variety of substances, but particularly with ketamine (Blackmore, 2003; Luke and Kittenis, 2005). A wide range of other anomalous experiences are also reported with psychedelics, such as NDEs and "encounters" with deceased persons or with nonhuman entities (Luke and Kittenis, 2005).

Despite the wealth of reports of psychedelic-induced psychic phenomena in the nonexperimental data, there is no certainty that these experiences are veridical events. The same arguments apply here as they do for and against the veracity of reports of non-drug-induced spontaneous psi experiences (for a review see Stokes, 1997). For example, in a study using the AEI, participants reporting false memories of a news event were significantly more likely to believe in and to have reported psychic experiences; however, this factor was independent of reported drug use (Wilson and French, 2006). Nevertheless, aside from the questionable value of nonexperimental data in this area, the similarity in reports from those in exploratory, therapeutic, and accidental contexts with those from traditional, ceremonial, and ritualistic contexts (i.e., the shamanic use of these substances) provides some comparative bases for speculation regarding the credibility of these data. In contrast, other traditional psychoactive substances, such as alcohol, coffee, and coca leaves are not often reported to induce spontaneous psychic experiences, and neither are there folk beliefs that suggest they do so.

Experimental Research

Given that these nonexperimental data provide only limited evidence for psi, despite their often impressive quality and quantity, it is somewhat disarming that the few experimental research projects conducted have not demonstrated more compelling evidence for the induction of psi events. However, the relative success of these few experiments appears to vary in relation to the type of methods used, with the most successful making more use of experienced participants and interesting tasks. In preparing this chapter, we could locate only 17 separately published studies utilizing a variety of parapsychological test paradigms (e.g., Ganzfeld, psychometry, card-guessing) and a variety of substances (primarily LSD and psilocybin, but also *Amanita muscaria* mushrooms, ayahuasca, cannabis, and mescaline). Most of these experiments were conducted during the peak of psychedelic research that occurred during the 1960s and were largely exploratory in nature, making it difficult to fully assess their efficacy in inducing ESP, while no PK experiments have been attempted to our knowledge. In addition, many of these experiments lacked an adequate control condition, many have been confounded by deleterious order effects, and others lacked the blind use of decoy targets in the judging process—all methodological flaws that make critical probability estimates of their worth impossible to ascertain.

In the one ESP-card experiment we found that did use a good control condition, scores in a psilocybin condition were significantly different from chance and were also superior to those obtained in the control condition, although not significantly so (Asperen de Boer, Barkema, and Kappers, 1966). Nevertheless, it is apparent that most of the other experiments using ESP-card type symbol guessing procedures did not differ from chance expectation (Don, McDonough, Warren, and Moura, 1996; Kugel, 1977; Masters and Houston, 1966; Pahnke, 1971; Palmer, Tart, and Redington, 1976; Rush and Cahn, 1958; Tart, Palmer, and Redington, 1979; Tinoco, 1994; Whittlesey, 1960). Perhaps this could be due to their use of the repetitive symbol-guessing procedures, which have been widely criticized for being far too mundane to interest participants under the influence of psychedelics (Grof, 1980; Masters and Houston, 1966; Pahnke, 1971; Parker, 1975; Rogo, 1976; Stafford and Golightly, 1967; Smythies, 1960; Tart, 1968; Whittlesey, 1960). Even so, one experiment using amanita muscaria (Puharich, 1959, 1962) demonstrated that forced-choice procedures could be successful with picture-sorting tasks, although there is a concern that this published research study was not peer reviewed (Krippner, 2006).

However, more engaging free-response procedures have demonstrated at least some success in two of the three studies we located that used psychometry (Asperen de Boer et al., 1966; Osis, 1961; Smythies, 1960, 1987), although these lacked any control condition for comparison. Of these, the Osis experiment was unique in that it used psychedelically naïve mediums as participants. However, as was typical of many of these experiments, most of these participants succumbed to the mystical rapture of their first visionary drug experience, leaving only one of the six participants to focus on the ESP task and to obtain above-chance scores. However, by far the best indication of possible psychedelically induced ESP, notwithstanding some methodological concerns, comes from the positive results of four out of six of the reported free response clairvoyance and telepathy experiments. Free response tests allow the participants to make a guess as to a hidden target's identity by describing or drawing their guess as to the target. Wezelman and Bierman (1997) obtained significant results with psilocybin but not with cannabis; later, Bierman (1998) had reported an unsuccessful ESP test with psilocybin. Positive, or at least suggestive, results with psychedelics had been reported by Cavanna and Servadio (1964);

Masters and Houston (1966); and Puharich (1962), even though statistical analysis was not utilized in most of these studies.

At the present time the evidence for psychedelically evoked ESP is nascent and inconclusive, although we think promising. Far more research is required to make any firm conclusions, although the recent political climate surrounding psychedelic experimentation has made such research difficult to pursue; the most recent experiments were conducted in the Netherlands where the drug laws and attitudes have been more liberal than elsewhere (Bierman, 1998). Psychedelic studies in the United States have been primarily clinical in nature; support for studies of extraordinary experiences probably would not be viewed favorably by Institutional Review Boards and other research gatekeepers (Friedman, 2006).

Neurochemical Models of Paranormal Experience

Now we return to our main topic, namely asking what neurochemical models might explain the types of anomalous phenomena we speculate could be related to the use of psychedelic substances. First, we think it is highly likely that all altered states of consciousness, including potentially ESP-conducive states, involve alterations in brain chemistry. As such, psychoactive drugs may have a part to play in helping us understand the neurochemistry underlying those states. Indeed, several psychedelic-neurochemical models have been proposed based upon the subjective psychic experiences occurring with certain substances and their specific neurochemical action. Additionally, it is entirely feasible that veridical psi events are mediated in the brain through the action of specific endogenous (made within the body) molecules (Vayne, 2001). This does not simply imply, reductionistically, that neurochemicals are the sole cause of these psi events but, rather, that they may be a part of the process. As the novelist Aldous Huxley often said in relation to mystical experiences and the use of psychedelics, they are the occasion rather than the cause (Dunaway, 1998).

Brain as Filter Model

Aldous Huxley (1954) also was prominent in promoting Henri Bergson's (1896/ 1990) theory of the brain as a filter of memory and sensory experience, acting to reduce the wealth of information available to awareness lest people become overwhelmed by a mass of largely useless and irrelevant data not needed for the survival of the organism. It was Bergson who suggested that, if these filters were bypassed, humans would be capable of remembering everything that had ever been experienced and perceiving everything that has happened everywhere in the universe (e.g., as in clairvoyance). It was also Huxley who applied this theory to psychedelics by suggesting that these mind-manifesting drugs override the "reducing valve" of the brain, allowing humans access to both psychic and mystical experiences.

Huxley's (1954) rather basic conception never received a more formal operationalization of the specific drug actions that may be involved, but research into the neurochemistry of psychedelics lends some support to his notion. For instance, Vollenweider and Geyer (2001) proposed that information processing in cortico-striato-thalamo-cortical (CSTC) feedback loops is disrupted by psychedelics via 5-HT (serotonin) receptor agonism (specifically 5-HT_{2A} receptors), thereby inhibiting the "gating" of extraneous sensory stimuli and inhibiting the ability to attend selectively to salient environmental features. Furthermore, psychedelics are also thought to induce presynaptic release of glutamate from thalamic afferents, leading to a simultaneous overload of internal information in the cortex. It is thought that these combined information overload effects are at least partly responsible for the "hallucinogenic" experience with these drugs, which are known to induce greatly altered or amplified incoming sensory information, as is indicated by an increased startle effect (Vollenweider, 2001). This disruption of the sensory gating function by psychedelics could also underpin the neurochemistry of ESP, whether elicited with any number of psychedelics (Luke and Kittenis, 2005) or without the intervention of such exogenous chemicals. Indeed like psychedelics, psi experiences and events have variously been conceptualized in relation to an inhibition of the ordinary sensory inhibition, often in conjunction with elevated psychosis and creativity, such as with the concepts of latent disinhibition (Holt, Simmonds-Moore, and Moore, 2008), transliminality (Thalbourne, 2000; Thalbourne and Houran, 2005), boundary thinness and schizotypy (Simmonds and Roe, 2000), and self-expansiveness (Friedman, 1983; Pappas and Friedman, 2007). It may be noted that psychedelics have also been long associated with both creativity (e.g., Dobkin de Rios and Janiger, 2003; Krippner, 1985) and psychosis (Osmond and Smythies, 1952).

Despite the simplistic appeal of the antireducing valve action of psychedelics as a neurochemical model of psi, considerable gaps still remain in our current understanding of the neuropharmacological action of psychedelics in humans. Since the early 1970s, practically all psychedelic research has been conducted with animals and there remain no definitive generalizations that can be made about the main neurotransmitter receptor sites involved, as psychedelics vary considerably in their chemical makeup and their ligand affinity (a ligand is a molecule, such as a neurotransmitter, that triggers a response in target protein). For instance, dissociative drugs such as ketamine are commonly N-methyl-D-aspartate (NMDA) receptor antagonists, whereas the simple tryptamines, such as psilocybin, are apparently 5-HT_{2A} agonists. Speculations about the cause of the hallucinogenic effects of psychedelics generally include the activation of 5-HT_{1A}, 5-HT_{2A}, 5-HT_{2C}, dopamine, and glutamate pathways, although it is generally believed that psychedelics primarily work by stimulating 5-HT_{2A} receptors, particularly those expressed in the neocorticol pyramidal cells (Nichols, 2004). Electrophysiology and receptor studies have revealed that both NMDA antagonists (e.g., ketamine) and classic serotonergic psychedelics (e.g., LSD) may actually enhance glutamatergic transmission via non-NMDA receptors in the frontal cortex. This may indicate a common mode of chemical action in the brain responsible for such similar experiences with these divergent molecules (Vollenweider, 2004); this serotonin/glutamate receptor-complex model of drug action is receiving high-profile attention again for psychedelics as a possible comparative model of psychosis (e.g., González-Maeso et al., 2008).

β-Carboline and Tryptamine Model

Advancing on older suggestions made about the pineal gland's involvement in psi (e.g., Miller, 1978; Sinel, 1927), Roney-Dougal (1986, 1989, 1991, 2001) has developed an endogenous neurochemical-perspective of psi based on the action of the pineal gland and several hallucinogenic substances found in ayahuasca, the Amazonian brew reported to induce a range of psychic experiences. The common neurotransmitter serotonin is known to be most active in the pineal gland where it follows a circadian rhythm and is converted at night into melatonin (5-methoxy tryptamine, or 5MT) and the β-carboline, pinoline (6-methoxy tetrahydro-β-carboline, or 6-MeO-THβC), which regulate sleep cycles (Callaway, 1988). The pineal may also create other β-carbolines, such as 6-methoxyharmalan, a harmala alkaloid. These β-carbolines block the neuronal uptake of serotonin (5-hydroxytryptamine, or 5-HT) making it available for use, and inhibit the enzyme monoamine oxidase (MAO), which breaks down certain tryptamines such as serotonin, *N,N*-dimethyl tryptamine (*N,N*-DMT, or simply DMT), and 5-methoxy *N,N*-dimethyl tryptamine (5-MeO-DMT). MAO inhibiters, such as pinoline or the harmala alkaloids, make serotonin available at the pineal where, with the aid of pineal enzymes (methyl transferases), it can also be converted into 5-MeO-DMT, DMT, and bufotenine (5-hydroxy-*N,N*-dimethyltyptamine, 5-HO-DMT), which are endogenous visionary substances also found in certain ingredients (such as *Psychotria viridis*) of ayahuasca brews and other shamanic visionary substances. Some of these visionary substances may even be of animal origin, such as the Sonoran desert toad (Rudgley, 2000). In vivo biosynthesis of DMT might also occur through the conversion of the common, nutritionally essential, amino acid tryptophan, following its conversion to endogenous tryptamine (Callaway, 2006; Jacob and Presti, 2005; Shulgin and Shulgin, 1997).

However, these endogenous visionary tryptamines are not orally active, as they are denatured by the MAO enzymes present in the stomach, but ayahuasca brews also contain plant additives (such as *Banisteriopsis caapi*) containing a range of harmala alkaloids that inhibit MAO and allow the complementarily ingested visionary tryptamines to be active in the brain. It is this action of the β-carbolines (particularly harmine) in ayahuasca that is these days considered their primary purpose as admixtures in the brew (e.g., McKenna, 2004), though this may not always be the case as subjectively potent ayahuasca decoctions occasionally do not actually contain DMT when analyzed (Callaway, 2005). Nevertheless, the harmala alkaloids are also known to induce visions themselves, likely due to their hyperserotonergic action and the subsequent production of the endogenous vision-inducing molecules 5-MeO-DMT and 5-HO-DMT (Callaway, 2006), and this may account for why harmala alkaloids are less effective and slower than DMT or DMT/harmala alkaloid combinations at inducing visions. Based on their known psychoactivity, Roney-Dougal (1986, 1989, 1991, 2001) originally implicated β-carbolines, such as the endogenous pinoline and the exogenous harmala alkaloids, as inducing psi-conducive states, either naturally during dreams (Callaway, 1988) or artificially by causing waking dream states. However, Roney-Dougal (2001) also later acknowledged that the β-carbolines may primarily exert their visionary effects by potentiating the effects of ingested visionary tryptamines like DMT or 5-MeO-DMT when consumed in combination with them, as in ayahuasca. In essence, ayahuasca contains two types of visionary chemicals, one type (β-carbolines, e.g., harmine) that helps to both potentiate the effects of, and create the other type (tryptamines, e.g., DMT), potentially mimicking the nocturnal chemistry of the pineal and its supposed control over natural visionary states such as dreams (Callaway, 1988), mystical experiences, and NDEs (Strassman, 2001).

Roney-Dougal (1989, 1991, 2001) suggested that the pineal gland and its neurobiology is important in the occurrence of psi events and points to the association made by yogis between the pineal gland and the *ajna* chakra, the yogic psychic center that allegedly controls psi experiences in those with "awakened kundalini" (Miller, 1978; Satyananda, 1972). Further to this point, Naranjo (1987) noted that both kundalini and ayahuasca experiences, being similar in many respects, also feature the same serpentine imagery, further speculating that they probably have the same neurochemistry and result in the same bioenergetic activation.

There is also some possibility that pineal gland activity or DMT production can be stimulated by certain esoteric yogic practices, such as *kechari*, which involves pressing the tongue into the far rear roof of the mouth to stimulate the production of *amrit*, a yogic nectar that reputedly evokes DMT-like ecstasies, which is supposedly secreted in the brain following prolonged practice (Motoyama, 2001; Satyananda, 1996). Some support for this speculation comes from Strassman's (2001) observation that the pineal gland is formed in utero from the tissue of the roof of the mouth rather than in the brain, and later migrates to its unique ventricle position just outside the blood-brain barrier, directly above a critical cerebrospinal fluid byway, and this may mean that pineal stimulation via the roof of the mouth may be possible. Furthermore, manifestation of very specific body vibrations said to be classic kundalini symptoms are supposedly quite reliably induced with substances such as DPT (*N,N*-dipropyl-tryptamine) and 4-Acetoxy-DIPT (*N,N*-diisopropyl-4-acetoxy-tryptamine), which are even more obscure psychedelic tryptamines than DMT, but close relatives of it (Toad, 1999a, 1999b). Similarly, Grof (2001) has reported what he termed "spontaneous kundalini arousal" occurring during psychedelic psychotherapy sessions.

Roney-Dougal (1989, 1991, 2001) also indicated that the pineal gland is sensitive to the same fluctuations in geomagnetic activity that appear to be associated with spontaneous psi phenomena, possibly related to melatonin fluctuations (Persinger, 1988). That the pineal gland is central to psi is further supported by anthropological research that suggests that DMT and the harmala alkaloids found in ayahuasca are psi conducive, along with clinical research that suggests that pinoline and melatonin regulate sleep cycles and dreaming, during which spontaneous psi experiences most often occur (Roney-Dougal, 1986, 1989, 1991, 2001). Some tentative support for the notion that ESP performance is directly predicted by pineal gland activity is also evident with experimental research that demonstrated prepubescent children score better on ESP tests at 3 AM, when the pineal's nocturnal chemicals (melatonin, etc.) are at peak concentrations in the brain, rather than at 9 PM (Satyanarayana, Rao, and Vijaylakshmi, 1993). This effect was not evident with a comparable group of pubescent children, as might be expected because the pineal is less active after infancy. Durwin (2001) has further suggested that the total isolation in the dark undergone for either the first 9 or 18 childhood years of the lives of trainee shamans of the Andean Kogi causes pineal gland deformation (presumably by melatonin/pinoline overproduction) that is responsible for their renowned divinatory skills.

Roney-Dougal (2001) also drew parallels between the ostensibly psi-conducive nature of the shamanic trance state, psychotic states, psychedelic states, and the dream state, which she suggested all belong to the same continuum, perhaps somewhat akin to Thalbourne's (1998) concept of transliminality, and that they all show suggestive evidence of being regulated by the same neurobiological processes.

DMT Model

The discovery of trace amine receptors in the brain for which DMT shows greater affinity than does serotonin—its more common neuroamine cousin—has led to a resurgence of interest in brain DMT in the mediation of mental health (Jacob and Presti, 2005). After extensive research investigating the phenomenological effects of administering intravenous injections of DMT, Strassman (2001) has independently hypothesized a role for DMT similar to that suggested by Roney-Dougal. Strassman echoes the same neurobiological action of the pineal as Roney-Dougal, and similarly proffered that psychotic, dream, meditation, and mystical states all occur through the overproduction of DMT, implicating DMT as a reality thermostat. However, Strassman indicated the action of DMT, not β-carbolines, as primary in producing these states and alternatively proposed that the pineal gland and endogenous DMT are central during extraordinary events such as birth, death, and NDEs. To support this view, Strassman noted that the anatomy of the pineal, suspended in cerebrospinal fluid outside of the blood-bathed brain, is independent enough to resist activation by normal stresses and yet is optimally situated to deliver DMT directly to the middle brain regions where DMT-sensitive serotonin receptors are involved in mood, perception, and thought. Furthermore, access to the brain in this way eliminates the need for DMT transportation in the blood—where it would be broken down by MAO enzymes anyway—thereby negating the need for a pumping heart for delivery. Jacob and Presti (2005) also noted that DMT is virtually unique among endogenous neurotransmitters in that it is a molecule small enough to have blood-brain barrier permeability. That melatonin exerts its influence slowly over a period of a day or more and so does not need the pineal's unique location further supports the supposed postmortem function of DMT. Strassman further speculated that the pineal may continue to produce postmortem DMT for a few hours. He also noted that the NDE has both psychedelic and mystical qualities, and that the DMT experience often shares the same features as an NDE. Some of his DMT study participants reported NDEs and death-rebirth experiences, with many others reporting a newfound fearlessness of death. However, that the participants may have been inadvertently primed for these experiences cannot be ruled out because they were told in the briefing to expect feelings of death or impending death. Nonetheless, a recent survey found that DMT users sometimes do report death-like and near-death-type experiences (Luke and Kittenis, 2005).

To Strassman's surprise, many of the participants in his DMT study reported contact with sentient beings during the experience, often described as elves, dwarves, imps, gremlins, clowns, reptilian beings, and aliens, but also as spirits, gods, or just as a presence, which were commonly supremely powerful, wise, and loving. Such prevalent encounter experiences with DMT use are seemingly so unique and reliable (e.g., Meyer, 1994) as to have had the impish characters popularly dubbed the "self-transforming machine elves" (McKenna, 1991, p. 16), and whose tangible reality has been hotly debated by other researchers of DMT experiences (see Kent, 2005; Luke, 2008; Pickover, 2005; Rodriguez, 2007; Strassman, 2001). Strassman suggested that fluctuations in endogenous DMT levels were also responsible for the frequent reports elsewhere of alien abduction, which share the newfound fearlessness of death and visions of energy tunnels, or cylinders of light, in common with DMT experiences. Following personal experiences with DMT-containing ayahuasca, Severi (2003) likewise noted the similarity between NDEs, traditional psychedelic-induced shamanic initiations, alien abduction experiences, and heightened psychic sensitivity, as have previous researchers (e.g., Harvey-Wilson, 2001; McKenna, 1991; Ring, 1989, 1992). However, Baruss (2003) pointed out that, despite the similarities, DMT and alien abduction experiences lack specific similarities, such as the absence with DMT of the classic "grays" (alleged small gray aliens). Nevertheless, Hancock (2005), also having experienced DMT and ayahuasca, argued that there are substantial similarities between aliens and elves, whether induced through DMT or else appearing in historic-folkloric legends and testimonies, speculating that the latter also have a DMT-induced etiology and, adopting the theory proposed by Vallee (1969), that these elves are the prototype encounter/abduction experiences. It should be noted that few experiencers ever doubt the reality of their encounters with either aliens (Mack, 1999) or DMT entities (Strassman, 2001), and many actually consider them to be "more real" than most ordinary experiences.

Additionally, like alien abduction reports, Strassman noted that his DMT study participants reported being probed and having objects inserted into them by these beings; however, it should be noted that this may have been induced by the medical nature of his experiments and the use of intravenous injections and equipment for monitoring vital signs. Incidentally, although neither Strassman nor other researchers pointed this out, it is apparent that some of the DMT experiences reported in his study, particularly the negative ones, shared several features in common with sleep paralysis (e.g., Cheyne, 2001), particularly the following: sense of presence; reports of one's chest being crushed; whistling, whining, and whirring sounds; and the terrifying paralysis of both body and vocal cords (Strassman, 2001). Both alien abduction experiences and NDEs are also associated with sleep paralysis (Sherwood, 2002). Furthermore, experiential reports from research programs in the 1950s and 1960s (outlined in Shulgin and Shulgin, 1997) indicate that the endogenous 5-HO-DMT (bufotenine), a very close relative to DMT with similar neurochemistry, is seemingly quite reliable in causing feelings of constriction in the throat and the crushing of one's chest, much like sleep paralysis, possibly indicating 5-HO-DMT as a cochemical factor in such experiences, along with DMT.

Additionally in South America and the Caribbean, the psychedelic cohoba snuff is made from one of the few traditionally used plants in which bufotenine is active (*Piptadenia peregrina*) and is used specifically to contact spirits (Cohen, 1970), perhaps somewhat like the sensed presences of sleep paralysis and some DMT experiences. However, Ott (2001) pointed out that the circulatory crises in the earlier bufotenine research were most likely due to psychological factors caused by the enforced nature of the experiments—conducted as they were on psychiatric patients and prisoners with limited consent—because such experiences were absent during Ott's own extensive self-experimentation. Furthermore, exogenous 5-HO-DMT is thought to be converted into the psychoactive 5-MeO-DMT before exerting its mind-altering effects; nevertheless, the concept of endogenous tryptamines as factors in the cause of sleep paralysis begs further investigation.

In evaluation of the role of the pineal gland and endogenous psychedelics in the activation of psi and NDEs, it has yet to be shown that psi phenomena can be produced with these substances under controlled conditions. In addition, both psi experiences and NDEs might be induced with other psychoactive substances, as outlined earlier, although this criticism has been countered by Strassman (2001) with the possibility that other psychedelic substances may also stimulate the pineal gland and endogenous DMT by their action. However, this proposal is little more than conjecture. Furthermore, although there is good support for the hypothesis that DMT is made in the human pineal, this is yet to be proven and remains speculative, like many of Strassman's and Roney-Dougal's suppositions. Nevertheless, despite their incompleteness, the pineal/β-carboline/DMT models of psi experiences and NDEs do offer unique neurochemical perspectives on psychic experiences around which further research can be framed. Additionally, although neither author has speculated on the others' ideas, their models are compatible with each other and may give clues to answering the question of why visionary molecules such as DMT are made within humans at all.

Ketamine Model

A proliferation of reported cases of NDEs with the use of ketamine (Jansen, 1997a, 1999, 2001) and the similarity of aspects of the ketamine experience to that of the NDE (Rogo, 1984), despite Morse's (1997) contentions that the evidence for this is weak, has led to the development of an alternative neurochemical model of NDEs based upon the action of this psychoactive substance (Jansen, 1990, 1997a, 2001). A dissociative anaesthetic—also reported to induce experiences of telepathy, precognition, kundalini, communication with the dead, and an increase in synchronicities (e.g., Case, 2003; Jansen, 2001; Wyllie, 1981)—ketamine acts by binding to the phencyclidine (PCP) site of the NMDA receptor, blocking the action of the neurotransmitter glutamate. Jansen (2001) indicated that potentially life-threatening circumstances (e.g., hypoxia, ischemia, hypoglycemia, temporal lobe epilepsy) can initiate a glutamate flood, which results in neurotoxicity through the overactivation of the NMDA receptors. This NDE trigger may be accompanied by a flood of neuroprotective agents that also bind to the NMDA receptor preventing damage, in much the same way as ketamine. Like Grinspoon and Bakalar's (1979) speculation that the brain synthesizes a chemical similar to ketamine in times of stress, Jansen proposed that "endopsychosins," which bind to the same receptor site as ketamine, would be discovered as the neuroprotective agents that cause an altered state of consciousness, like that caused by ketamine, termed the NDE.

Although parsimonious, Jansen's (1997a) ketamine model of NDE has been both duly criticized and well defended. It has been argued that, unlike NDEs, ketamine trips frequently induce fear (Strassman, 1997) and are not considered veridical (Fenwick, 1997). However, as Jansen (1997b) likewise contested, it is becoming increasingly recognized now that NDEs are also commonly reported to be distressing or traumatic (Atwater, 1994; Montanelli and Parra, 2000) and, furthermore, ketamine experiences are also more often than not reported to induce a sense of peace and pleasantness (Corazza, 2008; Luke, 2007). In support of the perceived reality of the ketamine experience, there are documented accounts of people who have had an NDE and then later a ketamine experience who reported the experiences being the same (Jansen, 2001). In support of this, Grof (1994) found that several cancer patients had NDEs during psychedelic therapy that were very similar to later spontaneous NDEs.

In further criticism of Jansen's model, it has been argued that the clarity and clear memory of the NDE experience is not consistent with cerebral dysfunction

(Fenwick, 1997; Greyson, 2000). However, it is arguable that Jansen's model does not stipulate the necessity of cerebral dysfunction for an NDE, merely the threat or even just the perceived threat of it, and Jansen (1997b) pointed out "there is no reason to suspect that the NDE mechanism would never be activated spontaneously" (p. 87). Furthermore, Jansen (1997b) regarded clarity of consciousness as a nebulous term in the discussion of altered states, as the term is loaded toward the ordinary state of consciousness. Greyson (2000) further contested that no endopsychosins have yet been identified, and Jansen (2001) conceded that this may initially have been a false lead and has suggested a number of alternative endogenous NMDA antagonists as candidates: *N*-acetyl-aspartyl-glutamate, kynurenic acid, and magnesium, all of which protect brain cells from excitotoxic damage (Jansen, 2004). Nevertheless, Thomas (2004), following Jansen in his search, has identified technical flaws with these speculated endogenous "NDE-ogens" and has instead proposed the neuromodulator agmatine as the most likely candidate.

In further criticism of the model, Parker (2001) noted that one-drug/one-experience theories were abandoned in the 1970s and that, along with Greyson (2000), he further noted that ketamine appears to have multiple effects in the brain and multiple experiential features, some of which include those of the NDE. Jansen (1997b) earlier countered this latter criticism with the proposal that factors of set and setting are paramount in determining experience with all ASCs, be they NDEs or ketamine-induced states, so experiences are expected to vary. Parker (2001), like Siegel (1980), added that other drugs also produce features of the NDE, although Jansen (1997b) has asserted that these NDE features are typical with ketamine but are not typical with other drugs, except for PCP and ibogaine (Bianchi, 1997; Jansen, 2001), which are NMDA antagonists (or more specifically called NMDA-PCP receptor blockers).

However, in support of Parker's criticism, Roll and Montagno (1985) have noted the similarity between NDEs and LSD experiences, as reported by Grof (1994). Reports of NDE also occur with the use of other dissociatives, like dextromethorphan (DXM; White, 1997), and carbogen (Meduna, 1950), as well as with high doses of hashish (Siegel and Hirschman, 1984), and tryptamines like 5-MeO-DMT (Shulgin and Shulgin, 1997) and the ayahuasca (often translated as "the vine of the soul") derivative, DMT (Strassman, 2001). Yet, Strassman (2001) did not find Jansen's model incompatible with his own DMT model of NDE, but rather asked why a neuroprotective agent like ketamine should also be psychedelic, as there is no obvious benefit to the NDE other than enabling consciousness to have awareness of its departure from the body.

Recently, electrophysiology and receptor studies have revealed that both NMDA antagonists, such as ketamine, and classic hallucinogens, such as LSD, may actually enhance glutamatergic transmission via non-NMDA receptors in the frontal cortex. This may indicate a common mode of chemical action in the brain responsible for such similar experiences with these divergent molecules, though further investigation is required (Vollenweider, 2004). Given the similarities between NDEs, ketamine experiences, and other drug experiences, Rogo (1984) proposed that the NDE-like effects of ketamine are more often interpreted as NDEs because it has so often been used in a medical setting, further suggesting that ketamine-induced NDEs are less prevalent with recreational use than with anaesthetic use, though this has not been systematically investigated to our knowledge. To our knowledge, the only systematic investigation of the ketamine hypothesis, besides Jansen's, is that of Corazza (2008) who compared 36 cases of NDEs reportedly caused by a cardiac arrest or other life-threatening circumstances with 36 cases of apparent NDEs induced by ketamine. Both groups showed a high degree of similarity in certain features, with a roughly equal prevalence among the groups of experiences involving altered perceptions of time, speeded up visions, and the occurrence of ESP, but the ketamine group members were more likely to report unity with the universe, and the cardiac groups were more likely to report dissociation from the body, visions of light, and encounters with deceased or religious beings. However, Corazza asserted that the evidence indicates that NDEs can be induced through ketamine, although they may not be identical to those occurring naturally.

Overall, despite oversimplification and generalization, the ketamine model of NDE offers the most complete neurobiological explanation of the NDE so far and, as with the DMT model, does not necessarily assume the position of materialist reductionism to explain the data, although some commentators (e.g., Sakellarios, 2005) have erroneously assumed that it does. Furthermore, the model can easily be tested and refined. For instance, there is evidence to suggest that the noncompetitive antagonism at the nonglycine site of the NMDA receptor in particular is linked to the event of dissociative anesthesia and altered sensory perceptions that are familiar to ketamine. This would indicate that relatively novel substances like HA-966 (1-hydroxy-3-amino-pyrrolidone-2), which acts in this particular neurochemical manner (Bonta, 2004), could induce NDEs in blind experimental conditions comparable to those occurring ordinarily, though this remains to be seen. In research with monkeys, HA-966 induced EEG patterns characteristic of sleep despite the animals remaining completely alert, which may be related to Jansen's (2004) observation that the same 60 percent of the general public that do not recall their dreams also do not recall their ketamine experiences during anesthesia, a proportion apparently equivalent to the number of people who do not report having had some kind of NDE.

Discussion

There is a surfeit of nonexperimental evidence (e.g., from anecdotal, anthropological, clinical, historical, and survey sources) linking neurochemistry, particularly through psychedelic substances, to a number of extraordinary anomalous phenomena often seen as relevant to parapsychological study. However, only a modicum of experimental research using rigorous research methods supports this possible connection. In order to facilitate exploring this further, we have outlined the existing evidence for possible neurochemical pathways to psi and related phenomena, as well as four plausible neurochemical models germane to explaining psychic experiences, namely the brain as filter, β-carboline and tryptamine, DMT, and ketamine models. We conclude that no one psychedelic model may be the correct one, as psychedelics may work in many ways (e.g., dissociatives are both NMDA antagonist, as well as μ-opioid agonists). Last, we want to emphasize that demonstrating these possible connections would not imply a reduction of these extraordinary phenomena as being simply materialistic, as the scope of these phenomena begs a wider interpretation. Nevertheless, increased understanding of these possible connections could further a more holistic approach that bridges neurobiological explanations with a number of other explanations, including those from transpersonal psychology.

References

Asperen de Boer, S. R. van, Barkema, P. R., and Kappers, J. (1966). Is it possible to induce ESP with psilocybin? An exploratory investigation. *International Journal of Neuropsychiatry, 2*, 447–473.

Atwater, P. M. H. (1994). *Beyond the light: What isn't being said about near-death experience.* New York: Carol.

Baruš, I. (2003). *Alterations of consciousness: An empirical analysis for social scientists.* Washington, DC: American Psychological Association.

Bergson, H. (1990). *Matter and memory* (N. M. Paul and W. S. Palmer, Trans). New York: Zone Books. (Original work published 1896.)

Bianchi, A. (1994). I mistici del vegetale: Piante psicotrope e stati alterati di coscienza nella selva Amazzonica [A mystical vegetation: Psychotropic plants and altered states of consciousness in the Amazon jungle]. *Quaderni de Parapsicologia, 25*(2), 43–58.

Bianchi, A. (1997). Comments on "The ketamine model of the near-death experience: A central role for the *N*-methyl-D-aspartate receptor." *Journal of Near-Death Studies, 16*, 71–78.

Bierman, D. J. (1998, October). *The effects of THC and psilocybin on paranormal phenomena.* Paper presented at Psychoactivity: A Multidisciplinary Conference on Plants, Shamanism, and States of Consciousness, Amsterdam.

Blackmore, S. J. (1982). Have you ever had an OBE?: The wording of the question. *Journal of the Society for Psychical Research, 51*, 292–302.

Blackmore, S. J. (1984). A postal survey of OBEs and other experiences. *Journal of the Society for Psychical Research, 52*, 225–244.

Blackmore, S. J. (2003). *Consciousness: An introduction.* London: Hodder & Stoughton.

Blackmore, S. J., and Harris, J. (1983). OBEs and perceptual distortions in schizophrenic patients and students. In W. G. Roll, J. Bellof, and R. A. White (Eds.), *Research in parapsychology 1982* (pp. 232–234). Metuchen, NJ: Scarecrow Press.

Blewett, D. B., and Chwelos, M. D. (1959). *A handbook for the therapeutic use of LSD-25: Individual and group procedures.* Saskatchewan, Canada: Authors.

Bonta, I. L. (2004). Schizophrenia, dissociative anesthesia and near-death experience; three events meeting at the NMDA receptor. *Medical Hypotheses, 62*, 23–28.

Callaway, J. C. (1988). A proposed mechanism for the visions of dream sleep. *Medical Hypotheses, 26*, 119–124.

Callaway, J. C. (2005). Various alkaloid profiles in decoctions of *Banisteriopsis capii. Journal of Psychoactive Drugs, 37*, 151–155.

Callaway, J. C. (2006). Phytochemistry and neuropharmacology of ayahuasca. In R. Metzner (Eds.), *Sacred vine of the spirits: Ayahuasca* (pp. 94–116). Rochester, VT: Park Street Press.

Case, J. (2003). The community K-hole. *Entheogen Review, 12*(2), 58.

Cavanna, R., and Servadio, E. (1964). *ESP experiments with LSD 25 and psilocybin.* New York: Parapsychology Foundation.

Cheyne, J. A. (2001). The ominous numinous: Sensed presence and 'other' hallucinations. *Journal of Consciousness Studies, 8*(5–7), 133–150.

Cohen, S. (1970). *Drugs of hallucination.* St. Albans, Hertshire, U.K.: Paladin.

Corazza, O. (2008). *Near-death experiences: Exploring the mind-body connection.* London: Routledge.

Devereux, P. (1997). *The long trip: A prehistory of psychedelia.* New York: Penguin/Arkana.

Dobkin de Rios, M. (1972). *Visionary vine: Hallucinogenic healing in the Peruvian Amazon.* Prospect Heights, IL: Waveland Press.

Dobkin de Rios, M. (1990). *Hallucinogens: Cross-cultural perspectives.* Bridport, U.K.: Prism.

Dobkin de Rios, M., and Janiger, O. (2003). *LSD, spirituality, and the creative process: Based on the groundbreaking research of Oscar Janiger, MD.* Rochester, VT: Park Street Press.

Don, N. S., McDonough, B. E., Warren, C. A., and Moura, G. (1996). Psi, brain function, and "ayahuasca" (telepathine). *Proceedings of papers presented at the 39th Annual Convention of the Parapsychological Association, San Diego, California* (pp. 315–334). Durham, NC: Parapsychological Association.

Dunaway, D. (1998). *Aldous Huxley recollected: An oral history.* Walnut Creek, CA: Rowman Altamira.

Durwin, J. (2001). *Dreamtime: Psycho-biological methodology and morphogenesis in the shamanic tradition.* Unpublished manuscript, Arizona State University.

Eisner, B. G. (1995). Physical and psychical loading (Abstract). *Journal of Scientific Exploration, 9*, 45.

Fenwick, P. (1997). Is the near-death experience only N-methyl-D-aspartate blocking? *Journal of Near-Death Studies, 16*, 42–53.

Friedman, H. (1983). The Self-Expansiveness Level Form: A conceptualization and measurement of a transpersonal construct. *The Journal of Transpersonal Psychology, 15*, 37–50.

Friedman, H. (2006). The renewal of psychedelic research: Implications for humanistic and transpersonal psychology. *The Humanistic Psychologist, 34*, 39–58.

Gallagher, C., Kumar, V. K., and Pekala, R. J. (1994). The anomalous experiences inventory: Reliability and validity. *Journal of Parapsychology, 58*, 402–428.

González-Maeso, J., Ang, R. L., Yuen, T., Chan, P., Weisstaub, N. V., López-Giménez, J. F., Zhou, M., Okawa, Y., Callado, L. F., Milligan, G., Gingrich, J. A., Filizola, M.,

Meana, J. J., and Sealfon, S. C. (2008). Identification of a serotonin/glutamate receptor complex implicated in psychosis (letter to editor). *Nature, 452,* 93–97.

Gorman, P. (1992). Journeys with ayahuasca, the vine of the little death. *Shaman's Drum, 29,* 49–58.

Greyson, B. (2000). Near-death experiences. In E. Cardeña, S. J. Lynn, and S. Krippner (Eds.), *Varieties of anomalous experience: Examining the scientific evidence* (pp. 315–352). Washington, DC: American Psychological Association.

Grinspoon, L., and Bakalar, J. (1979). *Psychedelic drugs reconsidered.* New York: Basic Books.

Grinspoon, L., and Bakalar, J. B. (1998). *Psychedelic drugs reconsidered* (2nd ed.). New York: The Lindesmith Centre.

Grof, S. (1975). *Realms of the human unconscious: Observations from LSD research.* New York: Viking Press.

Grof, S. (1980). *LSD psychotherapy.* Pomona, CA: Hunter House.

Grof, S. (1990). Survival after death: Observations from modern consciousness research. In G. Doore (Ed.), *What survives? Contemporary explanations of life after death* (pp. 22–33). Los Angeles: Tarcher.

Grof, S. (1994). Alternative cosmologies and altered states. *Noetic Sciences Review, 32,* 21.

Grof, S. (2001). *LSD psychotherapy* (3rd ed.). Sarasota, FL: Multidisciplinary Association for Psychedelic Studies.

Hancock, G. (2005). *Supernatural: Meetings with the ancient teachers of mankind.* London: Century.

Harman, W. (1963). Some aspects of the psychedelic drug controversy. *Journal of Humanistic Psychology, 3*(2), 93–107.

Harvey-Wilson, S. (2001). Shamanism and alien abductions: A comparative study. *Australian Journal of Parapsychology, 1*(2), 103–116.

Holt, N. J., Simmonds-Moore, C. A., and Moore, S. L. (2008, March). *Psi, belief in the paranormal, attentional filters and mental health.* Poster presentation at the Bial Foundation Symposium, Porto, Portugal.

Holzinger, R. (1964). LSD 25: A tool in psychotherapy. *Journal of General Psychology, 71,* 9–20.

Houran, J., and Williams, C. (1998). Relation of tolerance of ambiguity to global and specific paranormal experience. *Psychological Reports, 83,* 807–818.

Huxley, A. (1954). *The doors of perception.* London: Chatto & Windus.

Jacob, M. S., and Presti, D. E. (2005). Endogenous psychoactive tryptamines reconsidered: An anxiolytic role for dimethyltryptamine. *Medical Hypotheses, 64,* 930–937.

Jansen, K. L. R. (1990). Neuroscience and the near-death experience: Roles for the NMDA-PCP receptor, the sigma receptor, and the endopsychosins. *Medical Hypotheses, 31,* 25–29.

Jansen, K. L. R. (1997a). The ketamine model of the near-death experience: A central role for the NMDA receptor. *Journal of Near-Death Studies, 16,* 5–26.

Jansen, K. L. R. (1997b). Response to commentaries on "The ketamine model of the near-death experience." *Journal of Near-Death Studies, 16,* 79–95.

Jansen, K. L. R. (1999). Ketamine (K) and quantum psychiatry. *Asylum: The Journal for Democratic Psychiatry, 11*(3), 19–21.

Jansen, K. [L. R.] (2001). *Ketamine: Dreams and realities.* Sarasota, FL: Multidisciplinary Association for Psychedelic Studies.

Jansen, K. [L. R.] (2004). What can ketamine teach us about ordinary and altered states of consciousness? *Consciousness Research Abstracts from the Toward a Science of Consciousness Conference, Tucson, Arizona*, 90.

Kensinger, K. M. (1973). *Banisteriopsis* usage among the Peruvian Cashinahua. In M. J. Harner (Ed.), *Hallucinogens and shamanism* (pp. 9–14). Oxford: Oxford University Press.

Kent, J. (2005). The case against DMT elves. In C. Pickover (Ed.), *Sex, drugs, Einstein, and elves* (pp. 102–105). Petaluma, CA: Smart Publications.

Kjellgren, A., and Norlander, T. (2000–2001). Psychedelic drugs: A study of drug-induced experiences obtained by illegal drug users in relation to Stanislav Grof's model of altered states of consciousness. *Imagination, Cognition and Personality, 20*, 41–57.

Kolp, E., Friedman, H., Young, M. S., and Krupitsky, E. (2006). Ketamine Enhanced Psychotherapy: Preliminary clinical observations on its effectiveness in treating alcoholism. *The Humanistic Psychologist, 34*, 399–422.

Kolp, E., Young, M. S., Friedman, H., Krupitsky, E., Jansen, K., and O'Connor, L. (2007). Ketamine Enhanced Psychotherapy: Preliminary clinical observations on its effectiveness in treating death anxiety. *International Journal of Transpersonal Studies, 26*, 1–17.

Krippner, S. (1985). Psychedelic drugs and creativity. *Journal of Psychoactive Drugs, 17*(4), 235–245.

Krippner, S. (2006, January). *LSD and parapsychological experiences.* Paper presented at LSD: Problem Child and Wonder Drug, an International Symposium on the Occasion of the 100th Birthday of Albert Hofmann, 13–15 January, Basel, Switzerland.

Krippner, S., and Achterberg, J. (2000). Anomalous healing experiences. In E. Cardena, S. J. Lynn, and S. Krippner (Eds.), *Varieties of anomalous experience: Examining the scientific evidence* (pp. 353–395). Washington, DC: American Psychological Association.

Kugel, W. (1977). Call-time as a new parameter in statistical ESP experiments. In J. D. Morris, W. G. Roll, and R. L. Morris (Eds.), *Research in parapsychology 1976* (pp. 138–140). Metuchen, NJ: Scarecrow Press.

Laidlaw, R. W. (1961). New understanding of mediumistic phenomena. *Proceedings on Two Conferences on Parapsychology and Pharmacology* (pp. 25–26). New York: Parapsychology Foundation.

Levine, J. (1968). Psychopharmacology: Implications for psi research. In R. Cavanna and M. Ullman (Eds.), *Psi and Altered States of Consciousness: Proceedings of an International Conference on Hypnosis, Drugs, Dreams, and Psi* (pp. 88–106). New York: Parapsychology Foundation.

Luke, D. (2007). Lecture report: Inducing near-death states through the use of chemicals—Dr. Ornella Corazza. *Paranormal Review, 43*, 28–29.

Luke, D. (2008). Disembodied eyes revisited. An investigation into the ontology of entheogenic entity encounters. *Entheogen Review, 17*(1), 1–10.

Luke, D. P., and Kittenis, M. (2005). A preliminary survey of paranormal experiences with psychoactive drugs. *Journal of Parapsychology, 69*, 305–327.

Luna, L. E., and White, S. F. (Eds.). (2000). *Ayahuasca reader: Encounters with the Amazon's sacred vine.* Sante Fe, NM: Synergetic Press.

Mack, J. E. (1999). *Passport to the cosmos: Human transformation and alien encounters.* New York: Three Rivers.

Masters, R. E. L., and Houston, J. (1966). *The varieties of psychedelic experience.* London: Turnstone.

McGovern, W. (1927). *Jungle paths and Inca ruins*. New York: Grosset & Dunlap.

McKenna, D. (2004). Clinical investigations of the therapeutic potential of ayahuasca: Rationale and regulatory challenges. *Pharmacology and Therapeutics, 102*, 111–129.

McKenna, T. (1991). *The archaic revival: Speculations on psychedelic mushrooms, the Amazon, virtual reality, UFOs, evolution, shamanism, the rebirth of the Goddess, and the end of history*. San Francisco: Harper.

Meduna, L. J. (1950). The effect of carbon dioxide upon the functions of the brain. In L. J. Meduna (Ed.), *Carbon dioxide therapy*. Springfield, IL: Charles Thomas.

Metzner, R. (Eds.). (2006). *Sacred vine of the spirits: Ayahuasca*. Rochester, VT: Park Street Press.

Meyer, P. (1994). Apparent communication with discarnate entities induced by dimethyltryptamine (DMT). In T. Lyttle (Ed.), *Psychedelics* (pp. 161–203). New York: Barricade Books.

Miller, R. A. (1978). The biological function of the third eye. *The Continuum, 2*(3).

Montanelli, D. G., and Parra, A. (2000). Conflictive psi experiences: A survey with implications for clinical parapsychology [Abstract]. *Journal of Parapsychology, 64*(3), 248.

Morse, M. L. (1997). Commentary on Jansen's paper. *Journal of Near-Death Studies, 16*, 59–62.

Motoyama, H. (2001). *Theories of the chakras: Bridge to higher consciousness*. New Delhi, India: New Age Books.

Myers, S. A., Austrin, H. R., Grisso, J. T., and Nickeson, R. C. (1983). Personality characteristics as related to the out-of-body experience. *Journal of Parapsychology, 47*, 131–144.

Naranjo, C. (1987). "Ayahuasca" imagery and the therapeutic property of the harmala alkaloids. *Journal of Mental Imagery, 11*, 131–136.

Nichols, D. E. (2004). Hallucinogens. *Pharmacology and Therapeutics, 101*, 131–181.

Osis, K. (1961). A pharmacological approach to parapsychological experimentation. *Proceedings of Two Conferences on Parapsychology and Pharmacology* (pp. 74–75). New York: Parapsychology Foundation.

Osmond, H. (1961). Variables in the LSD setting. *Proceedings of Two Conferences on Parapsychology and Pharmacology* (pp. 33–35). New York: Parapsychology Foundation.

Osmond, H., and Smythies, J. (1952). Schizophrenia: A new approach. *Journal of Mental Science, 98*, 309–315.

Ott, J. (2001). Pharmanopo-psychonautics: human intranasal, sublingual, intrarectal, pulmonary and oral pharmacology of bufotenine. *Journal of Psychoactive Drugs, 33*(4), 403–407.

Pahnke, W. N. (1968). The psychedelic mystical experience in terminal cancer patients and its possible implications for psi research. In R. Cavanna and M. Ullman (Eds.), *Psi and Altered States of Consciousness: Proceedings of an International Conference on Hypnosis, Drugs, Dreams, and Psi* (pp. 115–128). New York: Parapsychology Foundation.

Pahnke, W. N. (1971). The use of psychedelic drugs in parapsychological research. *Parapsychology Review, 2*(4), 5–6 and 12–14.

Palmer, J. (1979). A community mail survey of psychic experiences. *Journal of the American Society for Psychical Research, 73*, 221–251.

Palmer, J., Tart, C. T., and Redington, D. (1976). A large-sample classroom ESP card-guessing experiment. *European Journal of Parapsychology, 1*, 40–56.

Pappas, J., and Friedman, H. (2007). The construct of self-expansiveness and the validity of the Transpersonal Scale of the Self-Expansiveness Level Form. *The Humanistic Psychologist, 35*, 323–347.

Parker, A. (1975). *States of mind: ESP and altered states of consciousness.* London: Malaby Press.

Parker, A. (2001). What can cognitive psychology and parapsychology tell us about near-death experiences? *Journal of the Society for Psychical Research, 65,* 225–240.

Persinger, M. A. (1988). Increased geomagnetic activity and the occurrence of bereavement hallucinations: Evidence for melatonin-mediated microseizuring in the temporal lobe? *Neuroscience Letters, 88,* 271–274.

Pickover, C. (2005). *Sex, drugs, Einstein, and elves.* Petaluma, CA: Smart Publications.

Puharich, A. (1959). *The sacred mushroom: Key to the door of eternity.* Garden City, NY: Doubleday.

Puharich, A. (1962). *Beyond telepathy.* Garden City, NY: Doubleday.

Ring, K. (1989). Near-death and UFO encounters as shamanic initiations: Some conceptual and evolutionary implications. *ReVision, 11*(3), 14–22.

Ring, K. (1992). *The Omega Project: Near-death experiences, UFO encounters and mind at large.* New York: William Morrow.

Rodriguez, M. A. (2007). A methodology for studying various interpretations of the *N,N*-dimethyltryptamine-induced alternate reality. *Journal of Scientific Exploration, 21,* 67–84.

Rogo, D. S. (1976). *Exploring psychic phenomena: Beyond mind and matter.* Wheaton, IL: The Theosophical Society in America.

Rogo, D. S. (1984). Ketamine and the near-death experience. *Anabiosis: The Journal of Near-Death Studies, 4,* 87–96.

Roll, W. G., and Montagno, E. (1985). System theory, neurophysiology, and psi. *Journal of Indian Psychology, 4,* 43–84.

Roney-Dougal, S. M. (1986). Some speculations on a possible psychic effect of harmaline. In D. H. Weiner and D. H. Radin (Eds.), *Research in parapsychology 1985* (pp. 120–123). Metuchen, NJ: Scarecrow Press.

Roney-Dougal, S. M. (1989). Recent findings relating to the possible role of the pineal gland in affecting psychic ability. *Journal of the Society for Psychical Research, 55,* 313–328.

Roney-Dougal, S. M. (1991). *Where science and magic meet.* London: Element Books.

Roney-Dougal, S. [M.] (2001). *Walking between the worlds: Links between psi, psychedelics, shamanism, and psychosis.* Unpublished manuscript, Psi Research Centre, Glastonbury, U.K.

Rudgley, R. (2000). *The encyclopedia of psychoactive substances.* New York: Thomas Dunne.

Rush, J. H., and Cahn, H. A. (1958). Physiological conditioning for psi performance [Abstract from the Proceedings of the first convention of the Parapsychological Association, August, 1958, New York]. *Journal of Parapsychology, 22,* 300.

Sakellarios, S. (2005). *Another view of near death experiences and reincarnation: How to respond to reductionistic thinking.* Retrieved November 25, 2005, from http:/www.omplace.com/articles/Reductionist_thinking.html.

Satyananda Saraswati, Swami. (1972). *The pineal gland (ajna chakra).* Bihar, India: Bihar School of Yoga.

Satyananda Saraswati, Swami. (1996). *Kundalini tantra* (2nd ed.). Munger, Bihar, India: Yoga Publications Trust.

Satyanarayana, M., Rao, P. V. K., and Vijaylakshmi, S. (1993). Role of pineal activity in ESP performance: A preliminary study. *Journal of Indian Psychology, 11,* 44–56.

Schultes, R. E., and Hofmann, A. (1992). *Plants of the Gods: Their sacred, healing, and hallucinogenic powers.* Rochester, VT: Healing Arts Press.

Severi, B. (2003). Sciamani e psichedelia. [Shamans and psychedelics]. *Quaderni de Parapsychologia, 34*(1), 36.

Shannon, B. (2002). *The antipodes of the mind: Charting the phenomena of the ayahuasca experience.* Oxford: Oxford University Press.

Sherwood, S. (2002). Relationship between the hypnogogic/hypnopompic states and reports of anomalous experiences. *Journal of Parapsychology, 66,* 127–150.

Shulgin, A. T., and Shulgin, A. (1997). *TIHKAL: The continuation.* Berkeley, CA: Transform Press.

Siegel, R. K. (1980). The psychology of life after death. *American Psychologist, 35,* 911–931.

Siegel, R. K., and Hirschman. A. E. (1984). Hashish near-death experiences. *Anabiosis: The Journal of Near-Death Studies, 4,* 70–86.

Simmonds, C. A., and Roe, C. A. (2000). Personality correlates of anomalous experiences, perceived ability and beliefs: Schizotypy, temporal lobe signs and gender. *Proceedings of presented papers from the 43rd annual convention of the Parapsychology Association* (pp. 272–291). Durham, NC: Parapsychological Association.

Sinel, J. (1927). *The sixth sense: A physical explanation for clairvoyance, telepathy, hypnotism, dreams and other phenomena usually considered occult.* London: T. Werner Laurie.

Smythies, J. R. (1960). New research frontiers in parapsychology and pharmacology. *International Journal of Parapsychology, 2*(2), 28–38.

Smythies, J. R. (1987). Psychometry and mescaline. *Journal of the Society for Psychical Research, 54,* 266–268.

Stafford, P. G., and Golightly, B. H. (1967). *LSD the problem-solving psychedelic.* London: Tandem.

Stokes, D. M. (1997). Spontaneous psi phenomena. In S. Krippner (Ed.), *Advances in parapsychological research* (Vol. 8, pp. 6–87). Jefferson, NC: McFarland.

Stolaroff, M. J. (2004). *The secret chief revealed: Conversations with a pioneer of the underground psychedelic therapy movement.* Sarasota, FL: Multidisciplinary Association for Psychedelic Studies.

Strassman, R. J. (1997). Endogenous ketamine-like compounds and the NDE: If so, so what? *Journal of Near-Death Studies, 16,* 27–41.

Strassman, R. [J.] (2001). *DMT: The spirit molecule: A doctor's revolutionary research into the biology of near-death and mystical experiences.* Rochester, VT: Park Street Press.

Tart, C. T. (1968). Hypnosis, psychedelics, and psi: Conceptual models. In R. Cavanna and M. Ullman (Eds.), *Psi and altered states of consciousness: Proceedings of an International Conference on Hypnosis, Drugs, Dreams, and Psi* (pp. 24–41). New York: Parapsychology Foundation.

Tart, C. T. (1970). Marijuana intoxication: Common experiences. *Nature, 226,* 701–704.

Tart, C. T. (1993). Marijuana intoxication, psi, and spiritual experiences. *The Journal of the American Society for Psychical Research, 87,* 149–170.

Tart, C. T., Palmer, J., and Redington, D. J. (1979). Effects of immediate feedback on ESP performance: A second study. *Journal of the American Society for Psychical Research, 73,* 151–165.

Thalbourne, M. A. (1998). Transliminality: Further correlates and a short measure. *Journal of the American Society for Psychical Research, 92,* 402–419.

Thalbourne, M. [A.] (2000). Transliminality and creativity. *The Journal of Creative Behavior, 34,* 193–202.

Thalbourne, M. A. (2001). Measures of the sheep goat variable, transliminality, and their correlates. *Psychological Reports, 88,* 339–350.

Thalbourne, M. A., and Houran, J. (2005). Patterns of self-reported happiness and substance use in the context of transliminality. *Personality and Individual Differences, 38,* 327–336.

Thomas, S. (2004). Agmatine and near-death experiences. Retrieved November 25, 2005, from http://www.neurotransmitter.net/neardeath.html.

Tinoco, C. A. (1994). Testa de ESP empacientes sob efeito da ayahuasca [Controlled ESP test in patients under the influence of ayahuasca]. *Revista de Brasileira de Parapsicologia, 14,* 42–48.

Toad (1999a). DPT primer. *The Entheogen Review, 8*(1), 4–10.

Toad (1999b). 4-Acetoxy-DIPT primer. *The Entheogen Review, 8*(4), 126–131.

Tornatore, N. V. (1977a). The paranormal event in psychotherapy as a psychotherapeutic tool: A survey of 609 psychiatrists. In J. D. Morris, W. G. Roll, and R. L. Morris (Eds.), *Research in parapsychology 1976* (pp. 114–116). Metuchen, NJ: Scarecrow Press.

Tornatore, N. [V.] (1977b, July). The paranormal event in psychotherapy: A survey of 609 psychiatrists. *Psychic Magazine,* pp. 34–37.

Usha, S., and Pasricha, S. (1989a). Claims of paranormal experiences: I. Survey of psi and psi-related experiences. *Journal of the National Institute of Mental Health and Neurosciences* (India), *7,* 143–150.

Usha, S., and Pasricha, S. (1989b). Claims of paranormal experiences: II. Attitudes toward psychical research and factors associated with psi and psi-related experiences. *Journal of the National Institute of Mental Health and Neurosciences* (India), *7,* 151–157.

Vallee, J. (1969). *Passport to Magonia.* Chicago: Henry Regnery.

Vayne, J. (2001). *Pharmakon: Drugs and the imagination.* London: Liminalspace/El Cheapo.

Vollenweider, F. X. (2001). Brain mechanisms of hallucinogens and entactogens. *Dialogues in Clinical Neurosceince, 3,* 265–279.

Vollenweider, F. X. (2004). Brain mechanisms of hallucinogens. *Consciousness Research Abstracts from the Toward a Science of Consciousness Conference, Tucson, Arizona,* 91–92.

Vollenweider, F. X., and Geyer, M. A. (2001). A systems model of altered consciousness: Integrating natural and drug-induced psychoses. *Brain Research Bulletin, 56,* 495–507.

Weil, G., Metzner, R., and Leary, T. (Eds). (1965). *The psychedelic reader.* New York: University Books.

Wezelman, R., and Bierman, D. J. (1997). Process orientated Ganzfeld research in Amsterdam. *Proceedings of the 40th Parapsychology Association Annual Convention held in conjunction with the Society for Psychical Research,* 477–492.

White, W. E. (1997). Altered states and paranormal experiences. In W. E. White, *The Dextromethorphan FAQ: Answers to frequently asked questions about DXM* (version 4). Retrieved April 2, 2002, from http://www.erowid.org/chemical/dxm/faq/dxm_paranormal.shtml.

Whittlesey, J. R. B. (1960). Some curious ESP results in terms of variance. *Journal of Parapsychology, 24*(3), 220–222.

Wilson, A. J. C. (1949). Ayahuasca, peyotl, yage. *Proceedings of the Society for Psychical Research, 49,* 353–363.

Wilson, K., and French, C. C. (2006). The relationship between susceptibility to false memories, dissociativity, and paranormal belief and experience. *Personality and Individual Differences, 41*, 1493–1502.

Winkelman, M. J., and Roberts, T. B. (Eds.). (2007). *Psychedelic medicine: New evidence for hallucinogenic substances as treatments.* London: Praeger.

Wyllie, T. (1981). Phencyclidine and ketamine: A view from the street. Unpublished manuscript. Available at http:/www.timothywyllie.com/PCP.htm.

Two Artists

Postscript

Stanley Krippner and Harris L. Friedman

Einstein once stated, "The most beautiful emotion we can experience is the mysterious. It is the fundamental emotion that stands at the cradle of all true art and science" (in Zuckerman, 2009, p. 52). The chapters in this book contain a wealth of findings relating neurobiology to extraordinary experiences, which remain mysterious but now seem at least potentially more accessible with the rapidly emerging new technologies opening access to heretofore inaccessible neurobiological data. However, our efforts are not meant to erode these mysteries of mind by reducing them to mere neurobiological mechanisms devoid of deeper meaning but, rather, to provide lines of converging evidence that help to illuminate these mysteries.

Neurobiology is that branch of biology that deals with the anatomy and physiology of the nervous system (Kesner and Martinez, 2007). To appreciate its relevance to the "mysterious minds" that are the foci of this book, it is helpful to make a short survey of the field and its development over the years. In ancient times, neurobiological functions were explained metaphorically. For example, Plato (1987) described the mind as a "wax block" on which experiences are "imprinted" (pp. 99–100). This wax tablet was said to have been the gift of Mnemosyne, the Greek goddess of memory (who is acknowledged in the English language term, "mnemonic devices"). A later metaphor compared the mind to an aviary; this metaphor is still used when people speak of placing the memory of an experience in a "pigeonhole." With the invention of photography in the nineteenth century, people began to speak of a "photographic mind"; later metaphors for mental functioning were derived from the telephone switchboard, the phonograph, and the computer, for example, "connections," "recording," and "downloading." And, of course, the psychoanalytic metaphor of "psychic energy" that can be pent-up or released is based on the most impressive machine of its day, the steam engine.

With the establishment of psychology as an independent discipline, and with subsequent advances in neurology, the nervous system became the focus for understanding mental activity. The Spanish neurologist Santiago Ramon y Cajal (1894) studied the development of "neural branching" among the vertebrates, including the human being. Ramon y Cajal spoke metaphorically as well, describing neural connections as a "system of telegraphic wires" and a "garden planted with innumerable trees" (pp. 467–468). Despite the insights made by such eminent scientists as William James and Ivan Pavlov, by the middle of the twentieth century, psychology and neurology were still using metaphors for descriptive purposes since there were no known neurobiological mechanisms for learning, memory, problem solving, and other mental functions (Rosenzweig, 2007, p. 12).

The Search for Neural Mechanisms

Rosenzweig (2007), in his insightful historical perspective on neurobiology, noted that "by 1950, the search for neural mechanisms of cognitive skills seemed to have reached an impasse" (p. 12). However, within the next few years, data obtained from a variety of electrophysiological and neurochemical techniques led to remarkable advances in the field. One of these was Hebb's (1949) postulate of neural plasticity and the changes in the brain's synapses that accompanied learning, an insight that echoed a formulation by William James (1890), who had written:

> When two elementary brain processes have been active together or in immediate succession, one of them, on recurring, tends to propagate its excitement into the other. (p. 566)

By the 1990s, Rosenzweig observed, the idea that activity could lead to new neural connections was well accepted: "neurons that fire together, wire together" (p. 13).

Hebb's hypothesis of use-dependent neural plasticity was confirmed by a number of investigators including Rosenzweig himself. Rosenzweig and his associates (e.g., Rosenzweig, Krech, and Bennett, 1961) demonstrated that both informal activities (e.g., playing with moving objects) and formal activities (e.g., running mazes) in varied environments led to measurable changes in the neurochemistry and microanatomy of rats' brains. Replications and extensions of this work, as well as parallel research in which the occlusion of a kitten's eye, led to a reduction of cortical cells responding to that eye (Wiesel and Hubel, 1965), demonstrating that training or differential experience could produce measurable changes in the brain.

Crick and Watson's discovery of the structure of DNA led to major advances in several fields including neurobiology. Not only was it possible to study gene expression in cognition, personality, and health, but to manipulate and modify specific genes (Rosenzweig, 2007, p. 26). The impact of genetics on neurobiology has been so profound that Gazzaniga (2008) humorously observed, "In biology, follow the genes" (p. 85), suggesting that the ultimate uniqueness of the human brain is due to its DNA sequence and emphasizing how research in genetics has revolutionized the neurosciences.

Data from both genetic expression and environmental effects on behavior led to the discovery that protein synthesis is required for some types of memory storage through "gene messengers," such as RNA. Memory and learning functions also appear to be modulated by opioid antagonists, while opioid agonists tend to impair memory formation. These reports of hypothetical "memory molecules" led McConnell (1986, pp. 411–412) to propose an explanation for his experiments with planaria. McConnell had been training planaria to turn right or left, reporting that untrained planaria that cannibalized the trained organisms learned the skill more quickly than noncannibal planaria; soon, McConnell claimed that positive results had been reported by scientists in a dozen different countries.

Similar reports were forthcoming from rat studies; when RNA extracted from trained rats was injected into untrained rats, the latter responded to training more rapidly than would be expected (Babich, Jacobson, Bubash, and Jacobson, 1965). In addition, Ungar and Oceguera-Navarro (1965) reported that trained responses in rats could be transferred to untrained rats by peptides extracted from the brain. However, later virtually all laboratories that tried to replicate these three lines of work failed to do so (e.g., Byrne et al., 1966; Rosenzweig, 1996). One of Ungar and Oceguera-Navarro's coexperimenters, reported that when a peptide, scotophobin, was injected into mice forced to remain in a black box, the mice developed an elevated blood corticosteroid level, while mice in a lighted box did not. Scotophobin seemed to be interacting with a particular environmental stimulus to elevate stress and caused the animal to attempt an escape from the stress-inducing situation. In other words, scotophobin may have been a modulatory, extrinsic agent, one that masked the researchers' conclusions that intrinsic factors were at work (Rosenzweig, 2007).

The failure to replicate any of these three reported effects is pertinent to the discussion of controversies surrounding psi research reviewed in this book (Parker, Chapter 4; Watt and Irwin, Chapter 3). In the case of purported intrinsic neurobiological changes, many similar scenarios were suggested to discount these findings, including methodological defects, experimenter effects, and extrinsic agents among them. However, charges of fraud were not leveled against McConnell, Babich, and his associates, or Ungar and Oceguera-Navarro for the failure to replicate their findings.

Advocates have detected instances of fraud in psi research, but not the convoluted scenarios made by some counteradvocates of psi research (e.g., Hansel, 1966/1980; Price, 1955). More accurate criticisms could be based on failures of replicability as well as other methodological concerns, such as the independence of studies, and the appropriateness of the statistics used to analyze them. All of these critiques could, however, be equally applied to many other areas of science and we conclude, given the vast number of successful studies on psi, that it is premature to foreclose on the promise that psi studies might hold for scientific inquiry.

Alcock (Chapter 2) is on target when he writes that before we can discuss a neurobiology of psi, we need to know first what psi is, advice that needs to be carefully considered by both parapsychology's advocates and counteradvocates. As was the case with the scotophobin research, some unknown modulatory agent may be discovered that will explain many of the positive results appearing in the parapsychological literature. If so, something of scientific value will have been learned; if not, the search for explanatory mechanisms for purported psi phenomena needs to continue. At the moment, the strongest likelihood for such mechanisms may well lie in the domain of neurobiology.

Rosenzweig (2007) observed that the electrical recording of sleep stages led to major advances in neurobiology. Several studies of rats and other nonhuman animals indicate that brain activity during sleep is related to memory formation and consolidation (e.g., Skaggs and McNaughton, 1996); sleep occurring after a learning task seems to reinforce the new relationships between neurons developed in that task. Advances in research technology have made it possible to study this effect in humans as well; Aton and his associates (Aton, Seibt, Dumoulin, Jha, et al., 2009) suggested that their data have provided strong support for the idea that consolidation of memories is one of the key functions of sleep. In their experiments, in which one eye was deprived of daytime stimulation, sleep consolidated ocular dominance plasticity by strengthening responses of the human brain's cortex to stimulation of the nondeprived eye. Further, sleep deprivation interfered with ocular dominance plasticity, but when the cortex was triggered to remodel in wakefulness, changes in the synapses were further modified and consolidated by reactivation and a series of signaling cascades during sleep. Nonetheless, there is so much that needs to be learned about the functions of sleep that Gazzaniga (2008) wrote that "the mysterious process of sleep ... has eluded understanding" (p. 2). Similarly, advances in neurobiological research technology germane to psi, which has eluded understanding even more than has sleep, offers great promise.

But neurobiological advances can also be used in unfortunate ways, merely reinforcing prejudices against psi. In fact, the highly publicized neuroimaging study by Moulton and Kosslyn (2008) that found no differences in participants' reactions to "psi" and "nonpsi" stimuli rests on the assumption that psi would have "left a footprint that could be detected by fMRI [functional magnetic resonance imaging]" (p. 189). Their overall results produced what they concluded "the strongest evidence yet obtained against the existence of paranormal mental phenomena" (p. 182). Although Roll and Williams (Chapter 1), Neppe (Chapter 7), and Watt and Irwin (Chapter 3) hold that their study was flawed in many ways and dispute their conclusion, we agree with their statement that neurobiological methods have "much to offer should researchers wish to investigate further the possible circumstances in which psi might exist" (p. 191).

Costly Signaling Theory

One avenue for approaching an understanding of neurobiological processes as possibly related to psi is "costly signaling theory" (CST). If there is a possibility that psi might be grounded in neurobiological processes, it seems reasonable that it would serve some adaptive function(s). Most human activity can be related to antecedents in other animals (Gazzaniga, 2008). Monkeys, apes, and humans still use orofacial gestures as their main natural way to communicate. The lip smacks and tongue smacks of monkeys persist in humans, where they form syllables in speech production. In this regard, both humans and other animals engage in a wide range of signaling behaviors. Human signaling includes speech and language exchanges, emotional displays, clothing styles, tattoos, gestures, postures, and various other types of body language (McNamara, 2004). CST maintains that, in order for signaling displays between two or more individuals (whether people or other species) to be workable or believable by both parties, they must be reliable, authentic, and fairly impervious to fakery. Only signals that cannot be faked can be trusted to carry authentic information. However, unfakeable signals are difficult to produce (i.e., "costly"). Their production costs are their certification of honesty (e.g., costly signals are required by peacocks during mating season under those conditions that require reliable and honest signaling. Namely, the peacocks' expensive, in terms of resources, display of plumage could be faked, but it would serve no useful purpose justifying the cost if the male peacock was incapable of mating).

Moreover, CST proposes that signalers (e.g., peacocks, humans) who are handicapped in some way (e.g., due to age, health, status, etc.) usually do not send false costly signals because the price (in terms of effort, energy, time, etc.) would be too high. In other words, they are already paying dearly (e.g., metabolically, motorically, behaviorally) to signal and the additional costs of false signaling would be prohibitive. If a signal were to be successfully faked, the fakery is usually committed by an individual whose health or status would not be compromised by the extra cost. Ultimately, however, it would be to no avail and not serve an adaptive function in the evolution of the species.

The proponents of CST have proposed that costly signals played an important role in evolution; these signals not only facilitated communication and cooperation among individuals, but they were a survival mechanism for the species as a whole. Costly signaling is especially crucial when organisms with conflicting interests are in communication. From an evolutionary perspective, the purpose of both parties is better served when the signals are honest, even though they require effort. For example, an alert bird may give a warning call to a stalking fox. It is communicating something quite useful to the fox, namely that the bird has detected the predator's presence; hence, the fox might as well give up the hunt because that predator is unlikely to catch the bird. In terminating the hunt, the predator and the bird have served mutual, though conflicting, interests.

Biological signals, such as the peacock's resplendent feathers and the bird's warning calls, are considered "honest" by CST proponents if they are useful and adaptive (Dall, 2005; Pentland, 2008). As it is sometimes difficult to determine the adaptive function of such costly signals in nonhuman animals, so this may be difficult to determine for humans. This is especially pertinent to infants whose neonatal crying promotes their survival (Madkour, Barakat, and Furlow, 1997) and whose rapid eye movement (REM) sleep has been identified as a costly signal that attracts parental attention (i.e., infants who did not manifest REM failed to obtain as much concern from their parents and were at risk for being abducted by predators; McNamara, 2004). Among adults, REM activity serves a somewhat different purpose, apparently facilitating cognitive development and memory consolidation (Domhoff, 2003). However, overlaid functions are not uncommon in human evolution; the organs used for speech are also used to facilitate the movement of food and drink from the mouth to the stomach.

McNamara and Szent-Imrey (2008) have applied CST to reports of anomalous healing, stating "our biology, apparently, can produce remarkable cures" (p. 209), an observation also made by Krippner (1994) in his discussion of data from psycho-neuroimmunology research.

McNamara and Szent-Imrey noted the overlap of anomalous healing reports with descriptions of the placebo response. Benedetti, Mayberg, Wager, Stohler, and Zubieta (2005) proposed that the placebo response

> is a psychobiological phenomenon that can be attributed to the patient's subjective expectation of clinical improvement on the one hand and to classical conditioning mechanisms on the other. Hence, the placebo response involves a powerful suppression of negative emotions and the expectation that relief is on the way, as well as belief in the efficacy of the forthcoming cure . . . Indeed, this is consistent with the placebo effect literature, which has revealed increased activation of several areas of the brain's frontal lobe with concomitant decreased activation in the amygdala. (p. 210)

The efforts involved in placebo responses, and by implication in anomalous healings, may be seen as "costly signals." Sickness is less easily faked than voluntary signals. The informational and affective content of the illness creates a mental set in the patient that signals other people concerning the qualities of the person who is ill. Frank and Frank (1991) listed expectation, hope, belief, and faith as critical elements in both psychotherapy and healing. In addition to using a placebo model to understand psi-like experiences, the psychology of faith could be a promising avenue for investigating reported extrasensory perception (ESP) and psychokinesis (PK) experiences.

In their discussion of anomalous healing, McNamara and Szent-Imrey (2008) commented, "There are no detailed scientific models of faith. What is faith? Who has it? How does one acquire it?" (p. 210). They proceeded to propose such a model, one based on CST and its premise that for signals between two parties to be workable or believable by both of the parties, they must be reliably unfakeable. They held that signals that cannot be faked easily can be trusted to carry honest information. Many of these costly signals are referred to in the CST literature as "handicaps." For a signal to qualify as a handicap, the net benefits for displaying a signal must be higher for low quality individuals. A low quality signaler may send a fake signal suggesting high quality, but low quality signalers generally do not send false signals because the net costs are too high.

In the case of anomalous healing, there may be any number of low quality signalers (e.g., charlatans, pseudopsychics, unstable individuals suffering from grandiosity), who send out false signals but, nevertheless, often obtain cures because of the placebo effect (Macknik et al., 2008). Nonetheless, these false signals resemble honest signals (sent out by healers endorsed by their community) in regard to the effort involved (e.g., exhortations, exorcisms, trance). Quite often, considerable effort is involved by the charlatan (e.g., space needs to be rented, publicity needs to be obtained, sometimes, to impress the participants, technology needs to be devised to overhear audience members discuss their ailments before the performance or to allow a confederate to send cues to the charlatan).

Those charlatans whose signals are not costly may sell "miracle medicine," "holy relics," or "blessed talismans." With a sophisticated audience, these low cost signals would be dismissed, demanding that the charlatan invest time and effort in producing fake signals. Boyer and his associates (1964) administered Rorschach Inkblots to a group of Apache healers, some of whom had received community sanction and some of whom had not. Members of the latter group, presumably more likely to be charlatans, manifested signs of psychopathology while the mental health of the former group was superior to that of the community as a whole. These data suggest that community members were able to discriminate between healers whose costly signals were honest and those whose signals failed to pass the test.

Community discrimination is essential when dealing with folk healers whose interventions are especially dramatic. Consider the "trance surgeries" described by Don (Chapter 6) in which the healers' psychophysiological data indicated that they were in a hyperaroused state when they performed their interventions. Not only was this hyperarousal a costly signal, but the surgeries themselves demonstrated extreme effort on the part of both the clients and the healers, some of whom used instruments (ranging from a scalpel to a circular saw) that demanded mutual focus and trust. CST would conceptualize the total healing session as one involving any number of costly signals—the healer's hyperarousal, the use of potentially lethal tools, and the client's hope, trust, and faith. After each successful surgery, both healer and client would be considered more "fit" by community members.

McNamara and Szent-Imrey (2008) suggested that sickness itself might be a costly signal. It removes the acutely ill person from social circulation allowing him or her to assume a "sick role" (Frank and Frank, 1991). Those clients who survive the ordeal may be seen as having become more "fit" and treated with greater respect and deference by community members. Some of these "fit" clients may even see their sickness as a "call to heal" and undergo training on the part of experienced healers. Krippner's (1989) study of Brazilian folk healers revealed that many of them interpreted their malady and subsequent recovery as signs that they should become healers themselves. The price paid by these "wounded healers" was costly, but led to "fitness" that was admired by the community, especially in the case of women who lived in societies where their importance typically was devalued.

The two mediums from Recife, Brazil, discussed by Hageman et al. (Chapter 5) could very well exemplify this syndrome. One of them was virtually deaf, while the other endured a barrage of "spiritual calls" that many Western psychotherapists would have considered hallucinations and delusions. In the psychophysiological tests reported by Hageman et al., both mediums manifested "high risk" incongruences between their mind and body systems, confirming Wickramasekera's (1989) prediction that individuals with mediumistic capacities put themselves at risk for psychogenic symptomatology. In this case the cost of the signals was measured by psychophysiological instrumentation and psychological tests; responses from the two mediums in question indicated that mediumship involves both absorption and dissociation.

Krippner, Wickramasekera, and Tartz (2001) proposed that community support and regimens for healthy living alleviated the risk that the mediums took in continuing their practice. The phenomena associated with mediumship not only may serve as an example of costly signals, but of Gazzaniga's (2008) conclusion that "We have evolved to connect deeply with other human beings. Our awareness of this fact can and should bring us even closer to one another" (p. 272). This "deep connection" may have reduced the risks involved in the mediums' costly efforts (induced dissociation and absorption, ritualized movement, etc.) to produce honest signals.

We would suggest that reported psi phenomena strongly resemble reports of anomalous healing as well as dramatic placebo responses. Whatever else they may be, putative ESP and PK are costly signals. In parapsychological circles, considerable traction has been gained by the proposal that reports of ESP and PK often are instrumental responses, that is, they are purposeful and serve an adaptive function.

For example, Stanford (1990) proposed that psi is both need relevant and goal-oriented. In his psi-mediated instrumental research (PMIR) model, Stanford hypothesized that psi occurs when, under certain conditions, an individual has some need for those experiences to occur. As Roll and Williams (Chapter 1) observed, psi generally operates outside of an individual's awareness and occurs in order to facilitate some need or desire that has been encoded in memory. According to Stanford, data from the outside world imposes a structure upon the mind and brain that are received and interpreted. The reduction of sensory input (as in a dream or Ganzfeld experiment) leads to a reduction in the constraints on brain activity resulting in greater randomness, hence increasing the likelihood of psi effects.

Robert (a pseudonym) dreamed that he and his family members were driving up a steep hill when the car went out of control and crashed against the side of a mountain. He reported, "The back door flies open and my sister and I are thrown out of the car with no harm. My parents remain inside the car and within moments they are killed" (Krippner, Bogzaran, and de Carvalho, 2002, p. 124). Two weeks later, some of his relatives were coordinating a holiday by the sea and invited Robert, his sister, and his parents to join them. Robert's father declined the offer, stating it would conflict with Robert's academic schedule. On their way to the coast, the relatives collided head on with a truck and Robert's aunt and uncle died instantly. Their son and daughter were badly injured but survived the crash (p. 124). Was this a coincidence, a case of distorted memory, or an example of PMIR? If the latter, the dream would have been a costly signal that could have had a lifesaving function. Had it occurred in many indigenous societies; the entire vacation might have been cancelled because of the signal that family members were endangered, even though the specific family members involved were not correctly identified in the dream.

The focus of this book is on the neurobiology of mediums, psychic claimants, and other remarkable people. We are primarily interested in their experiences, that is, the subjective aspects of their work (their feelings, the ritual context, and attributed meanings). Kelly et al. (2007) lamented that "practically nothing of significance is presently known about the great trance mediums (or for that matter about exceptional psi subjects of any other kind) in terms of relevant characteristics of physiological function, personality, or cognitive style" (p. 628). Additionally, Krippner and Achterberg (2000) have differentiated between "experiences" (the subjective experience of a healer and a client during a healing session) and "events" (e.g., the outcome of a healing session) (pp. 356–357). Alcock's well-stated criticisms of parapsychological data are directed to purported psi events, rather than to a cataloging and assessment of psi experiences, which has been undertaken by several mainstream psychologists (see the appropriate chapters in Cardeña, Lynn, and Krippner, 2000). This book attempts to address the omissions cited by Kelly et al., acknowledging that the existence of psi-related events is more controversial than is that of psi-related experiences.

In the meantime, we are proposing that CST may have explanatory value for both psi experiences and putative psi events, as it links human behavior to evolutionary theory. Both the discoverers of evolution, Charles Darwin and Alfred Wallace, concluded that, according to the principles of natural selection, for any characteristic to be selected in a competitive environment, it has to provide a survival advantage to the individual. We are proposing that psi experiences served an adaptive value and psi events, if they occur, served one as well.

In summary, psi experiences could be looked upon as signaling devices that enhance coordination and cooperation between members of a group or species. But they are costly signals in that they are difficult to produce, undependable, and hard to replicate. Yet their net effect is to leave the experients more "fit" than they were before the experiences, whether the experiences were anomalous, coincidental, or deceptive in nature. The benefits of these experiences include social bonding, warning in times of danger, healing intractable sickness, solace following the death of a loved one, and locating lost or hidden objects of value. Hence the benefits of psi experiences may outweigh their costs. CST holds that cost authenticates a signal, and that the "fitness cost" ensures its adaptive role for individuals, for groups, or for entire species. When a costly signal is wasted, the solidarity—and survival—of a group is put at risk. As a result, mediums, healers, and other psychic claimants emerged around the world to manage and utilize costly signals for the benefit of their communities. Thinking of a ghost is an experience, not an event, yet there are experimental data demonstrating that the experience tends to facilitate cooperation between members of a group, even in Western society (Norenzayan and Shariff, 2007). ESP and PK might or might not be events but, as experiences, they appear to have had adaptive value and it is doubtful that they will ever go away. And CST contextualized how such experiences, and possibly events, may serve adaptive functions.

The Possible Role of Mirror Neurons

One of the most important discoveries in the neurosciences has been that of "mirror neurons," specialized neurons in the brain that appear to respond to behaviors of others by triggering a similar arousal pattern in an observer, such that presumably the experiences of both are mirrored. Those found in the premotor and posterior parietal cortex respond to other people's intentions and to actions, while those found in the anterior insular and anterior cingulate respond to emotions of others (Rizzolatti, Fogassi, and Gallese, 2006). Such mirroring abilities may have facilitated imitation and empathy among homonoids; further, mirror neuron assisted exchanges between early humans may have facilitated the advent of reflective self-consciousness.

Preuss (2001), among others, has proposed that the cerebral cortex is the most complex entity known to science. Gazzaniga (2008) described the human brain as, "a bizarre device, set in place through natural selection for one main purpose—to make decisions that enhance reproductive success" (p. 29), adding that "humans are just getting a toehold on understanding their abilities" (p. 389). The abilities, both actual and purported, described in this book may be adaptive; furthermore, they demonstrate the complexity of the brain and its decision-making capacities.

The human brain contains about 100 billion neurons, each of which can make contact with thousands, even tens of thousands, of other neurons. The contacts, or synapses, are believed to be the main means by which neurons communicate with each other (Gazzaniga, 2008). Pribram (1991) emphasized the importance of events in and around the synapse, pointing out that the complex microlevel electrochemical patterns of activity in the rich dendritic fields of the neocortex are at the root of the malleability of brain processes. The question remains, however, as to how such events amplify upward into macrolevel processes of inflection that affect the overall activity of the brain, yielding to experiences of "collective consciousness" (Combs and Krippner, 2008, p. 269). It is also important to mention that other brain cells in addition to neurons, such as astrocytes, may be important in understanding overall brain functions, but neuroscientists are just beginning to understand the possible complexities involved.

Gazzaniga (2008) noted that human social behavior has biological origins and that humans are "social to the core" (p. 83). In the evolution of this type of communication, mirror neurons may well have played a prominent role (Combs and Krippner, 2008). Indeed, Freeman (2001), among others, proposed that the human brain evolved in communities and might even be considered a community organ. For example, the San people of the Kalahari Desert have maintained their cultural myths, songs, and rituals over time through altered state experiences in which they experience merging with the knowledge of their ancestors (Keeney, 2005).

Vyshedskiy's (2008) social brain hypothesis argues that the superior social organization of hominids influenced the development of a superior brain. Homo sapiens appear to have spread out of Africa about 50,000 years ago. By that time, Homo sapiens had clearly acquired mental synthesis as revealed by numerous symbolic objects, elaborated burials, objects of art, bone needles, exquisite sculptures, spectacular images on the walls of caves, and sophisticated musical instruments. Homo sapiens were able to spread all over the world in just 15,000 years, develop agriculture in about 35,000 years, domesticate animals in about 40,000 years, build cities in 45,000 years, and travel into space in only 50,000 years. All these accomplishments were achieved by humans because of the ability to mentally synthesize new conscious experiences in the process of mental synthesis and then use a synthesizing language to share their plans with fellow humans.

How was this mental synthesis possible? Mirror neuron research suggests that social codes are largely dictated by our biology (Iacoboni, 2008), yet the paradigm inaugurated by the discovery of mirror neurons was foreseen by Maurice Merleau-Ponty, Franz Brentano, Edmund Husserl, and other originators of phenomenology. They proposed going back to experience itself, instead of musing about abstractions (i.e., Aristotle's "instincts" were preferred over Plato's "ideal forms") (Iacoboni, 2008). Mirror neurons seem to bind people to each other mentally, emotionally, and ethically. Iacoboni (2008) pointed out that "when we see someone suffering or in pain, mirror neurons help us to read his or her facial expression and actually make us feel the suffering or the pain of the other person" (p. 5). He suggested that these reactions "are the foundation of empathy and possibility of morality, a morality that is deeply rooted in our biology" (p. 5). Murphy (1958) has made the discussion of this problem relevant to contemporary society, noting that many of the current problems facing humans are group problems. "This makes the individualists among us squirm," he wrote, "but there is still a reality here to be faced: the group character, the corporate character, of the thinking process . . . . Can we use this corporate character and find strength in it, rather than simply protest against it?" (p. 159).

The most basic property of mirror neurons is that they are helpful for recognizing the actions of other people, and may even discriminate between intentions (Iacoboni, 2008). Freeman's (2001) dynamical view of the brain conceptualizes networks of neural activity playing against significant regions of neural tissue that forms chaotic-like attractor patterns that constantly update and evolve as they are impacted by new experiences. Krippner and Combs (2000) have found this way of understanding chaotic brain activity useful for clarifying how subtle residual feelings and thoughts might also be responsive to subtle nonlocal and nontemporal influence. Stokes (1987) has surveyed "nonlocal" theories in the parapsychological literature, and noted their similarity to Jungian notions of a collective unconscious. Again, the search for a mechanism is essential and candidates include Eccles's (1970) quantum level synaptic events, Hameroff and Penrose's (1996) quantum entanglement, and Laszlo's (2009) quantum shift in the global brain—all of which are in their initial stages of development. Nonetheless, Roll and Williams (Chapter 1) have taken the position that ESP and PK fit easily within the framework of quantum physics, at least in some of its models and interpretations.

These theoretical frameworks may lay the groundwork for explaining the data reported by Freedman (Chapter 8). His discussion of extraordinary brain activity in the frontal lobes during psi experiments might illustrate the subtle influences to which the brain is responsive, influences he purports to have measured during his initial experiment and its replication. These frameworks also are consistent with the neurobiological model proposed by Roll and Williams (Chapter 1) and the effects of neurochemical influences on the brain as described by Luke and Friedman (Chapter 9).

The importance of mirror neurons to the understanding of mysterious minds is the possibility that they lead to an intersubjective experience or shared consciousness. Whether or not these experiences are also events, mirror neurons assist people to "read" their world, especially the people they encounter (Gazzaniga, 2008). Social and cultural factors also play their part in these experiences, leading people to conclude that they are not separated isolated entities. These feelings and interactions could have been highly adaptive in the course of human evolution and, even in an era that ignores their presence, may continue to shape the future of humanity (Combs and Krippner, 2008).

Beyond Neurobiology

This book has emphasized the importance of neurobiology and the neurosciences in fathoming the "mysterious minds" of remarkable people. As we previously noted, by 1950 the search for neural mechanisms of cognitive skills seemed to have reached an impasse (Rosenzweig, 2007). That impasse has since been breached through the amazing developments within neurobiology, which comes under many labels (cognitive neuroscience, affective neuroscience, social neuroscience, neuroethics, neuroeconomics, neuropolitics, neurotheology, etc.). For example, Vyshedskiy (2008) has provided a lucid description of conscious experience from the perspective of neurobiology and the neurosciences. In his model, conscious experiences are represented by synchronous activity of large groups of cortical neurons: neural assemblages.

> Enhanced connections between neurons in a neuronal ensemble enable the self-organization property of the ensemble and form the basis of memory . . . . Substantially the same neurons are activated during a conscious experience of physical objects and a conscious experience of imaginary objects. (p. 163)

Vyshedskiy (2008) concluded that at the core of all these truly human functions lies the process of mental synthesis. This allows people to imagine the results of their actions. All unique human cognitive abilities are based on the fundamental process of mental synthesis: auto-critique, self-reflection, storytelling, understanding a story, creativity. It is the identification of the process of mental synthesis at the core of multiple human traits that allows this model to bridge cognitive psychology and neuroscience, and to describe the human experience on the neuronal level.

On the neuronal level, mental synthesis involves synchronization of multiple neuronal ensembles with attention. This process enables humans to synthesize never-before-seen mental images, to mentally plan their actions and test for possible outcomes, to engineer machinery and design cities, and to create a conscious experience that they have never experienced before. As William James wrote, consciousness is not a thing but a process. In humans, it is the process of mental synthesis, that of voluntary creation of new mental constructs by the synchronization of multiple ensembles of neurons coding for previous experiences.

One solution to the mysteries of the mind was proposed by Rosenberg (2009), who stated,

> There is no separate mind from the brain, the mind is the brain. Cartesian logic of a separate mind and brain is an archaic philosophical concept displaced by current functional magnetic resonance imaging, DBS [deep brain stimulation] studies, years of meticulous clinical-neuropathologic studies, and experimental neurophysiological animal studies that have proven that consciousness and mind are embedded into specific neuroanatomical arousal and behavioral circuits. . . . It is now clear that coma, consciousness, and cognition are neural-directed constructs and probably result from mathematical computations yet to be discovered. (p. 1173)

The key phrase here is "yet to be discovered," a phrase that the Nobel Laureate Sir John Eccles (1970) probably would have included in his category of "promissory materialism." Alcock (1990) once described parapsychology as a belief system rather than a science, but Rosenberg's statement, including the term "proved," certainly expresses a belief. Because science is an open system, nothing can ever be "proved" or "proven." Hypotheses can be confirmed or refuted, studies can be replicated or fail to be replicated, but the word "proof" is better reserved for mathematics and logic.

We remain unconvinced that there is a firm solution to the so-called "mind-body problem" as yet; namely, can the "mind" simply be reduced to the brain? Most quantum mechanical models of consciousness assume such a reductionary monism and place the mechanisms of mind-body interactions on the level of the neural synapse, the gap between neurons to which we have referred several times in this postscript and clearly within the brain. Eccles (1970), for example, speculated that mind affects brain activity by affecting the way chemicals are released into the synaptic gap producing voluntary behavior.

Although mainstream quantum physics does not have a theoretical basis for purported nonlocal communication (ESP) or perturbation (PK), it does provide for instantaneous correlations. As Roll and Williams (Chapter 1) have pointed out, this is what quantum entanglement is all about. Whether ESP and PK are related to entanglement or not is still subject to debate, but what entanglement shows is that there are well-accepted aspects of the physical world that are completely compatible with a basic mystery underlying psi experiences, namely that objects only *appear* to be separate. If such objects also involve the human mind, then in principle humanity is connected with the rest of the universe. The disciplined study of spiritual and transcendent events has been taken up by a few parapsychologists who have investigated alleged cases of reincarnation, information obtained while "out of the body" or "near death," and data provided by mediums (e.g., Kelly et al., 2007; Tart, 2009). Hageman et al. (Chapter 5) propose that neurobiological mechanisms that are common to humanity may underlie mediumistic phenomena. In any event, mediumistic phenomena are not necessarily associated with psychosocial dysfunction. In addition, the worldview of the Brazilian mediums studied by Hageman et al. (Chapter 5) and Don (Chapter 6) is one that is clearly at odds with a reductionistic perspective of mind and body. It is "transpersonal" in nature, holding that there are psi-related events that transcend the limitations on mind-brain interactions imposed by mainstream science.

Like Roll and Williams (Chapter 1), Kelly et al. (2007) attempted to bridge these oppositional views, holding that a transpersonal perspective is consistent with the principles of quantum physics, as well as with many of the observations of neuroscience. Many of these issues were pioneered by quantum physicist E. H. Walker (1974, 1987) who postulated a nonphysical mind that could exert a measurable influence in the physical world. Because of the nonlocal properties of quantum phenomena, the mind may operate as a second nervous system affecting another person's brain (as in telepathy) or distant physical processes (as in PK).

Pfeiffer and Mack (2007) collected several other models that attempt to reconcile purported psi events with quantum physics, neurobiology, and the neurosciences. Kelly et al. (2007) asserted,

> We still have no real understanding of the ultimate nature of the relationship between brain processes and mental activity, and certainly no solution of Chalmers' [1996] "hard problem"—why conscious experiences with their specific qualitative characteristics should arise at all in connection with the associated patterns of brain activity. It is not clear which aspects of the "cognitive unconscious" go with the brain, which with the associated psyche and how their respective contributions get coordinated. (p. 629)

According to this model, the "psyche" is a second and distinct type of existent (itself possible at least in part physical in some extended sense) with which the body is somehow associated. Indeed, the authors continue, "There is no such thing as matter as classically conceived" (p. 630). Henry Stapp (2005), a quantum physicist, added that this perspective allows the physical world to become an evolving structure of information, and of propensities for experiences to occur, rather than a mechanically evolving mindless material structure.

It is in this spirit that Nöe (2009) has campaigned for an "ecological approach" for the study of consciousness, arguing that minds are more than brains. His ecological approach would require the joint cooperation of the neurosciences, the behavioral sciences, linguistics, mathematics, robotics, artificial intelligence, philosophy, and perhaps other disciplines that would further the understanding of the brain, the body, and their places in the world. We have tried to share such an ecological vision, hoping that this book will make a contribution to the development of a transdisciplinary field of inquiry that will normalize the "paranormal," demystify the "mysterious," and fathom the far reaches of the "mind."

Indeed, if brain and mind, both individually and collectively, and world are as inseparable as we think they might be, while not ruling out any of the many varieties of mind-body monism or dualism, the vexing problems that cause such sharp divisiveness between advocates and counteradvocates of psi may turn out to be based primarily on semantic differences resulting from underlying metaphoric (or worldview) assumptions in construing what is considered ontologically possible.

We started this chapter by pointing out how the use of metaphor characterized the early history of neurobiology. We end the chapter by suggesting that the role of metaphor may continue to play an important explanatory role. With further neurobiological advances, as well as advances in other areas of science such as quantum physics, we anticipate many of the deepest mysteries of the mind will be greatly clarified and these extant sharp divides will soften and perhaps merge over time.

References

Alcock, J. (1990). *Science and supernature: A critical appraisal of parapsychology.* Buffalo, NY: Prometheus.

Aton, S. J., Seibt, J., Dumoulin, M., Jha, S. K., Steinmetz, N., Coleman, T., Naidoo, N., and Frank, M. G. (2009). Mechanisms of sleep-dependent consolidation of cortical plasticity. *Neuron, 61*, 454–466.

Babich, F. R., Jacobson, A. L., Bubash, S., and Jacobson, A. (1965). Transfer of a response to naïve rats by injection of ribonucleic acid from trained rats. *Science, 149*, 656–657.

Benedetti, F., Mayberg, H. S., Wager, T. D., Stohler, C. S., and Zubieta, J. (2005). Neurobiological mechanisms of the placebo effect. *Journal of Neuroscience, 25*, 10390–10402.

Boyer, L. B., Klopfer, B., Brawer, F. B., and Kawai, H. (1964). Comparisons of the shamans and pseudoshamans of the Apaches of the Mescalero Indian reservation: A Rorschach study. *Journal of Projective Techniques, 28*, 173–180.

Byrne, W. L., Samuel, D., Bennett, E. L., Rosenzweig, M. R., Wasserman, E., et al. (1966). Memory transfer. *Science, 153*, 658–659.

Cajal, S. R. (1894). *La fine structure des centres nerveux. Proceedings of the Royal Society, London, 55*, 444–468.

Cardeña, E., Lynn, S. J., and Krippner, S. (Eds.). (2000). *Varieties of anomalous experience: Examining the scientific evidence.* Washington, DC: American Psychological Association.

Chalmers, D. (1996). *The conscious mind: In search of a fundamental theory.* New York: Oxford University Press.

Combs, A., and Krippner, S. (2008). Collective consciousness and the social brain. *Journal of Consciousness Studies, 15*, 264–276.

Dall, S. R. X. (2005). Information and its use by animals in evolutionary ecology. *Trends in Ecology and Evolution, 20*, 187–193.

Domhoff, G. W. (2003). *The scientific study of dreams: Neural networks, cognitive development, and content analysis.* Washington, DC: American Psychological Association.

Eccles, J. (1970) *Facing reality: Philosophical adventures of a brain scientist.* New York: Springer-Verlag.

Frank, J. D., and Frank, J. B. (1991). *Persuasion and healing* (3rd ed.). Baltimore, MD: Johns Hopkins University Press.

Freeman, W. (2001). *How brains make up their minds.* New York: Columbia University Press.

Gazzaniga, M. S. (2008). *Human: The science behind what makes us unique.* New York: HarperCollins.

Hameroff, S., and Penrose, R. (1996). Orchestrated reduction of quantum coherence in brain microtubules: A model for consciousness? In S. R. Hameroff, A. W. Kaszniak, and A. C. Scott (Eds.), *Toward a science of consciousness: The first Tucson discussions and debates* (pp. 507–540). Cambridge, MA: MIT Press.

Hansel, C. E. M. (1980). *ESP and parapsychology: A critical re-evaluation.* Buffalo: Prometheus Press. (Original work published 1966.)

Hebb, D. O. (1949). *The organization of behavior: A neuropsychological theory.* New York: John Wiley & Sons.

Iacoboni, M. (2008). *Mirroring people.* New York: Farrar, Straus and Giroux.

James, W. (1890). *Principles of psychology.* New York: Henry Holt.

Keeney. B. (2005). *Bushman shaman.* Rochester, NY: Destiny Books.

Kelly, E. F., Kelly, E. W., Crabtree, A., Gauld, A., Grosso, M., and Greyson, B. (2007). *Irreducible mind: Toward a psychology for the 21st century.* Lanham, MD: Rowman & Littlefield.

Kesner, R. P., and Martinez, J. L. (Eds.). (2007). *Neurobiology of learning and memory* (2nd ed.). New York: Elsevier.

Krippner, S. (1989). A call to heal: Entry patterns in Brazilian mediumship. In C. A. Ward (Ed.), *Altered states of consciousness and mental health: A cross-cultural perspective* (pp. 186–206). Newbury Park, CA: Sage.

Krippner, S. (1994). Psychoneuroimmunology. In R. J. Corsini (Ed.), *Encyclopedia of psychology* (2nd ed., Vol. 3, pp. 228–231). New York: John Wiley & Sons.

Krippner, S., and Achterberg. J. (2000). Anomalous healing experiences. In E. Cardeña, S. J. Lynn, and S. Krippner (Eds.), *Varieties of anomalous experience: Examining the scientific evidence* (pp. 353–395). Washington, DC: American Psychological Association.

Krippner, S., Bogzaran, F., and de Carvalho, A. (2002). *Extraordinary dreams and how to work with them.* Albany, NY: SUNY Press.

Krippner, S., and Combs, A. (2000). Self-organization in the dreaming brain. *Journal of Mind and Behavior, 21,* 399–412.

Krippner, S., Wickramasekera, I., and Tartz, R. (2001). Scoring thick and scoring thin: The boundaries of psychic claimants. *Subtle Energies and Energy Medicine, 11,* 43–63.

Laszlo, E. (2009). *Quantum shifts in the global brain.* Rochester, VT: Inner Traditions.

Macknik, S. L., King, M., Randi, J., Robbins, A., Teller, Thompson, J., and Martinez-Conde, S. (2008). Attention and awareness in stage magic. *Nature Reviews Neuroscience, 9,* 871–879.

Madkour, T. M., Barakat, A. M., and Furlow, F. B. (1997). Neonatal cry quality as an honest signal of fitness. *Evolution and Human Behavior, 18,* 175–193.

McConnell, J. V. (1986). *Understanding human behavior* (5th ed.). New York: Holt, Rinehart and Winston.

McNamara, P. (2004). *An evolutionary psychology of sleep and dreams.* Westport, CT: Praeger.

McNamara, P., and Szent-Imrey, R. (2008). What we can learn from miraculous healings and cures. In J. H. Ellens (Ed.), *Miracles: God, science, and psychology in the paranormal* (pp. 208–220). Westport, CT: Praeger.

Moulton, S. T., and Kosslyn, S. M. (2008). Using neuroimaging to resolve the psi debate. *Journal of Cognitive Neuroscience, 20,* 182–192.

Murphy, G. (1958). *Human potentialities.* New York: Basic Books.

Nöe, A. (2009). *Out of our heads: Why you are not your brain and other lessons from the biology of consciousness.* New York: St. Martin's Press.

Norenzayan, A., and Shariff, A. (2007). God is watching you: Supernatural agent concepts increase prosocial behavior in an anonymous economic game. *Psychological Science, 18,* 803–809.

Pentland, A. (2008). *Honest signals: How they shape our world.* Boston: MIT Press.

Pfeiffer, T., and Mack, J. E. (Eds.). (2007). *Mind before matter: Visions of a new science of consciousness.* Winchester, U.K.: O Books.

Plato. (1987). *Theaetus* (R. A. H. Waterfield, Trans.). Harmondsworth, U.K.: Penguin Books.

Preuss, T. M. (2001). The discovery of cerebral diversity: An unwelcome scientific revolution. In D. Falk and K. Gibson (Eds.), *Evolutionary anatomy of the primate cerebral cortex* (pp. 138–164). Cambridge, U.K.: Cambridge University Press.

Pribram, K. (1991). *Brain and perception: Holonomy and structure in figural processing.* Hillsdale, NJ: Erlbaum.

Price, G. R. (1955). Science and the supernatural. *Science, 122,* 359–367.

Rizzolatti, G., Fogassi, L., and Gallese, V. (2006). Mirrors in the mind. *Scientific American, 295*(5), 54–61.

Rosenberg, R. N. (2009). Consciousness, coma, and brain death—2009. *Journal of the American Medical Association, 301,* 1172–1174.

Rosenzweig, M. R. (1996). Aspects of the search for neural mechanisms of memory. *Annual Review of Psychology, 47,* 1–32.

Rosenzweig, M. R., (2007). Historical perspective. In R. P. Kesner and J. L. Martinez (Eds.), *Neurobiology of learning and memory* (2nd ed., pp. 3–55). New York: Elsevier.

Rosenzweig, M. R., Krech, D., and Bennett, E. I. (1961). Heredity, environment, brain biochemistry, and learning. In *Current trends in psychological theory* (pp. 87–110). Pittsburgh: University of Pittsburgh Press.

Skaggs, W. E., and McNaughton, B. L. (1996). Replay of neuronal firing sequences in rat hippocampus during sleep following spatial experience. *Science, 271,* 1870–1873.

Stanford, R. G. (1990). An experimentally testable model for spontaneous psi events: A review of related evidence from parapsychology and other sciences. In S. Krippner (Ed.), *Advances in parapsychological research* (Vol. 6, pp. 54–167). Jefferson, NC: McFarland.

Stapp, H. (2005). Quantum interactive dualism: An alternative to materialism. *Journal of Consciousness Studies, 12,* 43–58.

Stokes, D. M. (1987). Theoretical parapsychology. In S. Krippner (Ed.), *Advances in parapsychological research* (Vol. 4, pp. 77–189). Jefferson, NC: McFarland.

Tart, C. T. (2009). *The end of materialism: How evidence of the paranormal is bringing science and spirit together.* Oakland, CA: New Harbinger.

Ungar, G., and Oceguera-Navarro, C. (1965). Transfer of habituation by material extracted from brain. *Nature, 207,* 301–302.

Vyshedskiy, A. (2008). *On the origin of the human mind.* Toronto: MobileReference.

Walker, E. H. (1974). Consciousness as a hidden variable. *Physics Today, 24,* 39.

Walker, E. H. (1987). Measurement in quantum mechanics revisited. *Journal of the American Society for Psychical Research, 81,* 333–389.

Wickramasekera, I. (1989). Risk factors for parapsychological verbal reports, hypnotizability and somatic complaints. In B. Shapin and L. Coly (Eds.), *Parapsychology and human nature* (pp. 19–35). New York: Parapsychology Foundation.

Wiesel, T. V., and Hubel, D. H. (1965). Comparison of the effect of unilateral and bilateral eye closure on cortical unit responses in kittens. *Journal of Neurophysiology, 28,* 1029–1040.

Zuckerman, P. (2009, April/May). Aweism. *Free Inquiry,* 52–55.

About the Editors and Contributors

James E. Alcock, Ph.D., is Professor of Psychology at York University and has specialized in both social psychology and clinical psychology. His research interests focus on the psychology of belief and his books include *Parapsychology: Science or Magic*; *Science and Supernature*; *A Textbook of Social Psychology* (co-author); and *Psi Wars* (co-editor).

Leonardo Caixeta, M.D., Ph.D., is Associate Professor of Behavioral Medicine at the Federal University of Goiás, Brazil. His interests are parapsychological studies, particularly mediumship research as developed from his extensive contacts with Kardecian Spiritism, and transcultural psychiatry focusing on the indigenous and Afro-Brazilian populations of the Amazon.

Allan Combs, Ph.D., is a consciousness researcher and neuropsychologist at California Institute of Integral Studies and Professor Emeritus in Psychology at the University of North Carolina at Asheville. He is author of over 100 articles, chapters, and books on consciousness and the brain including the books *The Radiance of Being* and *Consciousness Explained Better*.

Norman S. Don, Ph.D., is a cognitive neuroscientist; his 60 publications focus on brain electrical activity and its relation to consciousness. He has conducted field work in Brazil as Director of Research for the Chicago-based Kairos Foundation, and was Co-Director of the Human Factors and Behavioral Toxicology Laboratory at the School of Public Health, University of Illinois at Chicago.

Morris Freedman, M.D., is Professor, Department of Medicine, and Director, Behavioural Neurology Section, Division of Neurology, University of Toronto. He is Head, Division of Neurology, Director of the Sam and Ida Ross Memory Clinic, and Scientist at the Rotman Research Institute. His research involves the study of brain-behavior relations with a focus on the mechanisms underlying cognitive impairment.

Harris L. Friedman, Ph.D., is Research Professor of Psychology, University of Florida, and Professor Emeritus, Saybrook University. A clinical psychologist, he studies transpersonal perspectives in psychology and social change, and has written over 100 professional publications. He is Editor of the *International Journal of Transpersonal Studies* and Associate Editor of *The Humanistic Psychologist*.

Joan H. Hageman, Ph.D., is the Chair of Research for the PsyMore Research Institute in Tampa, Florida. Her scientific publications and research interests focus on her multicultural research in human consciousness, spirituality and health, anomalous phenomena, hypnosis, dissociation, and the polypsychic nature of personality. These topics are covered in her book, *Spirituality: A Mind-Body-Spirit Cross-Cultural Perspective on Self-Healing*.

Harvey J. Irwin, Ph.D., has authored or co-authored over 100 papers in academic journals and four books, including the text, *An Introduction to Parapsychology*. He was a member of the School of Psychology, University of New England, Australia, for over 30 years, once serving as Head of the School. In 2002 the Parapsychological Association accorded Dr. Irwin its Outstanding Research Contribution Award.

Stanley Krippner, Ph.D., is Professor of Psychology, Saybrook University, and is the 2002 Recipient of the American Psychological Association's Award for Distinguished Contributions to the International Advancement of Psychology. He has served as president of two divisions in the American Psychological Association and is co-editor of its anthology *Varieties of Anomalous Experience: Examining the Scientific Evidence*.

David Luke, Ph.D., is Lecturer in Psychology at the University of Greenwich, Visiting Lecturer at the University of East London, and Research Associate at the Beckley Foundation, Oxford. His research interests and publications include such topics as parapsychology, parapsychopharmacology, cultural anthropology, meditation, yoga, and altered states of consciousness.

Alexander Moreira-Almeida, M.D., Ph.D., is Associate Professor of Psychiatry and Semiology at the School of Medicine, Federal University of Juiz de Fora, Brazil, and Founder and Coordinator of its Center for Research in Spirituality and Health as well as Director of its Center for Teaching, Research and Extension of the University Hospital. He has conducted postdoctoral work at Duke University.

Vernon M. Neppe, M.D., Ph.D., is Director of the Pacific Neuropsychiatric Institute in Seattle, Washington, and Adjunct Professor of Psychiatry and Human Behavior at St. Louis University, St. Louis, Missouri. He is a Fellow of the Royal Society (South Africa), and a Distinguished Fellow of the American Psychiatric Association.

He is author of seven books and two plays, the developer of a philosophical paradigm (vortex N-dimensionalism), and a Forensic Specialist.

Adrian Parker, Ph.D., is Professor of Psychology at Gothenburg University, Sweden, where he teaches courses in altered states of consciousness and parapsychology. He held the Perriot Warrick Studentship for Psychical Research at Trinity College, Cambridge. He has published widely in clinical psychology and critical parapsychology; including his book, *States of Mind: ESP and Altered States of Consciousness*.

Julio F. P. Peres, Ph.D., obtained his doctorate in Neurosciences and Behavior at the Institute of Psychology, University of São Paulo, then conducted postdoctoral work at the Center for Spirituality and the Mind at the University of Pennsylvania. He conducts research in neuroimaging, memory, and altered states of consciousness at the Institute of Psychiatry, University of São Paulo, Brazil.

William G. Roll, Ph.D., is Professor of Psychology and Psychical Research at the State University of West Georgia. He was on the staff at the Duke University Parapsychology Laboratory from 1957 to 1964 and also served as Research Director at the Psychical Research Foundation. He is author or co-author of four books and has written more than 200 professional papers.

Caroline A. Watt, Ph.D., is Senior Lecturer in Psychology at the University of Edinburgh, a founding member of the Koestler Parapsychology Unit, and past president of the Parapsychological Association. She is co-author of *An Introduction to Parapsychology*, and has over 20 years of experience in teaching and research in parapsychology and related fields.

Ian Wickramasekera II, Psy.D., has served as president of the American Psychological Association's Society of Psychological Hypnosis. He is engaged in teaching and research and also maintains a private psychology practice. He has published several articles on the empathic nature of hypnosis, the psychophysiology of unconscious mentation, and psychotherapy from a Buddhist perspective.

Bryan J. Williams, of the University of New Mexico, is an affiliate member of the Parapsychological Association and the Society for Scientific Exploration. He was the 2003 recipient of the Charles T. and Judith A. Tart Student Incentive Award for Parapsychological Research sponsored by the Parapsychology Foundation in New York, and a co-recipient of the Foundation's Eileen J. Garrett Scholarship in 2008.

Index

No Discord
4.19